World Economic Situation and Prospects 2015

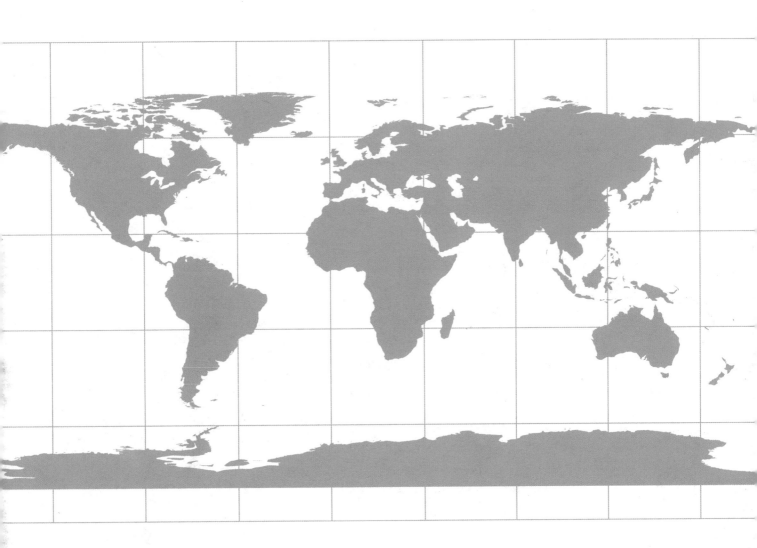

United Nations
New York, 2015

The report is a joint product of the United Nations Department of Economic and Social Affairs (UN/DESA), the United Nations Conference on Trade and Development (UNCTAD) and the five United Nations regional commissions (Economic Commission for Africa (ECA), Economic Commission for Europe (ECE), Economic Commission for Latin America and the Caribbean (ECLAC), Economic and Social Commission for Asia and the Pacific (ESCAP) and Economic and Social Commission for Western Asia (ESCWA)).

For further information, see http://www.un.org/en/development/desa/policy/wesp/index.shtml or contact:

DESA

Mr. Wu Hongbo, *Under-Secretary-General*

Department of Economic and Social Affairs
Room S-2922
United Nations
New York, NY 10017
USA

☎ +1-212-9635958
✉ wuh@un.org

UNCTAD

Dr. Mukhisa Kituyi, *Secretary-General*

United Nations Conference on Trade
and Development
Room E-9042
Palais de Nations
1211 Geneva 10
Switzerland

☎ +41-22-9175806
✉ sgo@unctad.org

ECA

Dr. Carlos Lopes, *Executive Secretary*

United Nations Economic Commission for Africa
Menelik II Avenue
P.O. Box 3001
Addis Ababa
Ethiopia

☎ +251-11-5511231
✉ ecainfo@uneca.org

ECE

Mr. Christian Friis Bach, *Executive Secretary*

United Nations Economic Commission for Europe
Palais des Nations
CH-1211 Geneva 10
Switzerland

☎ +41-22-9174444
✉ info.ece@unece.org

ECLAC

Ms. Alicia Bárcena, *Executive Secretary*

Economic Commission for Latin America
and the Caribbean
Av. Dag Hammarskjöld 3477
Vitacura
Santiago, Chile
Chile

☎ +56-2-22102000
✉ secepal@cepal.org

ESCAP

Dr. Shamshad Akhtar, *Executive Secretary*

Economic and Social Commission for Asia
and the Pacific
United Nations Building
Rajadamnern Nok Avenue
Bangkok 10200
Thailand

☎ +66-2-2881234
✉ unescap@unescap.org

ESCWA

Ms. Rima Khalaf, *Executive Secretary*

Economic and Social Commission for Western Asia
P.O. Box 11-8575
Riad el-Solh Square, Beirut
Lebanon

☎ +961-1-981301
@ http://www.escwa.un.org/main/contact.asp

ISBN: 978-92-1-109170-0
eISBN: 978-92-1-057135-7

United Nations publication
Sales No. E.15.II.C.2

Acknowledgements

For the preparation of the global outlook, inputs were received from the national centres of Project LINK and from the participants at the annual LINK meeting held in New York from 22 to 24 October 2014. The cooperation and support received through Project LINK are gratefully acknowledged.

The report was prepared under the general supervision of Pingfan Hong, Director of the Development Policy and Analysis Division (DPAD) in UN/DESA, and the coordination of Matthias Kempf, Economic Affairs Officer of the Global Economic Monitoring (GEM) Unit of DPAD in UN/DESA.

We gratefully acknowledge the team at **UN/DESA**: Grigor Agabekian, Clive Altshuler, Peter Chowla, Beir Cleghorne, Ann D'Lima, Cordelia Gow, Tim Hilger, Leah C. Kennedy, Mary Lee Kortes, Michael Lennard, Hung-Yi Li, Ingo Pitterle, Daniel Platz, Vladimir Popov, Hamid Rashid, Gerard Reyes, Ilka Ritter, Gabe Scelta, Benu Schneider, Oliver Schwank, Nancy Settecasi, Krishnan Sharma, Shari Spiegel, Alex Trepelkov, Sebastian Vergara, Sergio P. Vieira, Tianjao Wang and John Winkel; at **ECA**: Adam Elhiraika, Hopestone Chavula, Zivanemoyo Chinzara, Abbi Kedir, Mama Keita, Aboubacry Lom, Diderot Sandjong, Heini Suominen, Giovanni Valensisi, Zacharias Ziegelhofer; at **ECE**: José Palacín; at **ECLAC**: Luis Felipe Jimenez, Sandra Manuelito, Daniel Titelman, Jurgen Weller; at **ESCAP**: Shuvojit Banerjee, Sudip Ranjan Basu, Matthew Hammill, Yejin Ha, Daniel Jeongdae Lee, Muhammad Hussain Malik, Oliver Paddison, Kiatkanid Pongpanich and Vatcharin Sirimaneetham; at **ESCWA**: Abdallah Al Dardari, Mohamed Hedi Bchir, Nathalie Khaled, Jose Antonio Pedrosa Garcia and Yasuhisa Yamamoto; at **UNCTAD**: Alfredo Calcagno, Rajan Dhanjee, Pilar Fajarnes, Marco Fugazza, Samuel Gayi, Ricardo Gottschalk, Taisuke Ito, Alexandra Laurent, Mina Mashayekhi, Jörg Mayer, Nicolas Maystre, Ahmad Mukhtar, Alessandro Nicita, Janvier Nkurunziza, Victor Ognivtsev, Edgardo Torija Zane, Komi Tsowou, Guillermo Valles and Yan Zhang; and at **UNWTO**: Michel Julian, John Kester and Javier Ruescas.

Explanatory notes

The following symbols have been used in the tables throughout the report:

..	**Two dots** indicate that data are not available or are not separately reported.		-	**A minus** sign indicates deficit or decrease, except as indicated.
–	**A dash** indicates that the amount is nil or negligible.		/	**A slash** between years indicates a crop year or financial year, for example, 2014/15.
.	**A full stop** is used to indicate decimals.		–	**Use of a hyphen between years**, for example, 2015–2016, signifies the full period involved, including the beginning and end years.
-	**A hyphen** indicates that the item is not applicable.			

Reference to "dollars" ($) indicates United States dollars, unless otherwise stated.

Reference to "billions" indicates one thousand million.

Reference to "tons" indicates metric tons, unless otherwise stated.

Annual rates of growth or change, unless otherwise stated, refer to annual compound rates.

Details and percentages in tables do not necessarily add to totals, because of rounding.

Project LINK is an international collaborative research group for econometric modelling, coordinated jointly by the Development Policy and Analysis Division of UN/DESA and the University of Toronto.

For **country classifications**, see statistical annex.

Data presented in this publication incorporate information available as at **21 November 2014**.

The following abbreviations have been used:

ASEAN	Association of Southeast Asian Nations		ILO	International Labour Organization
BCBS	Basel Committee on Banking Supervision		IMF	International Monetary Fund
bpd	barrels per day		LDCs	least developed countries
BoE	Bank of England		MDGs	Millennium Development Goals
BoJ	Bank of Japan		MFN	most favoured nation
BRICS	Brazil, Russian Federation, India, China and South Africa		MNE	multinational enterprise
CIS	Commonwealth of Independent States		MTS	Multilateral Trade System
CPI	consumer price index		NTMs	non-tariff measures
DAC	Development Assistance Committee (of the Organization for Economic Cooperation and Development)		ODA	official development assistance
			OECD	Organization for Economic Cooperation and Development
DFQF	duty-free quota-free market access		OPEC	Organization of the Petroleum Exporting Countries
ECB	European Central Bank		pb	per barrel
ECOSOC	Economic and Social Council of the United Nations		QE	quantitative easing
EU	European Union		RTAs	regional trade agreements
FDI	foreign direct investment		SDGs	Sustainable Development Goals
Fed	Federal Reserve of the United States of America		SIDS	small island developing States
FSB	Financial Stability Board		SMEs	small and medium-sized enterprises
G8	Group of Eight		UNCTAD	United Nations Conference on Trade and Development
G20	Group of Twenty		UNFCCC	United Nations Framework Convention on Climate Change
GATS	General Agreement on Trade in Services			
GATT	General Agreement on Tariffs and Trade		UNWTO	World Tourism Organization
GCC	Cooperation Council for the Arab States of the Gulf		VAT	value added tax
GDP	gross domestic product		WGP	world gross product
IFFs	illicit financial flows		WTO	World Trade Organization

Executive summary

Prospects for global macroeconomic development

Global growth will improve slightly,
but continue at only a moderate level

The global economy continued to expand at only a moderate estimated pace of 2.6 per cent in 2014. Recovery was hampered by some new challenges, including a number of unexpected shocks, such as the heightened geopolitical conflicts in different parts of the world. Most economies have seen a shift in gross domestic product (GDP) growth to a noticeably lower path compared to pre-crisis levels, raising the spectre of longer-term mediocre economic growth. In the developed economies, although some improvements are forecast for 2015 and 2016, significant downside risks persist, especially in the euro area and Japan. Growth rates in developing countries and economies in transition have become more divergent during 2014, with a sharp deceleration in a number of large emerging economies, particularly in Latin America and the Commonwealth of Independent States (CIS). A number of these economies have encountered various country-specific challenges, including structural imbalances and geopolitical tensions. In the outlook period, the global economy is expected to expand at a slightly faster but still only moderate pace, with world gross product (WGP) projected to grow by 3.1 and 3.3 per cent in 2015 and 2016, respectively.

Sluggish employment creation and
weak wages remain major challenges

A major weakness in the macroeconomic picture remains the employment situation, as GDP growth continued to be subdued and below potential in many parts of the world, and therefore did not create a sufficient number of productive jobs. In the developed economies, unemployment figures remain elevated in several countries, especially in the euro area, while wage levels continue to be affected by the financial crisis. In developing economies, despite slower employment growth, unemployment rates have remained relatively stable since 2013, partly owing to lower labour force growth, although informality and vulnerable employment are still highly prevalent. However, high unemployment levels persist in various countries, especially in Northern Africa and Western Asia as well as in some of the economies in transition in South-Eastern Europe.

Benign global inflation encompasses deflation risks in the euro
area and high inflation in some developing countries

While the aggregate global inflation rate remains tame, this cannot mask a wide range of individual circumstances. Notably, inflation is elevated in about a dozen developing countries and economies in transition, while a growing number of developed economies in Europe are facing the risk of deflation. For the outlook period, global average inflation is projected to stay close to the level observed in the past two years, which was about 3 per cent. While aggregate average inflation for developed economies is expected to increase slightly until 2016, both developing economies and the economies in transition will register a decline in their aggregate inflation rates.

International trade and finance

Primary commodity prices trend lower, while trade growth will increase slightly

International prices of primary commodities have been on a downward trend in the past two years, and no measurable upturn is projected for 2015–2016. International prices of oil declined sharply in the second half of 2014 and are projected to continue softening in 2015–2016, as the growth of demand for oil is expected to remain weaker than the increase in supply of oil. Non-oil commodity prices have also been on a decreasing trend, although they still remain high relative to their long-term trend of the past decades.

Trade growth has been sluggish in the past few years, due mainly to the slow and uneven recovery in major developed countries and the moderate growth in developing countries. World trade is estimated to have expanded by 3.4 per cent in 2014, still well below pre-crisis trends. In the forecast period, trade growth is expected to pick up moderately along with improvement in global output, with the volume of world imports of goods and services projected to grow by 4.7 per cent in 2015 and 5.0 per cent in 2016. However, this projection is subject to various risks, including the possible disruptive effects on trade flows of any increase in geopolitical tensions in some subregions.

Capital inflows to emerging economies have declined moderately, with a slight increase expected later in the forecast period

Net private capital inflows to emerging economies have been on a moderate downturn since 2013, triggered by the tapering of the quantitative easing by the United States Federal Reserve, the deterioration in the growth prospects for these economies, and escalated geopolitical tensions. In 2014, net private inflows to this group of economies have declined, mainly because of capital flight from the Russian Federation amid a weakening economic situation and geopolitical strains. External borrowing costs continue to be relatively low for most emerging economies, but the risks for abrupt adjustments and increased volatility driven by changes in investor sentiment remain high. The outlook for capital inflows to emerging economies and developing countries remains moderately positive. Overall, net capital inflows are projected to stay at the same level in 2015 and slightly increase in 2016. But sudden shifts in investor sentiment due to geopolitical crises, the monetary policy change in the United States of America and a further divergence of the monetary policy stances of the major central banks might significantly affect portfolio flows. The divergence of monetary policy stances has already contributed to a significant strengthening of the dollar in the second half of 2014; a continuation of this trend could also underpin shifts in international trade patterns.

Risks and uncertainties

Monetary policy adjustments could create major macroeconomic instability

The global economic outlook is subject to a number of risks and uncertainties. These include a deviation of monetary policy from the policy path built into the current baseline projection. Weaker- or stronger-than-expected macroeconomic data could underpin a delay or acceleration in the normalization of policy interest rates in the United States, with a multitude of broader implications. In the case of a slower rise in interest rates, possible effects are higher volatility in financial markets and systemic instability risks stemming from excessive asset price levels. By contrast, a quicker tightening in monetary policy would result in higher credit spreads, accompanied by an increase in volatility as well as significant repercussions for global financial markets. This could imply significant international spillover effects, especially for emerging economies, in the form of a fall in market liquidity and an increase in bond yields.

The economic recovery in the euro area remains fragile

A further risk is the fragile economic situation in the euro area. While monetary policy measures have led to a significant improvement in the sovereign debt crisis, the economic recovery remains precariously weak. The underlying growth momentum has decelerated to the point where an exogenous event could return the region to recession. The current tensions regarding Ukraine and resulting sanctions have already had a serious negative impact on activity and confidence. The weak state of the recovery is characterized by continued low levels of private investment, extremely high unemployment in many countries—which becomes more entrenched as the ranks of the long-term unemployed increase—and by dangerously low inflation, which carries the risk of turning into deflation.

Emerging economies face a combination of domestic and external vulnerabilities

Many large emerging economies continue to face a challenging macroeconomic environment, as weaknesses in their domestic economies interact with external financial vulnerabilities. At present, the main risk for many emerging economies arises from the potential for negative feedback loops between weak activity in the real sector, reversals of capital inflows, and a tightening of domestic financial conditions amid an expected rise in interest rates in the United States. Although the baseline forecast projects a moderate growth recovery in 2015 and 2016 for almost all emerging economies, including Brazil, India, Indonesia, Mexico, the Russian Federation, South Africa and Turkey, and only a slight moderation in China, there are significant risks of a further slowdown or a prolonged period of weak growth. A broad-based downturn in emerging economies, particularly a sharp slowdown in China, would not only weigh on growth in smaller developing countries and economies in transition, but could also derail the fragile recovery in developed countries, particularly in the struggling euro area.

Geopolitical tensions constitute a major downside risk

Geopolitical tensions remain a major downside risk for the economic outlook. In addition to the severe human toll, the crises in Iraq, Libya, the Syrian Arab Republic and Ukraine have already had pronounced economic impacts at the national and subregional levels, although the global economic effect has so far been relatively limited. A major reason for the limited global impact is that any actual or feared conflict-related decline in oil supplies was offset by oil production increases. Nevertheless, subregional economic weakness caused by conflict and sanctions could lead to a more pronounced slowdown for the world economy. In addition to geopolitical tensions, crises scenarios such as the current Ebola outbreak also imply a major degree of uncertainty for individual countries and subregions.

Policy challenges

Monetary policy in the United States faces the challenge of achieving a smooth normalization

Monetary policy in the United States is charting its future path amid a host of challenges. The actual path of the policy interest rate will depend on a number of factors, especially the evolving macroeconomic picture regarding unemployment and inflation, as well as concerns about financial stability risks. At the same time, interest rates will be a major determinant, not just of the macroeconomic performance, but also the extent of financial stability risks and global spillovers. Policymakers must determine the optimal magnitude and timing of interest-rate changes while dealing with a difficult trade-off: to delay the policy tightening could create asset mispricing and financial stability risks; however, an unwarranted quick tightening could weaken the still unfledged recovery.

Developed countries confront a difficult fiscal policy trade-off

In the area of fiscal policy, developed countries find themselves in the difficult position of striking a balance between fiscal support for aggregate demand in the short run and ensuring fiscal sustainability in the long run. Many developing countries are facing the challenge of meeting the increasing demand for public finance for infrastructure, education and other services. Despite comparatively low public debt levels, developing countries also need to manage their external debt exposure, as refinancing external debt may prove to be costly in case of a sharp change in investor appetite towards emerging markets, a weakening of the exchange rate or higher levels of benchmark interest rates.

Coherent labour market policies are needed to address employment problems

Macroeconomic policies in many countries have been uncoordinated, creating only limited support for job creation. While expansionary monetary policies in developed economies may have averted otherwise larger falls in employment, the direct effects on employment growth are only limited. Monetary and fiscal policies should be combined with specific labour market policies. Policies should also be more amenable to the creation of businesses and jobs, for example, by streamlining administrative procedures. In many developing countries, in addition to greater economic diversification, continued efforts to expand formal employment and implement social protection programmes would also help in improving labour market conditions and supporting aggregate demand.

Strengthening international policy coordination and cooperation is imperative

In order to mitigate the myriad risks and meet the various challenges, it is imperative to strengthen international policy coordination and cooperation. In particular, macroeconomic policies worldwide should be aligned towards supporting robust and balanced growth, creating productive jobs, and maintaining economic and financial stability in the long run. Meanwhile, international policy coordination and cooperation is equally important for defusing geopolitical tensions and containing crises such as the Ebola pandemic. Other areas that make international and multilateral approaches indispensable include strengthening the resilience of the financial sector through further regulatory reforms, deepening cooperation on tax matters, reforming the governance of international financial institutions, expediting the WTO Doha Round negotiations, achieving concerted actions on combating climate change, delivering on the commitment of official development assistance to the least developed countries, and formulating and implementing a new post-2015 global development policy agenda, including the sustainable development goals.

Table of contents

Page

Boxes

Figures

Chapter I
Global economic outlook

Prospects for the world economy in 2015–2016

Global growth prospects

The global economy continued to expand during 2014 at a moderate and uneven pace, as the prolonged recovery process from the global financial crisis was still saddled with unfinished post-crisis adjustments. Global recovery was also hampered by some new challenges, including a number of unexpected shocks, such as the heightened geopolitical conflicts in various areas of the world. Growth of world gross product (WGP) is estimated to be 2.6 per cent in 2014, marginally better than the growth of 2.5 per cent registered in 2013, but lower than the 2.9 per cent projected in *World economic situation and prospects as of mid-2014*.[1] In the outlook period, premised on a set of assumptions (box I.1) and subject to a number of uncertainties and downside risks (see the section on uncertainties and risks), the global economy is expected to strengthen in the following two years, with WGP projected to grow by 3.1 and 3.3 per cent in 2015 and 2016, respectively (figure I.1 and table I.1).

Six years after the global financial crisis, gross domestic product (GDP) growth for a majority of the world economies has shifted to a noticeably lower path compared to pre-crisis levels. Excluding the three years from 2008–2010, which featured, respectively, the eruption of the financial crisis, the Great Recession and the policy-driven rebound,

Moderate global growth continues amid challenges and risks

Most economies have shifted to a lower growth path

Figure I.1
Growth of world gross product, 2008–2016ᵃ

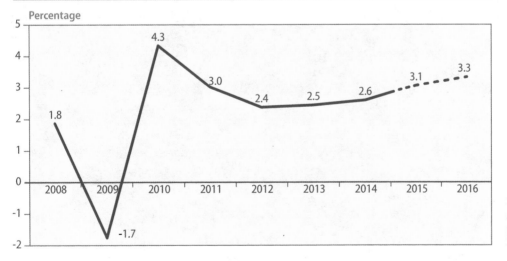

Source: UN/DESA.

a Growth rate for 2014 is partially estimated; rates for 2015 and 2016 are forecast.

---

1   United Nations, "World economic situation and prospects as of mid-2014 (E/2014/70)", available from http://www.un.org/en/development/desa/policy/publications/ecosoc/e_2014_70_wesp_mid.pdf.

Table I.1
Growth of world output, 2008–2016

Annual percentage change	2008-2011[a]	2012	2013[b]	2014[b]	2015[c]	2016[c]	Change from WESP 2014 forecast[d]	
							2014	2015
World	1.9	2.4	2.5	2.6	3.1	3.3	-0.4	-0.2
Developed economies	0.1	1.1	1.2	1.6	2.1	2.3	-0.3	-0.3
United States of America	0.2	2.3	2.2	2.3	2.8	3.1	-0.2	-0.4
Japan	-0.7	1.5	1.5	0.4	1.2	1.1	-1.1	0.0
European Union	-0.1	-0.4	0.0	1.3	1.7	2.0	-0.1	-0.2
EU-15	-0.2	-0.5	-0.1	1.2	1.5	1.9	-0.2	-0.3
New EU members	1.2	0.7	1.1	2.6	2.9	3.3	0.5	0.2
Euro area	-0.2	-0.8	-0.5	0.8	1.3	1.7	-0.3	-0.3
Other European countries	0.7	1.9	1.4	1.4	2.2	2.3	-1.2	-0.7
Other developed countries	1.5	2.6	2.2	2.6	2.6	2.6	0.0	-0.3
Economies in transition	1.9	3.3	2.0	0.8	1.1	2.1	-2.5	-2.9
South-Eastern Europe	1.6	-0.9	2.4	0.7	2.7	3.0	-1.9	-0.4
Commonwealth of Independent States and Georgia	1.9	3.5	2.0	0.8	1.1	2.1	-2.6	-2.9
Russian Federation	1.4	3.4	1.3	0.5	0.2	1.2	-2.4	-3.4
Developing economies	5.6	4.8	4.8	4.3	4.8	5.1	-0.8	-0.5
Africa	3.5	5.6	3.5	3.5	4.6	4.9	-1.2	-0.4
North Africa	1.8	6.6	1.4	1.6	3.9	4.3	-1.7	-0.4
East Africa	6.2	6.1	6.3	6.5	6.8	6.6	0.1	0.3
Central Africa	3.9	5.3	2.2	4.3	4.7	5.0	-0.4	0.7
West Africa	5.9	6.9	7.0	5.9	6.2	6.1	-1.0	-0.5
Nigeria	6.4	6.7	7.3	5.8	6.1	5.9	-1.1	-0.6
Southern Africa	3.3	3.4	3.0	2.9	3.6	4.1	-1.2	-0.8
South Africa	2.2	2.5	1.9	2.0	2.7	3.3	-1.3	-1.0
East and South Asia	7.2	5.6	5.9	5.9	6.0	6.0	0.0	0.0
East Asia	7.4	6.3	6.4	6.1	6.1	6.0	-0.1	0.0
China	9.6	7.7	7.7	7.3	7.0	6.8	-0.2	-0.3
South Asia	6.2	2.9	4.1	4.9	5.4	5.7	0.3	0.2
India	7.3	4.7	5.0	5.4	5.9	6.3	0.1	0.2
Western Asia	4.3	4.5	4.0	2.9	3.7	4.3	-1.4	-0.2
Latin America and the Caribbean	3.2	2.7	2.6	1.3	2.4	3.1	-2.3	-1.9
South America	3.8	2.2	2.8	0.7	1.9	2.8	-2.7	-2.2
Brazil	3.7	1.0	2.3	0.3	1.5	2.4	-2.7	-2.7
Mexico and Central America	1.6	4.2	1.8	2.6	3.5	3.8	-1.4	-1.2
Mexico	1.4	4.0	1.4	2.4	3.4	3.8	-1.6	-1.4
Caribbean	2.5	2.8	3.0	3.8	3.8	3.8	0.5	0.0
By level of development								
High-income countries	0.4	1.4	1.4	1.7	2.2	2.4	-0.4	-0.3
Upper-middle-income countries	5.7	4.9	4.9	4.3	4.8	5.2	-1.0	-0.6
Lower-middle-income countries	5.6	4.8	5.2	4.6	5.3	5.7	-0.4	-0.2
Low-income countries	5.7	4.9	4.9	4.4	4.9	5.3	-1.7	-1.2
Least developed countries	5.6	5.0	5.3	5.3	5.7	5.9	-0.3	0.1
Memorandum items								
World trade[e]	2.5	2.5	3.0	3.4	4.5	4.9	-1.3	-0.7
World output growth with PPP-based weights	2.7	2.9	3.0	3.1	3.5	3.8	-0.5	-0.5

Source: UN/DESA.

a Average percentage change.

b Actual or most recent estimates.

c Forecast, based in part on Project LINK and baseline projections of the UN/DESA World Economic Forecasting Model.

d See United Nations *World Economic Situation and Prospects 2014*.

e Average of exports and imports of goods and services.

Box I.1
Major assumptions for the baseline forecast

This box summarizes key assumptions underlying the baseline forecast for various important factors, including monetary and fiscal policies for major economies, exchange rates for major currencies, international prices of oil and other primary commodities. Policy assumptions for other countries can be found in the text of the regional outlook.

Monetary policy

The Federal Reserve of the United States (Fed) is assumed to gradually normalize the stance of monetary policy during 2015–2016, from the extremely accommodative "anti-crisis" mode to a more neutral position. It is assumed that the federal funds interest rate will remain within the range of 0.00 to 0.25 per cent until mid-2015. The Fed will then start to raise interest rates gradually in the third quarter of 2015 with the federal funds interest rate reaching 2.75 per cent by the end of 2016. It is also assumed that the Fed will maintain the assets acquired under the past quantitative easing policy on its balance sheet by reinvesting the matured principle through the end of 2015. After that point, the Fed will reduce the size of its balance sheet by letting the assets mature.

The European Central Bank (ECB) is assumed to keep its policy interest rates at their current levels through mid-2016, followed by a series of gradual increases. The ECB is expected to extend its existing programme of providing unlimited short-term liquidity via its main refinancing operations until at least 2016. It is also following through by implementing three new programmes: the targeted longer-term refinancing operations and the asset-backed securities and covered bond purchase programmes. In total, these three programmes are expected to add close to one trillion euro to the ECB balance sheet so that it would return to the level prevailing in 2012, about three trillion euro.

The Bank of Japan (BoJ) is assumed to continue its Quantitative and Qualitative Monetary Easing programme until April 2016, although the strength of the programme may be reduced gradually. The policy rate of the BoJ is also assumed to stay within the range of 0.0 to 0.1 per cent until the end of 2016.

The People's Bank of China is expected to maintain its current monetary policy approach, which largely relies on short-term quantitative measures and targeted adjustments of liquidity. Overall, monetary conditions are expected to be neutral in 2015–2016.

Fiscal policy

Fiscal policy in the United States of America is expected to remain restrictive, but less severe than in 2014. Real federal government spending is forecast to decline by less than 1 per cent in 2015–2016. It is also assumed that the debt ceiling will be increased during the forecasting period.

In the euro area, fiscal policy in the majority of economies will continue to focus on reducing fiscal imbalances, but the degree of consolidation will be less onerous than in the past few years. The debt crisis countries will continue their adjustment programmes, and any shortfalls due to growth underruns will not be made up; rather, the timetable for achieving targets will be extended. It is also assumed that no countries will ask for formal assistance under the European Stability Mechanism.

In Japan, the focus continues to be on improving the budget situation. The original plan was to implement the second part of the consumption tax increase—raising the tax rate from 8 to 10 per cent— in October 2015, but the Government announced in November 2014 that it will postpone the tax increase for 18 months.

China is expected to maintain its current fiscal policy stance, which is based on robust expenditure growth and targeted easing measures to offset weaknesses. Accounting for recently adopted tightening measures on extrabudgetary activities, the overall fiscal policy stance has become more restrictive than the official budget figures suggest.

Exchange rates among major currencies

The dollar/euro exchange rate is assumed to average 1.34 in 2014 and to continue to depreciate, averaging 1.25 in 2015 and 1.21 in 2016.

The yen/dollar exchange rate is assumed to average 104.1 in 2014 and then 107.5 in 2015 and 105.5 in 2016.

The renminbi/dollar exchange rate is assumed to be 6.15 CNY/dollar in 2014 and 6.10 in 2015 and 6.05 in 2016.

Oil price

The Brent oil price is expected to average $102 per barrel (pb) in 2014. In 2015 and 2016, it is assumed to be $92 pb and $96 pb, respectively.

Source: UN/DESA.

four fifths of the world economies have seen lower average growth in 2011–2014 than in 2004–2007 (figure I.2). At issue is whether such a shift to a lower path of growth in most countries will become entrenched for a long period. According to some pessimistic views, major developed economies are highly likely to be entrapped in secular stagnation (see also box IV.1 in chapter 4), while policymakers in China have indeed taken growth of 7.0–7.5 per cent as the new normal for the Chinese economy, compared with the average growth of 10 per cent that China achieved in the previous three decades. Many other large emerging economies, particularly those outside of Asia, have also seen a much slower growth trajectory in recent years as domestic weaknesses interact with challenging international conditions.

Quarterly growth rates of developed countries have been volatile

A salient feature for major developed countries during 2014 has been the erratic movements in their quarterly GDP growth rates. For example, the economy of the United States of America oscillated from a decline of 2.1 per cent in the first quarter of 2014 to an increase of 4.6 per cent in the second quarter, while at the same time the economy of Japan swung from growth of 6.7 per cent to a contraction by 7.3 per cent. For the year as a whole, all major developed economies in North America, Europe and developed Asia have indeed aligned on an upward growth trajectory for the first time since 2011. Although the discrepancy in the growth rates of these economies has narrowed from the previous year (figure I.3), the growth picture remains diverse: while the United States has managed to

Figure I.2
Growth performance: pre-crisis (2004–2007) vs. post-crisis (2011–2014)

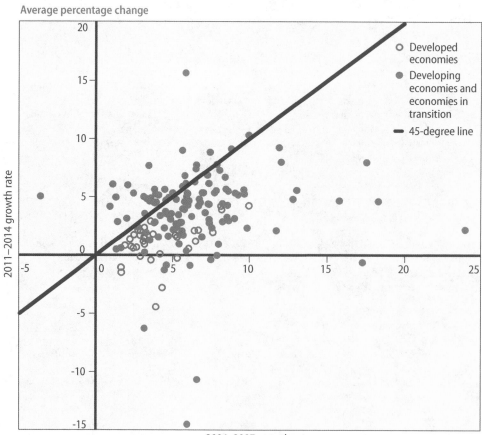

Source: UN/DESA.

maintain an annual growth rate above 2 per cent in 2014, the economic situation in Europe is precarious, particularly in the euro area, where growth is exceptionally weak, with some countries close to or already in recession. Meanwhile, in Japan, momentum generated by the fiscal stimulus package and monetary easing introduced in 2013 has receded. In the baseline outlook, further improvement is expected for developed countries, with growth projected to be 2.1 and 2.3 per cent for 2015 and 2016, respectively, compared with the 1.6 per cent estimated for 2014. However, downside risks remain significant, especially in the euro area and Japan, which have seen renewed weakness in 2014.

Growth rates in developing countries and economies in transition have become more divergent during 2014 (figure I.4), as a sharp deceleration occurred in a number of large emerging economies, particularly in Latin America and the Commonwealth of Independent States (CIS). A number of these economies have encountered various country-specific challenges, including structural imbalances, infrastructural bottlenecks, increased financial risks and ineffective macroeconomic management, as well as geopolitical and political tensions. In contrast, East Asia, including China, managed to register relatively robust growth, while India led South Asia to a moderate strengthening. In the baseline outlook, developing countries as a group are expected to grow at 4.8 and 5.1 per cent in 2015 and 2016, respectively, up from the 4.3 per cent estimated for 2014. Growth in the least developed countries (LDCs) is expected to continue exceeding the global average, at 5.7 per cent in 2015 and 5.9 per cent in 2016 (box I.2). The economies in transition as a group are expected to grow at 1.1 per cent and 2.1 per cent in 2015 and 2016, respectively, up from the 0.8 per cent estimated for 2014. As in the case of developed economies, the risks to this baseline outlook are mainly on the downside. Many developing countries and economies in transition appear vulnerable to a tightening of global financial conditions and to the risk of a sharper-than-expected slowdown in major emerging economies, as well as a further aggravation of geopolitical tensions and an escalation of the Ebola epidemic.

Developing countries and economies in transition have seen more divergent growth

Among the developed economies, the economy of the United States, after some erratic fluctuation in 2014, is expected to improve in 2015 and 2016, with GDP projected to expand by 2.8 and 3.1 per cent respectively, compared with an estimate of 2.3 per cent for 2014. While an increase in business investment will be the major driver, household consumption is also expected to strengthen, along with continued improvement in employment. The fiscal drag on growth is expected to remain, but with much milder intensity than in previous years. The policy interest rates are set to rise gradually after mid-2015, but the monetary policy stance will continue to be accommodative. The contribution from the external sector will be limited, as export growth is expected to be curbed by the strong appreciation of the dollar. The risks for the economy are mainly associated with the possibility of sizeable volatility in financial markets in response to the normalization of monetary policy, leading to adverse effects on the real economy.

The United States will see stronger growth

Western Europe continues to struggle. In the EU-15,[2] GDP growth is estimated to be only 1.2 per cent in 2014, with a slight pickup to 1.5 per cent and 1.9 per cent in 2015 and 2016, respectively. The region is held back by the travails of the euro area, where the level

A slight improvement in growth is expected in Western Europe

---

2   The EU-15 refers to the 15 countries that were members of the European Union (EU) prior to the accession of the new member States on 1 May 2004: Austria, Belgium, Denmark, Finland, France, Germany, Greece, Ireland, Italy, Luxembourg, the Netherlands, Portugal, Spain, Sweden, and the United Kingdom of Great Britain and Northern Ireland.

Figure I.3
Distribution of growth rates for developed economies

Source: UN/DESA.
Note: The boxplots show the
distribution of GDP growth rates
among developed countries
between the first and third
quartiles, that is within the
middle 50 per cent of the data.
The wider a box, the more
divergent are the growth rates.
The horizontal line in the box
represents the median, the
symbol indicates the mean. The
shading indicates a confidence
interval at 95 percent for
the median.

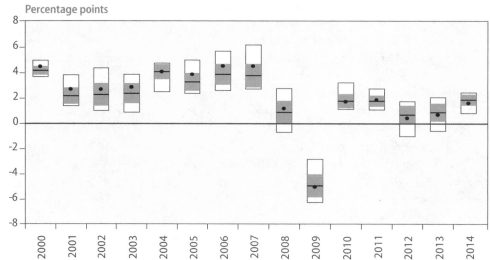

Figure I.4
Distribution of growth rates for developing economies

Source: UN/DESA.
Note: The boxplots show the
distribution of GDP growth rates
among developing countries
between the first and third
quartiles, that is within the
middle 50 per cent of the data.
The wider a box, the more
divergent are the growth rates.
The horizontal line in the box
represents the median, the
symbol indicates the mean. The
shading indicates a confidence
interval at 95 percent for
the median.

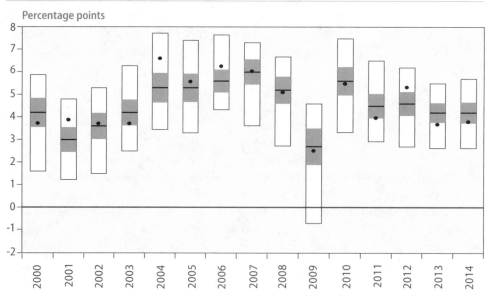

of GDP has yet to regain its pre-recession peak. Unemployment remains extremely high in many countries in the region and headline inflation is at alarmingly low levels. In the large economies, Italy is expected to contract for the third consecutive year and France has stagnated, while Germany started the year strongly, but has since slowed significantly. There is a ray of hope in that some of the crisis countries have resumed growth. Spain resumed positive growth in mid-2013 and has been strengthening since; Ireland and Portugal have

Box I.2
Prospects for the least developed countries

Growth in the economies of the least developed countries (LDCs) will continue to exceed the global average, with an expected acceleration from 5.3 per cent in 2014 to 5.7 per cent in 2015 and 5.9 per cent in 2016. Major drivers for this performance will be an anticipated improving external environment, which helps underpin growth through trade and financial flows; continued strong investment in infrastructure and natural resource projects; and, in some cases, the reconstruction after conflicts or natural disasters. Despite this positive headline performance, meaningful economic and social development remains a challenge for many LDCs, given a number of factors including: the often low starting point for growth; institutional shortfalls; the exposure to numerous risks, including public health crises such as the recent Ebola epidemic, or adverse weather patterns; and the lack of basic services and infrastructure despite, in some cases, significant public financial resources from commodity exports.

Within a wide range of performances, the highest growth rate among LDCs in 2015 is forecast for the Democratic Republic of the Congo. Major factors are a mining sector that is strengthening from investment in new capacities, infrastructure investment, and higher agricultural output due in part to better access to inputs. Similar dynamics are also playing out in other LDC forecasts for 2015. For example, in Ethiopia, the agricultural sector will underpin growth by 7.5 per cent, while in the United Republic of Tanzania, natural resource investment, notably in the gas sector, will lead to an economic expansion by 7.2 per cent. In Bangladesh, the economy will continue its multi-year streak of solid growth of more than 6 per cent in 2015 and 2016, driven by strong external demand for textile products and robust domestic demand.

By contrast, numerous LDCs face particularly pronounced growth challenges. The Ebola crisis (see box IV.3 in chapter IV) has taken a severe humanitarian toll in Guinea, Liberia and Sierra Leone and created a significant drag on economic growth. Even in the absence of an exceptional crisis, all three countries feature weak and strained public health systems, creating high vulnerability to crisis scenarios. Meanwhile, Equatorial Guinea will register a contraction of its economy by 1.6 per cent in 2015, which will mark the third consecutive year of declining gross domestic product (GDP). Falling oil output combined with lower oil prices is crimping other sectors of the economy, such as construction, with the lack of any positive offsetting factors, thus highlighting the vagaries of an overreliance on the natural resource sector. In Yemen, growth of GDP is estimated to have decreased by more than half to 2.1 per cent in 2014, with a moderate acceleration in growth to 3.7 per cent expected in 2015. Political instability has led to disruptions in oil output, reducing oil revenues by about one third in the first half of 2014. The non-oil sector has performed better, but still below potential, owing to the general instability.

Taken together, despite the overall solid headline growth picture for LDCs, the underlying situation and performance of many LDCs underscore numerous pressing problems and the need to reinforce effective policy measures in this regard. First, countries with strong reliance on resource-extracting industries need to further strengthen their efforts to diversify their economic structure and thus reduce their vulnerability to external shocks. This is especially relevant in the context of the decline in oil prices as well as the price of various other commodities. Effective policies in this respect, both in terms of funding and expertise, include the promotion of higher-value-added activities, the support of small and medium-sized enterprises and investment in better education programmes. Second, as illustrated by the Ebola outbreak, any meaningful and lasting development progress requires as a foundation the sufficient and stable provision of basic public services. This includes, first and foremost, not only a functioning health-care system, but also sufficient energy supply and viable transportation linkages. Last, the international community should redouble its efforts to deliver on the commitment of financial and other types of assistance to the LDCs.

Source: UN/DESA.

also returned to positive growth, but all three recoveries remain extremely fragile. The only example of more robust growth is outside the euro area in the United Kingdom of Great Britain and Northern Ireland.

The recovery in the new European Union (EU) member States gained further ground in 2014, thanks to recovering domestic demand, the gradual abandonment of fiscal austerity and a turnaround in the inventory cycle. While the region is confronted with a difficult

Domestic demand will increasingly drive growth in the new EU member States

external environment as prospects for the core euro area countries are downgraded, domestic demand is becoming an increasingly important driver of growth. Although household foreign-exchange-denominated debt still remains a major macroeconomic problem in some of the new EU members, private consumption is expected to strengthen in the outlook period and investment is benefiting from the expansion in public sector projects. Inflation in the region hit record lows in 2014, thanks to lower food and energy prices; it is estimated to have been negative in a number of countries and is expected to remain very low in 2015. Labour markets continued to improve, although progress was very uneven across the countries. In those with flexible currencies, interest rates were reduced to record lows and in 2015, monetary policy should remain accommodative. However, as deleveraging by foreign banks continues (although at a diminishing rate), the recovery in credit markets lags. The aggregate GDP of the new EU member States is expected to grow by 2.9 per cent in 2015 and 3.3 per cent in 2016, compared with an estimate of 2.6 per cent in 2014.

Private consumption constrained by higher taxes will weigh on Japan's growth

Japan is estimated to grow by only 0.4 per cent in 2014, technically falling into a recession in the second and third quarters. The drop in private consumption caused by the higher consumption tax is the main reason for the slowdown. Quantitative easing introduced in 2013 has predictably raised inflation expectations and the central bank further strengthened this policy in late-2014. Exports are expected to eventually benefit from the depreciation of the Japanese yen triggered by the monetary easing, while the planned cut in corporate taxes will support fixed investment. The growth rate is predicted to be 1.2 per cent in 2015 and 1.1 per cent in 2016.

Regarding other developed countries, GDP in Canada is estimated to register growth of 2.3 per cent in 2014 and is projected to grow by 2.6 per cent and 2.8 per cent in 2015 and 2016, respectively. Exports will likely expand at a robust pace and support growth. However, household indebtedness remains a concern and improvement in the labour market has been slow. GDP in Australia is estimated to grow by 3.0 per cent in 2014, before receding to 2.4 per cent and 2.3 per cent in 2015 and 2016, respectively. Exports and fixed investment in large natural resource projects will provide support for continued growth, while the slow improvement in the labour market will be a limiting factor. New Zealand became the first developed country to tighten its monetary policy stance after the Great Recession. GDP is estimated to grow by 3.0 per cent in 2014 and 3.3 per cent in 2015, with the solid expansion of investment in fixed structures as an important contributor.

Africa's growth will be driven by private consumption and investment

Among the developing countries, Africa's overall growth momentum is set to continue, with GDP growth expected to accelerate from 3.5 per cent in 2014 to 4.6 per cent in 2015 and 4.9 per cent in 2016. Growth in private consumption and investment are expected to remain the key drivers of GDP growth across all five subregions and all economic groupings. Net exports will continue to moderately pull down growth. Inflation in Africa will remain flat, at an average of 6.9 in 2015, in the light of moderating global prices for commodities, food, oil and industrial imports as well as prudent monetary policies. Fiscal balances will remain negative, owing to infrastructure spending, public wage bills and social sector projects. A number of internal and external risks remain, such as a continued slow recovery in the developed countries, a slowdown in China, tighter global financial conditions, the Ebola outbreak, political instability, terrorism and weather-related shocks.

East Asia will remain the fastest-growing region

East Asia remains the world's fastest-growing region, with GDP growth estimated at 6.1 per cent in 2014. In the outlook period, the region is projected to see stable growth of 6.1 per cent in 2015 and 6.0 per cent in 2016. China's transition to more moderate growth is expected to be partly offset by higher growth in other economies, where investment and exports will likely strengthen as activity in developed countries improves. Household consumption is expected to remain strong in most economies, supported by mild inflation, robust labour markets and generally low real interest rates, even as monetary conditions will likely become less accommodative, in line with the normalization of monetary policy in the United States. Fiscal policy is expected to remain mildly supportive of growth and most countries have sufficient space to provide additional stimulus, if necessary. The key downside risks for East Asia are related to the upcoming tightening of global liquidity conditions, which could result in weaker growth of domestic consumption and investment, and to a sharper-than-expected slowdown of the Chinese economy.

Economic growth in South Asia is set to gradually pick up from an estimated 4.9 per cent in 2014 to 5.4 per cent in 2015 and 5.7 per cent in 2016. While the recovery will be led by India, which accounts for about 70 per cent of regional output, other economies such as Bangladesh and the Islamic Republic of Iran are also projected to see stronger growth in the forecast period. Along with robust external demand, growth is expected to be underpinned by a moderate strengthening of domestic consumption and investment as countries benefit from improved macroeconomic conditions. With international oil prices declining, inflation has further eased across the region. If this trend continues, some central banks may have room to ease monetary policy. At the same time, several countries, notably India, are likely to make progress in implementing economic policy reforms, thus providing support to business and consumer confidence. There are, however, significant downside risks for the region due to the continuing fragility of the global economy and considerable country-specific weaknesses, including political instability and the agricultural dependency on the monsoon.

Stronger domestic demand will underpin growth in South Asia

Lower oil prices and armed conflicts in Iraq, Gaza and the Syrian Arab Republic hampered economic growth in Western Asia throughout 2014. The external environment was also not conducive to growth for non-oil exporting countries, given the relatively subdued economic growth in many developed economies. On the domestic front, the Cooperation Council for the Arab States of the Gulf (GCC) partially offset weaker external demand for oil by increasing fiscal spending, whereas other countries, such as Turkey, had to implement restrictive policies, either to limit their fiscal deficit or to avoid further depreciation of the national currency and inflation pressures. As a result, GDP growth has slowed to 2.9 per cent in 2014 from 4.0 per cent in 2013. During the forecast period, the aggregate economic situation is expected to pick up, although with only relatively modest GDP growth compared to previous years. Domestic demand will remain strong in GCC members, stimulated by ongoing public investment in infrastructure. Turkey will benefit from stronger external demand, provided that the depreciation of the national currency will continue to help the export sector, with GDP projected to grow by 3.7 per cent in 2015 and 4.3 per cent in 2016. The downside risks notably include any possible further fallout from the conflicts in Iraq and the Syrian Arab Republic. Moreover, should the Brent oil price come down to a level below $70 per barrel, it would hurt business confidence significantly in GCC countries.

Economic growth in Western Asia will moderately increase, with serious downside risks

Economic growth in Latin America and the Caribbean is projected to moderately improve from a meagre 1.3 per cent in 2014 to 2.4 per cent in 2015 and 3.1 per cent in 2016, albeit to varying degrees across countries and with significant risks to the downside. Investment demand is estimated to recover from the current sharp slowdown, as large public investment projects are expected to be implemented in countries such as Brazil, Chile and Mexico. Accommodative monetary policy is also expected to support economic activity in

Latin America and the Caribbean will see an uptick in growth

some countries. On the external front, a sustained recovery in the United States will continue to benefit the economies of Mexico and Central America through the trade, tourism and remittances channels. The downside risks are related to a larger-than-expected growth decline in China, further reductions in commodity prices and the potential financial spillovers from the normalization of the monetary policy stance in the United States.

Among the economies in transition, growth in the CIS slowed down sharply in 2014. The geopolitical tensions in the region resulted in a difficult external environment with high levels of uncertainty. Economic activity in the Russian Federation came to a standstill, which also lowered growth prospects for other economies in the region. In Ukraine, a severe output contraction followed years of sluggish expansion. Smaller CIS economies were affected by a contraction in the inflow of remittances. The prospects for 2015 are weak: near-zero growth is expected in the Russian Federation as the high cost of capital will deter private investment, and the possibility of deeper recession exists in Ukraine. However, some of the Central Asian energy exporters will continue to see strong growth. Inflation in the CIS accelerated in 2014, as currency depreciations created price pressures in many countries, including in the Russian Federation. Despite the slowdown in economic activity, the unemployment rate in the Russian Federation reached historical lows during the year. By contrast, labour market conditions worsened in Ukraine and in lower-income Central Asian countries. The aggregate GDP growth of the CIS and Georgia is expected to strengthen only modestly to 1.1 per cent in 2015 and 2.1 per cent in 2016, compared with the estimate of 0.8 per cent for 2014.

After returning to growth in 2013, overall economic activity in South-Eastern Europe slowed down in 2014, as significant floods in May caused severe damage in Bosnia and Herzegovina and Serbia. As a result, the economy of Serbia contracted in 2014. Economic performance in the rest of the region modestly improved. External demand remained the main driver of growth in early 2014. After contracting for two years, domestic demand also modestly recovered, with the notable exception of Serbia. Infrastructure, tourism and energy projects have supported economic expansion in the region. Growth is expected to pick up in 2015, boosted by reconstruction work in flood-affected areas and planned infrastructure projects, although high unemployment, ongoing fiscal adjustments and elevated indebtedness will constrain the speed of economic expansion. The aggregate GDP of South-Eastern Europe is expected to grow by 2.7 per cent and 3.0 per cent in 2015 and 2016, respectively, compared with the estimate of 0.7 per cent in 2014.

Employment trends

The global employment situation remains a key policy challenge, as GDP growth continued to be modest and below potential in many parts of the world. Globally, employment is estimated to have grown by 1.4 per cent in 2014, similar to the pace in 2013, but still lower than the 1.7 per cent rate in pre-crisis years. As a result, unemployment figures remain historically high in some regions, even though they appear to have stopped rising. The overall labour market situation is, however, more complex and challenging if a wider range of indicators are taken into consideration, such as labour force participation, long-term unemployment, wage levels (box I.3), involuntary part-time work and informality.

In developed economies, the job recovery has been insufficient to recuperate the losses from the financial crisis. The employment rate (employment-to-population ratio) declined significantly after the financial crisis in developed economies and remains below the pre-crisis level, with the exception of Japan.

The overall decline in employment rates since the beginning of the financial crisis is explained by weak labour demand, but also by structural factors and lower labour force participation. A case in point is the United States, where the labour force participation rate is near its lowest level in the past 10 years due to population ageing, an increase in skills upgrading and a higher number of discouraged workers.

Employment has been improving slowly in developed economies, although significant challenges remain. While the unemployment rate in the United States has decreased to below 6 per cent, the unemployment rate in the euro area remains elevated, with several economies in the euro area featuring extremely high unemployment. In addition, youth unemployment rates remain high in several European countries, with 53 per cent in Spain, 44 per cent in Italy and 35 per cent in Portugal, for example.

During the Great Recession, the duration of unemployment has been abnormally prolonged in many developed and developing economies (figure I.5), bringing long-term unemployment rates to record highs, including among youth. In the Organization for Economic Cooperation and Development (OECD) countries as a whole in the last quarter of 2013, one third of unemployed individuals had been out of work for 12 months or more. This equals 16.7 million people, or twice as many as before the financial crisis. Even in countries where unemployment rates have improved or remain low, long-term unemployment remains persistently high. For instance, in the second quarter of 2014 in the United States, the share of long-term unemployed in total unemployment was 23.6 per cent, still more than double the figure prior to the financial crisis; in the euro area, the share of long-term unemployed reached as high as 62 per cent in Italy and Ireland.

Long-term unemployment has become a more severe problem

In developing countries and economies in transition, the employment situation has not improved considerably either, with economic expansion decelerating in many economies. However, there have been noticeable improvements in some countries since the beginning of the financial crisis, including in some larger emerging economies. For example, Argentina, Brazil, Indonesia, the Russian Federation, Saudi Arabia and Turkey have recorded higher employment rates in 2014 than in 2007.

Employment growth slowed in developing countries and economies in transition

Despite slower employment growth, the unemployment rates have remained relatively stable since 2013, partially owing to a level of labour force growth in East Asia, South Asia and Latin America and the Caribbean that is lower than pre-crisis levels. In general, slower labour force growth can be attributed to ageing of the economically active population and to more young people enrolling in longer educational programmes. The highest unemployment rates of 2013 continue to be in North Africa and Western Asia, which registered 12.2 per cent and 10.9 per cent, respectively. In both cases, the unemployment rates remain higher than pre-crisis rates, and they are not expected to improve during the forecast period owing to extremely high structural unemployment, particularly among youth, and several armed conflicts that will require longer-term solutions.

Conversely, reported unemployment rates remained low across much of East Asia and South Asia in 2013, at 4.5 per cent and 4.0 per cent, respectively. Nevertheless, the unemployment rate in East Asia has been rising since the onset of the financial crisis, from 3.8 per cent in 2007, while the employment rate remains below the pre-crisis level, confirming relatively slow employment growth.

In the CIS and South-Eastern Europe, unemployment rates remain relatively high in general, with an average of about 8.2 per cent in 2013 and alarmingly high unemploy-

Box I.3

Wages remain weak in Organization for Economic Cooperation and Development countries

In addition to slower employment growth and higher unemployment rates, wages and earnings were also significantly affected by the financial crisis. During the period 2010–2013, the annualized real wage growth was about -0.1 per cent in the euro area, about 0.2 per cent in the United States of America and -0.1 per cent in Japan. When unemployment increases, wages and earnings normally decrease, and these adjustments in the labour market could eventually restore demand for labour and reduce unemployment. However, during the Great Recession, hourly wage adjustments were much more severe than in previous crises. Real wages have fallen faster for every percentage point of increase in unemployment than in the past, exacerbating social distress, depressing aggregate demand and curbing economic recovery and employment growth. In addition, wage growth has also been slow during the recovery period, particularly in the United States, prolonging the economic burden on lower-income workers.

According to an Organization for Economic Cooperation and Development (OECD) study for European economies,[a] in the absence of a minimum wage, income of newly hired workers fell about 3 per cent for every percentage point of increase in the unemployment rate. As wages are the main source of income for the majority of households, many face the challenge of poverty—especially low-skilled workers, whose real wage growth declined more dramatically than others. In the United States, for instance, the share of working poor in the overall working population increased from about 5 per cent in 2007 to about 7 per cent in 2012.

The fall in wages is not only a cyclical issue, but a long-term trend aggravated by the financial crisis. The gap between wage growth and productivity growth has widened. Real wages, which had been flat for a decade in many developed economies, decreased in the aftermath of the financial crisis, leading to an increase in the number of working poor and higher levels of income inequality.

Some evidence in the OECD study shows that introducing or increasing minimum wages are effective measures to curb working poverty and income inequality, while supporting aggregate demand. Such initiatives may also help to increase labour force participation. The main challenge, however, is to set the minimum wage at a proper level so that it does not reduce employment opportunities for those unemployed.

a Organization for Economic Cooperation and Development, *OECD Employment Outlook 2014*, Paris.
Source: UN/DESA.

Figure I.5

Share of long-term unemployed within the total unemployed population in major economies

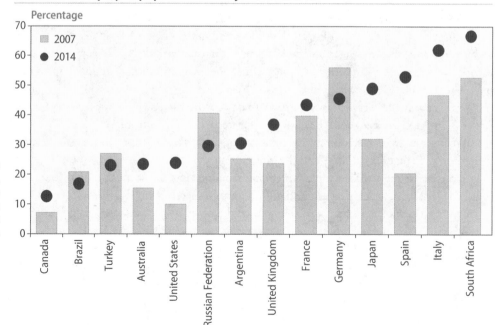

Source: OECD and ILO databases.
Note: Long-term unemployment refers to persons unemployed for one year or longer.

ment rates in most of South-Eastern Europe. Nevertheless, the unemployment rate was at historical lows in the Russian Federation, at 5.1 per cent in the first quarter of 2014, 0.2 percentage points lower than the previous year.

In many developing countries, the unemployment rate is, however, only a limited indicator to assess labour market conditions, given the high prevalence of informal and vulnerable employment. According to International Labour Organization (ILO) estimations, informal employment is widespread in Africa, Asia and Latin America and the Caribbean, with a cross-country average between 40 and 50 per cent. But significantly higher informality rates can be found in many economies, particularly in South and South-East Asia, reaching in some cases as high as 90 per cent of total employment. In India, for instance, despite some progress in reducing the share of workers in the informal sector, they still represented 82.2 per cent of the labour force in 2011–2012. In addition to informality, gender gaps in earnings and the employment rate are still widespread in many parts of the developing world, especially where informality is more pronounced. For instance, the participation rate of women in the labour force is below 40 per cent in almost all countries in South Asia, whereas for men, it tends to be about 75 per cent.

Inflation outlook

Global inflation remains tame, although inflation rates are still elevated in about a dozen developing countries and economies in transition, and some developed economies in the euro area are facing the risk of deflation. For the outlook period, global average inflation is projected to stay close to the level observed in the past two years, which was about 3 per cent. However, the trends at the subregional level vary. While average inflation for developed economies is estimated to have increased from 1.3 per cent in 2013 to 1.5 per cent in 2014 (mainly owing to the higher inflation in Japan), inflation in the EU is estimated to have decreased from 1.5 per cent in 2013 to 0.7 per cent in 2014 because of the sizeable output gap, the weakness of the recovery, and the strength of regional currencies until mid-2014. A fall into deflation is considered a downside risk for several euro area countries; if persistent, deflation may lead to greater reluctance by households and businesses to increase their current spending, thus weakening aggregate demand.

The average inflation rate for the economies in transition is estimated to have increased by 1.8 percentage points in 2014, with the increase in average inflation in the CIS countries more than offsetting the 3 percentage-point drop in inflation in the South-Eastern European countries. The significant depreciation of currencies for many CIS members played an important role in the acceleration of inflation in 2014. Regional inflation is predicted to be 8.1 per cent in 2014, but will decline to 7.4 per cent and 5.7 per cent in 2015 and 2016, respectively.

Average inflation for developing economies will fall slowly over the outlook period. In Africa, inflation will decline to 6.8 per cent in 2016, owing to increasingly prudent monetary policies as well as moderating import prices. While inflation for East Asia will stay near the recent levels of 2–3 per cent over the outlook period, a pronounced decrease is forecast for South Asia due to falling inflation in almost all countries, especially in India and the Islamic Republic of Iran. Regional average inflation for South Asia is projected to decrease gradually from 14.7 per cent in 2013 to 7.2 per cent in 2016. In Western Asia, inflationary pressures have been well contained, with the exception of the Syrian Arab Republic, Turkey

While global inflation remains subdued, the spectrum ranges from deflation risks in the euro area to high inflation in some developing countries

and Yemen. Those three countries are expected to face close to or higher than 10 per cent inflation over the outlook period and push the regional inflation rate from 4.4 per cent in 2013 up to 5.3 per cent in 2016. In Latin America and the Caribbean, aggregate regional inflation has increased in 2014, driven by Argentina and Venezuela (Bolivarian Republic of), but it is expected to recede moderately to 8.8 per cent in 2015.

Trends in international trade and finance[3]

International prices of primary commodities

Primary commodity prices will remain subdued

International prices of primary commodities have been on a downward trend in the past two years, and no measurable upturn is projected for 2015–2016.

The Brent oil price is projected to decline in 2015–2016 from the average price in 2014, as the gap between demand growth and supply growth is expected to continue. Oil demand growth has been slowing down throughout 2014, following sluggish economic growth in key economies, including Western Europe and Japan. In addition, weaker-than-expected GDP growth in China has also weighed on weaker demand, particularly during the second quarter of 2014. As a result, growth in oil demand was at its lowest level in more than two years. In 2015–2016, increasing demand in the United States is expected to partially offset the weaker demand from other developed economies. However, global demand growth for crude oil should continue at a moderate pace.

Non-oil commodity markets strengthened slightly during the first quarter of 2014, led by a surge in food prices, but eased thereafter. The Non-oil Nominal Commodity Price Index of UNCTAD[4] increased from 245 points in January to 252 points in March 2014 and decreased afterwards by 3 per cent to reach 244 points in August. The average value of the index over the period of January–August was about 6 per cent lower than a year ago, but remains high relative to its long-term trend of the past decades. Compared to 2013, major commodity groups registered an overall decline in their prices, with the exception of tropical beverages, which increased.

International trade flows

Trade growth will increase moderately

Slow and uneven recovery in major developed countries and moderated growth in developing countries have led to sluggish trade growth in the past few years. World trade is estimated to have expanded by 3.4 per cent in 2014, still well below pre-crisis trends. In the forecast period, trade growth is expected to pick up moderately along with improvement in global output, rising to 4.5 per cent in 2015 and 4.9 per cent in 2016.

Developed countries are expected to see some improvement in trade growth, with export growth rising from 3.5 per cent in 2014 to 4.4 per cent in 2015. Import growth will also progress at a similar rate. Further improvement is expected in 2016. In the United States, export growth has been strong in 2014, but will be restrained by the appreciation of the dollar in 2015 and 2016. Further stabilization in Western Europe will boost export

---

3   See also chapter II on international trade and chapter III on international finance.

4   The UNCTAD Non-oil Nominal Commodity Price Index covers these subgroups of commodities: food, tropical beverages, vegetable oilseeds and oils, agricultural raw materials, and minerals, ores and metals.

growth somewhat, although the deprecation of the euro may limit import growth in the euro area. Japan's exports are expected to grow moderately, partly owing to a weaker yen.

Exports of the CIS have been heavily affected by geopolitical tensions in the region and the global oil market. Export volumes for the region are estimated to register close to zero growth for 2014 and are expected to rise only moderately over the forecast period. Import growth will fare worse, falling by 3.4 per cent in 2014 and rising only slightly over the forecast period.

Growth of exports in developing countries is expected to increase from 3.9 per cent in 2014 to 4.6 per cent in 2015 and 5.5 per cent in 2016, while growth of imports will expand even more rapidly from 3.8 per cent in 2014 to 5.3 per cent in 2015 and 6.0 per cent in 2016.

International capital inflows to emerging economies

Net private capital inflows to emerging economies have been on a moderate downturn since 2013, triggered by the Fed tapering its quantitative easing programme, the deterioration in the growth prospects for these economies and escalated geopolitical tensions. In 2014, net private inflows to this group of economies are estimated to have declined by about 6.0 per cent from 2013, to a level of $1,160 billion, compared with the recent peak of $1,256 billion in 2012.[5] However, this decline is mainly explained by capital flight from the Russian Federation, amid a weak economic situation and escalating geopolitical tensions. In other emerging markets, capital inflows rebounded after a sharp contraction in early 2014, albeit to varying degrees and with significant fluctuations. Meanwhile, external borrowing costs continue to be relatively low for most developing regions (figure I.6). Despite this recent trend, the risks for abrupt adjustments and increased volatility driven by changes in investor sentiment remain high.

Among different types of capital flows, portfolio equity inflows rebounded significantly in 2014 from a sharp decline in 2013, reaching about $140 billion, driven by a renewed search for yield. By mid-2014, these flows increased significantly to Asia and Latin America, including countries such as Brazil, India, Indonesia and Mexico, but also to other markets such as South Africa and Turkey. By contrast, portfolio debt inflows continued to decline in 2014, to a level of $310 billion from $390 billion in 2013. Despite the decline over the past two years, debt inflows are noticeably higher than the pre-crisis peak levels. Moreover, the partial recovery of bond flows by mid-2014, after the sharp reduction in January and February, resulted in a reduction in external financing costs in some developing regions, like Asia and Africa.

Foreign direct investment (FDI) inflows have remained the most stable and relevant source of financing for developing countries. FDI maintains a relatively solid path across regions, standing at about $550 billion for the past three years and accounting for about half of the total net inflows to emerging economies. In addition, the importance of emerging economies and developing countries regarding FDI outflows continues to increase. In

Capital inflows to emerging economies have declined moderately

---

5   The data and definition of private capital inflows in this section are based on Institute of International Finance, "Capital flows to emerging market economies", IIF Research Note, 2 October 2014.

Figure I.6
Yield spreads on developing economies' bonds, January 2007–October 2014

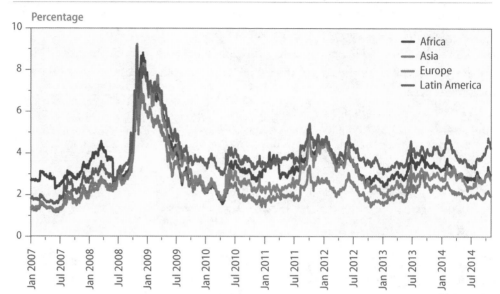

Source: JPMorgan Chase.

2013, these economies reached a record of $460 billion in FDI outflows, which constitutes about 39 per cent of global FDI outflows.[6]

Across different regions, emerging economies in Asia continue to receive the bulk of net capital inflows, accounting for about 60 per cent of the total in 2014, increasing from 51 per cent in 2013, with China alone absorbing some $500 billion. Emerging economies in Latin America accounted for 24 per cent, Africa and Western Asia combined for 8 per cent, and emerging economies in Europe for 7 per cent.

Capital flows will remain flat in 2015 and increase slightly in 2016

The outlook for capital inflows to emerging economies and developing countries remains moderately positive. Overall, net capital inflows are projected to stay at the same level in 2015 and slightly increase in 2016. However, abrupt changes in investor sentiment regarding geopolitical tensions, ongoing monetary policy shifts in the United States, and further divergence of the monetary policy stances of the major central banks might significantly affect portfolio flows. As was also illustrated towards the middle of 2013, a retrenchment in capital flows can have widespread impacts, especially in emerging economies, on exchange rates, foreign reserves, bond yields and equity prices.[7] Economic fundamentals seem to provide little insulation in this regard, and the magnitude of the short-term impacts appears to depend more strongly on the size of national financial markets. A sudden stop in capital inflows also stands to significantly affect growth, for example, through a tightening of bank lending.

6   UNCTAD, "Investment by South TNCs reached a record level", Global Investment Trends Monitor, No. 16 (28 April 2014).

7   Barry Eichengreen and Poonam Gupta, "Tapering talk: the impact of expectations of reduced Federal Reserve security purchases on emerging markets", World Bank Policy Research Working Paper, No. 6754 (December 2013), Washington, D. C.

Exchange rates

Starting in the third quarter of 2014, the dominant trend on foreign exchange markets has been the appreciation of the United States dollar. This trend has been fuelled by expectations that the Fed's monetary policy stance would increasingly diverge from that of other major central banks, notably the ECB and BoJ. The recent dollar strength has been broadly based, with considerable gains against the euro, the Japanese yen, the pound sterling and most emerging market currencies. The dollar index, which measures the value of the dollar relative to a basket of six developed-economy currencies, reached a four-year high in November 2014 (figure I.7).[8]

Against the euro, the dollar gained more than 10 per cent between May and November, climbing from 1.39 to 1.25 dollar/euro, after trading in a fairly narrow range in early 2014. The strong adjustment since May 2014 reflects a growing divergence in the economic performance and the monetary policies between the two areas. Faced with a slumping euro area economy and the threat of deflation, the ECB has taken additional steps to loosen monetary policy, including a further reduction of its main policy rates and the expansion of unconventional policies. The Fed, by contrast, ended its quantitative easing programme in October 2014 and appears set to increase interest rates by mid-2015, amid robust growth prospects and positive labour market trends. As this divergence is expected to continue in the forecast period, the dollar is assumed to strengthen further against the euro, although much more slowly than in the third quarter of 2014.

The dollar also appreciated notably against the Japanese yen in the third quarter of 2014, moving from 101 yen/dollar in July to a seven-year high of 115 yen/dollar in November. As with the euro area, this appreciation largely reflects different monetary policy paths, as the BoJ expanded its quantitative and qualitative easing programme in late October

The United States dollar appreciated substantially

Figure I.7
United States dollar index, February 2007–November 2014

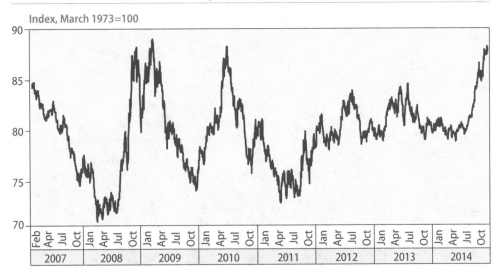

Index, March 1973=100

Source: UN/DESA, based on data from http://www.Investing.com (accessed on 25 November 2014). Note: A rising index indicates an appreciation of the United States dollar.

---

8   The basket of currencies includes the euro, the Japanese yen, the pound sterling, the Canadian dollar, the Swedish krona and the Swiss franc.

2014. The yen is expected to stay relatively weak in 2015 before appreciating slightly in 2016 as the BoJ starts to normalize its monetary policy.

With few exceptions, emerging-market currencies also weakened notably against the dollar in the third quarter of 2014, while remaining fairly stable against the euro and the yen. This follows a moderate strengthening against developed-economy currencies between February and June, when capital flows to emerging economies recovered amid relatively benign global financial conditions. The recent slide against the dollar reflects not only expectations of monetary policy tightening in the United States, but also renewed concerns over the short-term outlook for some emerging economies. In several countries—Brazil, the Russian Federation, South Africa and Turkey, for example—the growth forecasts for 2014 and 2015 have been revised downward sharply in the face of weak domestic demand, geopolitical tensions and falling commodity prices. Some of these economies also continue to record considerable external imbalances, including large current-account deficits, and appear vulnerable to a sudden shift in market sentiment or a tightening of global financial conditions. These factors will continue to weigh on emerging-economy currencies in the outlook period, although, given diverging macroeconomic trends, significant cross-country differences are expected.

The renminbi appreciated against the dollar

In contrast to most other emerging economy currencies, the Chinese renminbi appreciated against the dollar between May and early November, following a significant depreciation in early 2014. The People's Bank of China is expected to keep the average value of the renminbi relatively stable during the forecast period in a bid to maintain competitiveness and support growth.

Global imbalances

Global imbalances narrowed slightly

The size of global current-account imbalances narrowed slightly in 2014 as their pattern remained largely unchanged (figure I.8). The sum of the absolute values of current-account balances is estimated at about 3.5 per cent of WGP, down from a peak of 5.6 per cent in 2006.[9] A significant part of this narrowing appears to be driven by weaker demand in many economies since the global financial crisis along with a decline in potential output.[10] Moreover, several of the major contributors to the pre-crisis imbalances, including China and Japan on the surplus side and the United States and the euro area's peripheral countries on the deficit side, have seen structural shifts that tended to push their economies towards external balance.

The United States still has by far the largest current-account deficit in the world. For 2014, the deficit is estimated at $430 billion, slightly up from 2013. As a share of domestic GDP, the deficit stood at 2.5 per cent, well below the peak of 6.0 per cent registered in 2006. By contrast, China's surplus in 2014 remained the same as in 2013, at about 1.9 per cent of GDP, compared to 10.1 per cent in 2007, whereas the surpluses of fuel-exporting countries in Western Asia, such as Saudi Arabia and the United Arab Emirates, further declined, owing to lower oil prices. Germany, which has replaced China as the largest individual surplus country in the world, continued to see a significant current-account surplus

---

9   The total imbalances depicted in figure I.8 are smaller than the total (global) sum of current-account balances because some groups, such as the rest of the world, the EU without Germany, and East Asia without China, include both deficit and surplus countries.

10   See IMF, *World Economic Outlook: Legacies, Clouds, Uncertainties*, October 2014, chap. 4.

in 2014 as exports continued to outpace imports. Germany's current-account-to-GDP ratio for 2014 is estimated at about 7 per cent, exceeding the European Commission's early warning threshold of 6 per cent.[11] Japan, by contrast, recorded only a very small surplus of about 0.2 per cent of GDP, despite the weakening of the yen against the dollar.

In the outlook period, the total size of global imbalances, relative to WGP, is projected to remain fairly constant. From a global perspective, the magnitude of current-account imbalances does not appear to pose an imminent threat to the stability of the world economy. Nonetheless, there are important problems associated with the current pattern of imbalances and the ongoing adjustment processes. On the one hand, Europe's shift from a current-account deficit prior to the global financial crisis to a significant surplus in recent years has largely been the result of weak internal demand. This reflects deep recession in the euro area's peripheral economies, and a heavy reliance by northern countries, including Germany, on exports for growth. Due to a lack of investment at home, the region has become the world's largest capital exporter. This is exerting a considerable deflationary impact on the world economy at a time when global demand is still slacking. On the other hand, the ongoing high current-account deficits in some large emerging economies, such as Brazil, Indonesia, South Africa and Turkey, remain a concern, particularly in light of fickle short-term international capital flows and an upcoming normalization of United States monetary policy. A sudden change in market sentiment, similar to the experience of mid-2013, could trigger a painful adjustment process in the countries with large external deficits, through tighter monetary conditions and weaker aggregate demand.

New patterns in the global imbalances

Figure I.8
Global imbalances, 2000–2016

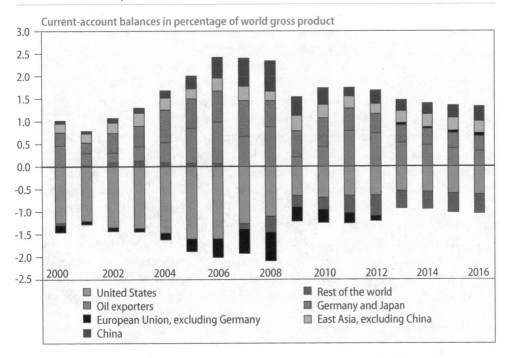

Current-account balances in percentage of world gross product

Legend:
- United States
- Oil exporters
- European Union, excluding Germany
- China
- Rest of the world
- Germany and Japan
- East Asia, excluding China

Source: UN/DESA, based on IMF World Economic Outlook, October 2014. Data for 2015–2016 are forecast.

---

11   Germany recently undertook a major revision of the national accounts. This has resulted in an upward shift in the level of GDP and, accordingly, in a reduction of the current-account-to-GDP ratio. The number cited here is from the data before the revision.

Risks and uncertainties in the global economy

Risks associated with the normalization of United States interest rates

The uncertainty associated with the normalization of monetary policy by the Fed can be captured in three different scenarios.[12] While the assumption for the baseline outlook as delineated above is a smooth process of interest-rate normalization, any unexpected changes in GDP growth, employment creation, inflation or other circumstances can trigger a deviation from the assumed interest-rate path. This, in turn, would lead to the sudden repricing of financial assets, higher volatility and possibly to global spillovers. In one scenario, higher inflation or financial bubble concerns would lead to a more rapid increase in the policy interest rate. Together with a rise in term premia, this would drive up credit spreads, accompanied by an increase in volatility and significant repercussions for global financial markets. By contrast, in another scenario, a renewed slowdown in growth prompts a delay in interest-rate hikes. This would set off higher volatility and possibly lead to additional financial instability risks in the light of asset pricing that is based for an even longer time on abundant liquidity rather than on economic fundamentals.

Any deviation from the expected interest-rate path could have major effects on financial markets...

Any deviation from the policy interest-rate path expected by financial markets could have major ramifications in financial markets. One reason for this is the decrease in market liquidity for corporate bonds due to a retrenchment of market-making banks. As a result, any sell-off in bond markets caused by an upward revision of interest-rate expectations would lead to a more pronounced fall in bond prices, higher yields and higher borrowing costs. A further reason lies in the increased role of financial actors that feature a higher redemption risk, such as mutual funds and exchange-traded funds. These actors, together with households, have seen a continuous increase in their share as holders of corporate bonds, while the share of insurance and pension funds has decreased.

...with spillover effects to other economies

A faster-than-expected normalization of interest rates in the United States can also create significant international spillover effects, especially a drying up of liquidity in emerging economies and an increase in bond yields. Historically, the yields on 10-year government bonds across advanced and major developing economies have exhibited a high degree of correlation, especially during phases of rising interest rates in the United States. The direction of causation typically flows from the United States to the other markets, with the term premium being the major adjustment component. This observation is especially relevant in the current context, with other central banks like the ECB remaining committed to a loose monetary policy stance. While this will keep expected short-term interest rates low, a cascading term-premium shock would still be likely to put upward pressure on long-term yields. Many emerging economies also remain vulnerable to the fallout from rising global interest rates. While certain economic fundamentals such as currency reserve ratios are overall in better condition than in the past, various factors have increased emerging markets' vulnerability, particularly to higher global interest rates. This includes, for example, rising levels of foreign-currency-denominated debt, particularly short-term debt in a number of cases.

---

12   See more detailed discussion in IMF, *Global Financial Stability Report: Risk Taking, Liquidity, and Shadow Banking: Curbing Excess While Promoting Growth,* October 2014; and *Global Financial Stability Report: Moving from Liquidity to Growth-Driven Markets,* April 2014.

Remaining fragilities in the euro area

The euro area sovereign debt crisis has subsided dramatically since the European Central Bank (ECB) announced its Outright Monetary Transactions facility in August 2012. It has yet to be activated, but its mere existence has broken the negative feedback loop between weak banks and weak government fiscal positions. Sovereign-bond spreads have narrowed significantly and some of the crisis countries have seen an improvement in their debt ratings.

The recovery in the euro area remains precarious

However, while the sense of crisis has dissipated, significant risks remain. The banking sector remains under stress. Lending conditions remain fragmented across the region, with firms in periphery countries, particularly small and medium-sized enterprises (SMEs), starved of credit. The recent Asset Quality Review and stress tests performed by the ECB and the European Banking Authority revealed that the capital shortfall was at the lower end of expectations and was manageable, thus eliminating a major source of tension in recent months. But it also revealed that the majority of problems were in periphery country banks.

The most significant risk, however, is the precarious nature of the euro area recovery. The underlying growth momentum in the region has decelerated to the point where an exogenous event could lead to a return to recession. The current tensions in Ukraine and resulting sanctions have already had a serious negative impact on activity and confidence. The weak state of the recovery is characterized by continued low levels of private investment, extremely high unemployment in many countries—which becomes more entrenched as the ranks of the long-term unemployed increase—and by dangerously low inflation, which could turn to Japan-style deflation. Aside from being exceptionally difficult to exit, deflation would also increase real government debt burdens and perhaps reignite the debt crisis as fiscal targets become increasingly difficult to achieve.

Vulnerabilities in emerging economies

Many large emerging economies continue to face a challenging macroeconomic environment, as weaknesses in their domestic economies interact with external financial vulnerabilities. Although the baseline forecast projects a moderate growth recovery in 2015 and 2016 for almost all emerging economies—including Brazil, India, Indonesia, Mexico, the Russian Federation, South Africa and Turkey—and only a slight moderation in China, there are significant risks of a further slowdown or a prolonged period of weak growth. A broad-based downturn in emerging economies, particularly a sharp slowdown in China, would not only weigh on growth in smaller developing countries and economies in transition, but could also derail the fragile recovery in developed countries, particularly in the struggling euro area.

At present, the main risk for many emerging economies arises from the potential for negative feedback loops between weak activity in the real sector, reversals of capital inflows and a tightening of domestic financial conditions amid an expected rise in the interest rates in the United States. The financial turmoil episodes of mid-2013 and early 2014 illustrated the dynamics of such feedback loops and underlined the policy dilemma some of the countries are facing. During these episodes, global investors reallocated their portfolios amid a reassessment of the Fed's monetary tightening path, concerns over global growth, higher

The possible interaction between weaker growth and tighter financing conditions presents a risk

uncertainty and country-specific shocks.[13] This resulted in strong portfolio capital reversals and rapidly depreciating currencies in emerging economies, particularly those with large external financing needs and macroeconomic imbalances, such as Brazil, Indonesia, South Africa and Turkey. Faced with significant downward pressure on domestic asset prices and currencies, the central banks in these countries hiked interest rates even as economic growth slowed. These moves, while helping to stabilize financial markets, have further slowed down activity in the real sector. During the course of 2014, the growth projections have been lowered sharply for Brazil, South Africa and Turkey and marginally for Indonesia.

Geopolitical tensions (especially the conflict between the Russian Federation and Ukraine), the weaker-than-expected performance of developed economies, and the growth moderation in China have also negatively impacted real activity in emerging economies over the past year. Contrary to expectations at the beginning of the year, average GDP growth in a group of 18 emerging economies declined further in 2014 to 4.1 per cent, down from 4.7 per cent in 2013 (figure I.9).[14] The current pace is less than half the rate recorded in the period 2004–2007, when these countries grew at an annual average rate of 8.5 per cent. When China is excluded, the slowdown is even more pronounced, indicating the magnitude of the recent slump. Without China, emerging market growth in 2014 averaged only 2.3 per cent, compared to 6.5 per cent in 2004–2007.

Much of the recent downturn in emerging economies outside Asia can be attributed to weak growth in investment and in total factor productivity. In many countries, investment in fixed capital has slowed considerably since 2011 even as global financial conditions remained unusually loose. As a result, the contributions of gross fixed investment to GDP

Figure I.9
Annual GDP growth in emerging economies, 2000–2014[a]

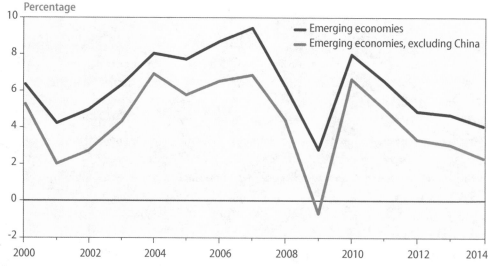

Source: UN/DESA.
a Growth rate for 2014 is partially estimated.

---

13   Changes in market expectations about the path of monetary tightening in the United States of America were the main factor behind the turbulence in mid-2013, whereas country-specific shocks, such as an unexpected devaluation in Argentina and a deterioration of the geopolitical situation around Ukraine, played the major role in early 2014.

14   The 18 emerging economies analyzed here are: Argentina, Brazil, Chile, China, Colombia, India, Indonesia, Malaysia, Mexico, Peru, the Philippines, Poland, the Russian Federation, South Africa, Thailand, Turkey, Ukraine and Venezuela (Bolivarian Republic of).

growth in most emerging economies outside Asia have been low or negative in the past two years. Investment-to-GDP ratios have remained below 20 per cent in several economies, such as Argentina, Brazil, South Africa and Turkey. Growth in total factor productivity fell to the lowest level in two decades in 2013, indicating increased challenges for emerging economies to achieve technological progress and efficiency gains. Given the expected normalization of monetary policy in the United States, it is likely that emerging markets will see a tightening of financial conditions in the forecast period. In the absence of a new reform push, this may further weaken real investment growth, particularly in the private sector. A key question in this regard is the degree to which the upcoming increase in United States interest rates will affect borrowing costs in emerging economies.

While fixed capital formation has remained subdued in recent years, many emerging economies have registered considerable credit growth, with increased leverage in the household and the corporate sector. Corporate sector debt as a share of GDP is particularly high in some faster-growing East Asian countries, such as China and Malaysia, but also elevated in many less dynamic economies, including Brazil, the Russian Federation, South Africa and Turkey. Preliminary evidence suggests that part of the new borrowing has been used for more speculative activities, as indicated by a marked increase in corporate cash holdings.[15] Rising interest rates, along with weakening earnings in the context of slowing economic growth, could put considerable pressure on corporate balance sheets. China's high and rapidly rising level of total debt poses a substantial risk factor, although almost all of the debt is held domestically and the country is partly insulated from changes to global financial conditions.

Private-sector debt in many emerging economies has increased significantly

An additional risk factor for several emerging economies, including Brazil, Colombia, Indonesia, Peru, South Africa and Turkey, are persistently large current-account deficits. According to recent projections, full-year current-account deficits in 2014 are expected to be about 3.5 per cent in Brazil and Indonesia, 4.0 per cent in Colombia, 5.0 per cent in Peru and close to 6.0 per cent in South Africa and Turkey. Among the economies with large external financing needs, those with weak economic fundamentals and large open capital markets appear to be most vulnerable to a tightening of global financing conditions and further portfolio reallocation.

Geopolitical tensions and risks

Geopolitical tensions remain a major downside risk for the economic outlook. In addition to the severe human toll, the crises in Iraq, Libya, the Syrian Arab Republic and Ukraine have already had pronounced economic impacts at the national and subregional levels, although the global economic effect has so far been relatively limited. A major reason for the limited global impact thus far is that global oil markets remained on an even footing, with any actual or feared conflict-related decline in oil supplies being offset by oil production increases, notably in the United States. Nevertheless, the world economy remains at risk to experience a more pronounced slowdown that could be caused by subregional economic weakness due to conflict and sanctions feeding into a broader global impact. A further risk lies in a drastic fall in oil output and exports by any of the major oil-exporting countries, which may set off a sharp adjustment in financial markets' risk perception, leading to higher risk premia and an increase in market volatility across different asset classes.

---

15   See Michael Chui, Ingo Fender and Vladyslav Sushko, "Risks related to EME corporate balance sheets: the role of leverage and currency mismatch", BIS Quarterly Review, September 2014.

The crisis in Ukraine has led to several rounds of sanctions between the Russian Federation and leading OECD economies. Over the course of 2014, those countries have introduced a series of increasingly tough sanctions against the Russian economy, affecting the defence, finance and energy sectors by restricting exports of arms, double-use technology and certain equipment for the oil industry, and by curbing access of Russian banks and companies to international capital markets. The measures have already imposed a serious toll on the Russian economy through worsening business sentiment and an outflow of capital, and have triggered a reciprocal response. In August of 2014, the Government of the Russian Federation decided to impose counter-sanctions against those countries—most notably imposing a one-year ban on imports of their food products, despite the fact that switching to alternative suppliers may imply high transaction costs and lead to higher inflation, which currently poses a serious macroeconomic threat to the Russian economy.

Weaker Russian import demand has already affected a number of EU economies, as the Russian market absorbs almost 5 per cent of the euro area's exports. The slowdown in the German economy in the second quarter is partially explained by lower exports of automotive components to the Russian Federation. Moreover, the restriction on supplying deep-water drilling equipment to sanctioned Russian companies affected Germany's producers. Financial difficulties experienced by the sanctioned oil companies will limit their investment plans and, consequently, sales of construction materials to those companies. Some countries, such as the Baltic States and Finland, will lose transit revenue. Globally, the tourism industry will suffer from the depreciation of the Russian currency.

The Russian ban on food imports, in turn, will mostly hurt those countries which are strongly exposed to trade with the Russian Federation, not only through direct losses by the agricultural sector, but also their consequential effects. Total EU food exports to the Russian market amount to approximately $11 billion annually. The forgone food exports would impact the entire logistics sector (including transport), put pressure on the states' budgets to compensate for farmers' losses, put banks exposed to agricultural borrowers at risk by increasing the number of non-performing loans, and constrain credit extended to farmers. For some East European countries (especially the Baltic States and Poland) and also for Finland and Norway, the Russian Federation absorbs a significant share of their food exports. For Poland, fruit and vegetable exports to the Russian Federation provided revenue of about $1 billion last year.

The loss of the Russian market may also have a multiplier effect on the region, through weaker aggregate demand in the affected countries, resulting from significant intraregional trade links. Although the EU members will be able to file a compensation claim with the EU, and the European Commission in late August announced support measures for dairy exporters and fruit and vegetable farmers, full coverage of losses is not likely. Nevertheless, at the macroeconomic level, the impact of the Russian food import ban still remains to be seen. By contrast, some countries, among them Argentina, Brazil, Serbia and Turkey, as well as some CIS economies, may benefit from the current situation, becoming alternative food product suppliers to the Russian Federation.

The conflict situations in Iraq, Libya and the Syrian Arab Republic have created considerable uncertainty in the oil market. In 2013, Iraq's oil production constituted 3.7 per cent of total world oil production, while Libya provided 1.1 per cent of global output. But despite the ongoing conflicts in these countries, crude oil prices actually declined, in contrast to similar episodes in the past that saw sharp increases in crude oil prices. This price behaviour is linked to the oil output trend in other oil producers, especially the United

States. Oil production there jumped by 12.5 per cent in 2013, following an increase by 13.0 per cent in the previous year. The United States oil output level in 2013 came close to that of the Russian Federation, which was surpassed only by Saudi Arabia. Taken together, this has increased the resilience of the global oil market to any crisis scenarios. However, a major downside risk remains the possible sudden and drastic stoppage of exports by a major supplier country. While such a scenario could eventually be compensated for by existing slack in global oil markets, the immediate reaction of financial markets could be severe, with possible negative repercussions for real economic activity as well.[16]

A further risk to the outlook lies in the future development of the Ebola epidemic. The current outbreak of the disease is the largest since the virus was first discovered in 1976, with the number of cases and deaths in this outbreak exceeding those of all previous outbreaks combined. In August of 2014, the World Health Organization declared the outbreak an international public health emergency; in September, the United Nations Security Council declared the epidemic a threat to international peace and security. The first cases of the current outbreak were identified in March 2014 and the majority of cases have so far occurred in three West African countries, namely Guinea, Liberia and Sierra Leone. The occurrence of the outbreak and the difficulties in addressing it have been underpinned by the weak health systems in these countries, both in terms of human and physical resources. In addition to the severe human toll the disease has taken, it has also imposed major economic costs in the affected countries through disruptions to travel and trade.

The Ebola outbreak has not only taken a severe human toll, but has also had major economic repercussions

Policy challenges

Fiscal policy stance

For major developed economies, including Japan, which earlier resorted to a fiscal stimulus, fiscal policy in 2014 was dominated by pursuing the goal of fiscal consolidation, both on the revenue and on the expenditure side. Consequently, the average size of the budget deficit in developed economies is expected to decline further in 2014. The implications of those consolidation policies for economic growth may not be so straightforward to assess, but in general they should have a mildly contractionary impact. In the outlook for 2015, fiscal tightening in most of the developed economies is likely to continue; but, since the most drastic post-crisis austerity measures have already been implemented, the countries should face less fiscal drag, unless the cyclical position of those economies deteriorates dramatically and undermines public revenues.

Fiscal consolidation will continue in developed economies

In the United States, several years of fiscal austerity noticeably reduced the size of the federal budget deficit (by approximately one half between 2010 and 2013) and improved public accounts at the state and local government level. Although the federal budget squeeze is expected to continue in 2015 (despite the increase in the public debt ceiling, agreed in February 2014), spending at the state and local government level may increase. Thus, the total impact of fiscal policy on growth may be largely neutral. Nevertheless, the long-term sustainability of the entitlement programmes is being questioned repeatedly and their reforms will remain on the agenda, although the sharp political divisions will most likely prevent reaching any consensus in the near term.

---

16 Oil market data is from BP Statistical Review of World Energy, June 2014, p. 8.

In the EU, where fiscal accounts has been severely damaged by the loss of tax income during the economic downturn, by countercyclical spending, and by bailouts of the banking system, fiscal consolidation has been progressing slowly, with only slight improvements in the fiscal positions of many countries. In some large economies, such as France, the Government mostly relied on tax increases. In 2014, many of the EU members are expected to violate the provision of the Stability and Growth Pact that stipulates a deficit limit of 3 per cent of GDP. In early October, the Government of France announced that it will shift its target date of complying with the 3 per cent threshold to 2017, two years beyond its initial target. The overall efficiency of the austerity measures in the periphery euro area countries is being debated; however, in these countries deficits have been reduced significantly and the prospective issuance of Eurobonds should mitigate near-term fiscal risks and promote greater fiscal discipline in the EU.

In Japan, the large fiscal stimulus enacted in 2013 has led to a swelling of the budget deficit to about 10 per cent of GDP. The public debt-to-GDP ratio, at over 220 per cent, has already been among the highest in developed countries and may be unsustainable in the long run. However, supportive factors include the fact that most debt is held domestically, the borrowing costs are currently low, and the real interest rate became negative after the monetary stimulus. Additionally, the consumption tax increases enacted in 2014 and planned for 2015 should gradually reduce the deficit.

In developing countries and economies in transition, fiscal developments in 2014 varied. Their budget deficits and public debt levels are generally lower than in developed economies. As commodity prices still remained weak, public revenues for a number of commodity exporters continued to underperform. In China, the fiscal deficit moderately expanded. Against the backdrop of the high indebtedness of local governments, spending by the central Government is likely to increase in the future.

The refinancing of external debt could pose challenges for developing countries

Despite comparatively low public debt levels, a more cautious attitude towards sovereign borrowing may be recommended for many developing countries. Refinancing external debt could prove to be costly should there be a sharp change of investor appetite for emerging markets, a weakening of the exchange rate, or higher levels of benchmark interest rates. However, the increasing inequality in many emerging economies will necessitate fiscal spending aimed at narrowing income gaps and promoting social mobility.

Monetary policy stance

The direction of monetary policies has become more divergent among different economies in the world. While some countries are in a position to raise interest rates, others intend to reduce interest rates, reflecting a diverse economic situation and different country-specific challenges facing different economies.

Monetary policy remained accommodative in developed economies

Major developed economy central banks continued to maintain accommodative monetary policy stances in 2014 against the backdrop of a weak recovery, deflationary pressures and limited support from the fiscal side. At its most recent meeting in September, the Fed decided to maintain the federal funds rate within the current range of 0.00–0.25 per cent for a "considerable time" after ending the asset-purchasing programme, especially if projected inflation continues to run below 2.0 per cent and inflation expectations remain well anchored.

In forward guidance issued in July, the ECB announced that interest rates would remain at present or lower levels for an extended period of time, given the subdued outlook for inflation in the medium-term, broad-based weakness in the real economy and weak monetary transmission. In September, in line with its forward guidance, the ECB kept the interest rates on refinancing operations, the marginal lending facility and the deposit facility unchanged at 0.05 per cent, 0.30 per cent and -0.20 per cent, respectively. In mid-October, the ECB will start buying covered bonds and asset-backed securities, which are expected to add 1.1 trillion euros to its balance sheet. The new round of asset purchases is expected to boost lending to SMEs, a priority sector for the ECB, to stimulate employment and growth in the euro area economies.

At its meeting in October, the Bank of England (BoE) kept the policy rate unchanged at 0.5 per cent and the asset-purchasing programme at 375 billion pounds. In its first forward guidance in August 2013, the BoE had signalled that it would leave interest rates unchanged at 0.5 per cent at least until the unemployment rate fell to 7.0 per cent. However, as unemployment fell below 7.0 per cent by April 2014, the BoE maintained that there was still room for non-inflationary growth in the economy before it needed to raise interest rates and that the increases in interest rates are likely to be gradual and limited.

The BoJ continued its Quantitative and Qualitative Monetary Easing Programme, as inflation remained well below the 2 per cent target. On 31 October 2014, the BoJ announced that it will increase the monetary base at an annual pace of about 80 trillion yen and purchase Japanese government bonds at an annual rate of about 80 trillion yen, with an average remaining maturity of about seven years. The BoJ kept its policy rate below 0.10 per cent; it has remained at this level since 2009.

In contrast to developed economies, developing- and emerging-economy central banks demonstrated considerable divergence in their monetary policy operations. The People's Bank of China cut its benchmark interest rate in November 2014, after previously reducing the short-term repo rate twice during 2014 in order to inject liquidity into the banking system. It also cut the reserve requirements for banks that lend to SMEs and rural sectors of the economy. On the other hand, the Central Bank of Brazil increased its policy rate three times during 2014 amid concerns about rising inflation. The central banks of India and South Africa raised interest rates during the first half of 2014, largely to stem capital outflows and prevent depreciation of their exchange rates, while the central bank of Indonesia has kept its policy rate unchanged at 7.5 per cent since November 2013 and the central bank of Turkey cut the policy rate by 50 basis points in May 2014.

Emerging economies featured more divergent monetary policy stances

Challenges in managing the normalization of monetary policy

Both the end of quantitative easing by the Fed in October 2014 and the forthcoming normalization of its policy interest rate assumed in the baseline forecast hold significant risks and uncertainties for the economic outlook. These relate to the design of the exit strategy, its timing, and how it is perceived by financial markets. The potential difficulties that can arise in this context already became clear in the spring of 2013, when the announcement by the Fed of its intention to taper its bond purchases set off a fall in the price of various financial assets and a spike in financial market volatility.

As the Fed has ended its quantitative easing (i.e., bond purchases), the focus has increasingly moved to the future trajectory of the policy interest rate. As outlined in the assumptions for the baseline forecast, the first interest-rate hike is expected in the third quarter of 2015, with further gradual increases bringing the policy rate to 2.75 per cent by the end of 2016. This projection is linked to the guidance given by the Fed that it will maintain the current near-zero level of interest rates for a considerable time after the end of the asset-purchasing programme, provided that inflation remains low.

The actual path of the policy interest rate will depend on a number of factors, particularly the emerging macroeconomic picture, in terms of unemployment and inflation, and concerns about financial stability risks. Interest rates will also be a major determinant not just of macroeconomic performance, but also the extent of financial stability risks and global spillovers. Policymakers face the challenge of determining the optimal magnitude and timing of interest-rate changes while dealing with a difficult trade-off: delaying the policy tightening could reinforce any asset mispricing and financial stability risks, while an unwarranted quick tightening could weaken the still fragile economic growth picture.

Complex macroeconomic data can complicate monetary policy

The difficulty of designing the optimal monetary policy path stems in large part from the uncertain nature of macroeconomic data. A case in point is the unemployment rate in the United States, which has fallen from a peak of 10 per cent in 2010 to below 6 per cent. However, at the same time, the percentage of employees working part-time but preferring to work full-time remains elevated, indicating significant underemployment. In addition, the labour force participation rate has decreased, meaning that more people have simply stopped looking for a job. This raises two issues for monetary policymakers. First, there is the need to consider a broader unemployment variable that adjusts the nominal unemployment rate for involuntary part-time work and for the decrease in the labour-force participation rate. Second, if the drop in the participation rate is cyclical, monetary policy can be a potent means for reducing the participation gap by letting the unemployment rate fall below its long-term natural rate. This would help in bringing people back into the job market, which would have the side effect of reducing (to a point) any inflation pressure from the undershooting of the unemployment rate.[17] However, an opposite argument can be made that a large part of the decline in the participation rate is actually structural, due, for example, to the ageing of the population;[18] in this case, targeting the participation rate with monetary policy would be inadequate and create upward wage pressures and inflation.

Policy challenges for strengthening employment and improving working conditions

As discussed earlier, employment rates, in comparison with pre-crisis levels, are still relatively low in many economies, requiring more supportive macroeconomic policies to foster employment creation. At the same time, long-term unemployment has increased and labour market conditions—wages in particular— have deteriorated, requiring more active labour market policies.

Macroeconomic policies and structural measures need to target employment creation

To date, macroeconomic policies in many developed economies have been uncoordinated and only had a limited impact on job creation. While expansionary monetary policies in developed economies may have averted otherwise larger falls in employment, they cannot directly stimulate employment growth. Moreover, fiscal austerity in many developed economies and, more recently, in some emerging economies, has led to a weak demand in the short run; further, economic uncertainty has deterred private investment

---

17   Christopher Erceg and Andrew Levin, "Labour force participation and monetary policy in the wake of the great recession", IMF Working Paper, WP/13/245, July 2013, p. 4.

18   Stephanie Aaronson, and others, "Labour force participation: recent developments and future prospects", Brookings Papers on Economic Activity, Fall 2014.

and perpetuated a vicious cycle of weak labour demand and constrained private consumption. Therefore, the main challenge for policymakers in many countries is to implement fiscal strategies that are more supportive of output growth and employment creation. On the monetary side, access to credit for SMEs will continue to be an essential tool, as they play a significant role in job creation. There is also the need to adequately coordinate monetary and fiscal policies to foster employment creation. On the structural side, policymakers in a number of countries need to create an environment that is more amenable to the creation of businesses and jobs—by streamlining administrative procedures, for example.

In addition to macroeconomic policies, specific labour market policies are also required in order to effectively address current challenges. This includes wage growth policies (box I.3), which would also help to support aggregate demand. Such policies are especially relevant as consumer demand has been constrained not only as a result of the financial crisis, but also because of a long-term decline of the labour share in total income. In addition, policymakers should minimize individual losses caused by structural economic changes, such as automation. Governments therefore need to find the right balance between recent labour market flexibility initiatives, which are expected to create more dynamic labour markets, and guaranteeing decent working conditions. In developed economies, in-work benefits and tax credits for low-paid workers have been efficient in limiting the risk of working poverty. In many developing countries, greater diversification of the economic structure and development of higher value-added sectors are needed to promote productivity and reduce unemployment and underemployment, as well as to increase formal employment. This can be achieved through more proactive industrial and innovation policies. Social protection programmes implemented in many emerging economies also recently proved to be effective in improving labour market conditions and supporting aggregate demand.

Long-term unemployment remains another major challenge for policymakers, including in countries where unemployment figures appear to have declined faster in recent years. Long-term unemployment, as discussed earlier, leads to the depreciation of human capital, negative health effects and higher risks of aggravating structural unemployment. Ultimately, it will limit a country's economic growth potential and require extended social programmes, straining budget resources. Because the long-term unemployed remain progressively on the margins of labour markets, wages can rise as the short-term unemployed cohort shrinks. Lower short-term unemployment could thereby lift inflation and push central banks to reverse their expansionary monetary policy by raising interest rates, which would aggravate job prospects for the long-term unemployed.

Concrete labour market policies to tackle long-term unemployment must be implemented, as conventional policies to stimulate aggregate demand will not be sufficient to reintegrate those trapped in extended joblessness. Empirical evidence[19] shows that long-term unemployment often leads to discrimination from employers, worker discouragement or skills depreciation. As a result, the long-term unemployed tend to leave the labour market altogether, mainly because they are discouraged by the relatively low prospects of finding a job. This is particularly evident for workers who are suffering from a chronic skill mismatch due to technological changes or industrial geographical reallocation, who therefore do not possess the skills required to reintegrate into today's labour market.

Specific labour market policies are also required to address the various challenges

Concrete policies are needed to address long-term unemployment

---

19   Alan B. Krueger, Judd Cramer and David Cho, "Are the long term unemployed on the margins of the labor market?", Brookings Papers on Economic Activity, Spring 2014.

In many cases, Governments should extend unemployment benefit schemes to minimize individual losses for those who face higher risk of long-term unemployment and poverty. In order to create incentives for individuals to continue seeking employment while benefiting from unemployment benefits, Governments could introduce a myriad of additional policies. Unemployment benefits, for instance, should be coupled with active labour market policies. Specific lessons from developed economies with lower unemployment rates during the crisis indicate that activation strategies for unemployed individuals should include job search assistance and training programmes, as well as institutional reforms to better coordinate unemployment schemes with employment services. However, in the aftermath of the financial crisis, many Governments face limited resources to ensure such adequate employment services.

Policy challenges in promoting international trade

At the ninth Ministerial Conference of the World Trade Organization (WTO), held in Bali in December 2013, agreements were reached on trade facilitation, agriculture, a package of decisions related to the LDCs, and a monitoring system on special and differential treatment provisions.

Among these agreements was the Trade Facilitation Agreement, the first multilateral agreement concluded in the WTO since its creation in 1995. The Agreement is expected to possibly induce a reduction in business costs equivalent to as much as 15 per cent of present costs and to raise global exports by as much as $1 trillion, in the most optimistic scenario.[20] In Africa, for example, a significant reduction in transaction costs may not only enhance Africa's trade with the rest of the world, but also support regional integration. However, a key WTO member failed to ratify the agreement by the deadline of 31 July 2014.

The agreements reached in Bali only encompassed a limited and least controversial subset of the issues of the Doha Round. WTO ministers were instructed to prepare, by December 2014, a clearly defined work programme to conclude the Doha Round.

There is recognition that tough issues lie ahead, particularly concerning industrial goods, services and agriculture, which are crucial for many developing countries. The list of unresolved issues contains many possible stumbling blocks. Even decisions in the package that are binding will require time and commitment from the parties in order to have a positive effect on international trade.

The multilateral trading system is becoming more fragmented

Since the Doha Round started more than a decade ago, the landscape of international trade and political order has changed considerably. For instance, the number of bilateral and regional trade agreements has increased substantially. Some of the multi-country agreements currently under negotiation, such as the Trans-Pacific Partnership and the Transatlantic Trade and Investment Partnership, might have a major impact on international trade, but developing-country considerations may not be taken into account in those negotiations. The multilateral trading system is faced with the danger of fragmentation. Bali has renewed the trust in the WTO, but it also reinforced views on the difficulty in achieving ambitious reforms at the multilateral level. This poses a challenge to the entire multilateral approach to development cooperation.

---

20   See Organization for Economic Cooperation and Development, "The WTO Trade Facilitation Agreement: potential impact on trade costs", Paris, February 2014.

International policy coordination and cooperation

In order to mitigate the risks and meet challenges as discussed above, it is imperative that international policy coordination is strengthened. In particular, macroeconomic policies worldwide should be aligned towards supporting robust and balanced growth, creating productive jobs, and maintaining economic and financial stability in the long run. Meanwhile, international policy coordination and cooperation is equally important for such areas as defusing geopolitical tensions and addressing wider health crises, as illustrated by the recent Ebola pandemic.

The new initiative of the Group of Twenty (G20) to raise their collective GDP by 2018 by more than 2 per cent above the trajectory projected in 2013 is positive for the global economy. The call by the International Monetary Fund (IMF) and the World Bank to increase global investment in infrastructure, including energy, is also very timely and will not only stimulate short-term growth and employment, but also lift long-term potential growth. However, broader international policy coordination is also needed to boost growth in the majority of developing countries, especially LDCs. In this regard, the international community should accelerate its concerted efforts to deliver on the official development assistance (ODA) commitment to the LDCs. ODA flows rebounded by 6.0 per cent in 2013 from the decline in 2011 and 2012, reaching a record level, but are still far below the United Nations target of 0.7 per cent of gross national income of the donor countries.

The international community has taken important steps to strengthen the resilience of the financial sector through regulatory reform. These reforms attempt to reduce the risk of future crises, but should balance the need for greater stability with ensuring sufficient access to financing, particularly for sustainable development. To date, reforms have focused on regulation of the banking sector. Further progress is needed on other aspects of the international regulatory agenda, including addressing shadow banking and systemically important institutions that are considered too big to fail. There is also a need for stronger cross-border resolution regimes with fair burden-sharing. The development and implementation of international financial regulation would also benefit from greater representation of and participation by developing countries.

Despite some progress, further efforts are needed in reforming international financial regulation

Progress continues to be made on international cooperation in tax matters. There is important ongoing work in this area in several international forums, including the OECD, the G20 and the United Nations system. Some steps have been taken, for example, against base erosion and profit-shifting, and towards developing a widely applicable system of automatic exchange of tax information between countries. In all areas of international tax cooperation, it will be critically important to ensure that the developing world, and in particular the poorest countries, are able to participate in, and benefit from, new developments. Domestic resource mobilization will be central to raising resources to finance sustainable development. Measures which aim to support the developing world in mobilising more domestic resources for development, such as through capacity-building, are critically important and have high development paybacks.

Timely implementation of the 2010 IMF quota and governance reforms would have been an important first step towards bolstering the credibility, legitimacy and effectiveness of the institution. Rapid adoption of the 2010 IMF reforms will pave the way for the next round of quota and voice reforms. Successful completion of further reforms will boost the coherence and stability of the global financial system. Additionally, United Nations Member States agreed in April 2010 that the next round of World Bank governance reforms in 2015 should move the institution towards equitable voting power and protect the voting

**It is imperative to ensure
a seamless transition
from the MDGs to
the SDGs**

power of the smallest poor countries. Agreement should be reached on these reforms in a timely fashion.

It also is crucial to enhance international policy coordination and cooperation in the global efforts to promote sustainable development. The United Nations Member States are formulating an ambitious and transformative post-2015 development agenda. The broad contours of this agenda are becoming clear, with an especially strong commitment to end poverty and ensure sustainable development for all. The Open Working Group of the General Assembly on Sustainable Development Goals (SDGs), initiated by the United Nations Conference on Sustainable Development (Rio+20), has proposed a set of 17 goals and 169 associated targets. While poverty eradication will remain at its core, the post-2015 development agenda is aimed at integrating the economic, social and environmental dimensions of sustainable development. It is generally agreed that the agenda should be firmly anchored in the values and principles as enshrined in the United Nations Charter and complete the unfinished business of the Millennium Development Goals (MDGs), while meeting the new challenges the world is facing, such as climate change. In addition, the Intergovernmental Committee of Experts on Sustainable Development Financing, established in the follow-up to the Rio+20 Conference, has delivered its report[21] proposing options for a sustainable development financing strategy. As the target date of the MDGs is approaching, it is imperative for the international community to ensure a seamless transition from the MDGs to the SDGs in 2015.

---

21   United Nations, "Report of the Intergovernmental Committee of Experts on Sustainable Development Financing (A/69/315)", available from http://sustainabledevelopment.un.org/index. php?menu=1558.

Chapter II
International trade

Trade flows

World trade flows, measured in terms of import volumes, continued to grow at a slow pace in 2014, expanding at about 3.3 per cent, slightly faster than in 2013 but still well below the long-term trend of the decades before the global financial crisis. In the two decades prior to the crisis, for instance, the annual growth of world trade, measured by imports in volume, was on average twice the growth of world gross product (WGP), although trade flows were characterized by much higher volatility than WGP (figure II.1). The eruption of the global financial crisis in 2008 and the subsequent Great Recession in 2009 led to a collapse in world trade flows, with the volume of world imports plummeting over 11 per cent in 2009, 5 times the percentage decline in WGP. Except for a strong rebound in 2010, world trade has been expanding at a sluggish pace during the recovery, at only about the same rate as WGP. In the forecast period, trade growth is expected to expand moderately, at a pace of 4.7 per cent in 2015 and 5.0 per cent in 2016. While this will be an improvement, the ratio of the growth of world trade to that of WGP will still be only 1.5, not a full recovery to the pre-crisis trend.

World trade continued to grow at a slow pace in 2014, but is expected to rise over the forecast period

Figure II.1
Growth of world trade and world gross product, 2001–2016[a]

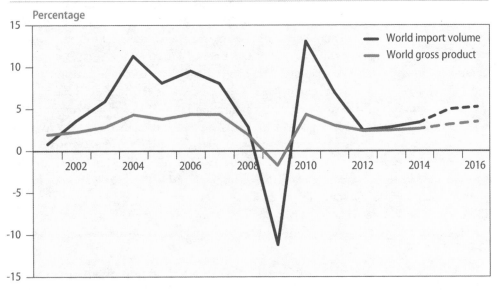

Source: UN/DESA.
a Growth rate for 2014 is partially estimated; rates for 2015 and 2016 are forecast.

At issue is whether the slowdown in trade growth relative to WGP in the years since the global financial crisis reflects a fundamental change in the structure of the global economy, or a transient and cyclical change in the relationship between trade and gross domestic product (GDP). The answer is probably that both cyclical and structural changes are at play.

The slow recovery in developed countries and decelerations in developing countries are blunting trade growth

Among the cyclical changes, the anaemic recovery in major developed countries, particularly the protracted recession in the euro area, has led to feeble import demand. As indicated in the next section, for example, European countries' imports from outside Europe are currently more than 7 per cent below the levels of 2008, and their imports from other European countries are also 8 per cent lower than the levels of 2008. Moreover, weak economic recovery in developed countries has had adverse effects on trade flows in developing countries, as developing countries contribute to more than 30 per cent of the exports to developed countries. In the medium term, stagnant wage growth in many developed countries, coupled with ageing populations, could increase downward pressure on import growth. Furthermore, as trade between developing countries represents a quarter of world trade, slowing growth in developing countries has also weighed on world trade growth.

An increase in post-crisis trade protection is restricting trade growth

After the eruption of the global financial crisis, a large number of countries adopted temporary protectionist measures on international trade and investment, restricting trade flows. For example, the Group of Twenty (G20) countries have adopted 1,244 trade-restrictive measures since October 2008, but only 282 of these had been removed by mid-October 2014.[1] Furthermore, between mid-May and mid-October 2014, G20 members put in place 93 new trade-restrictive measures. The continued accumulation of these restrictive measures remains of concern. This highlights the importance of renewed global efforts to reduce trade restrictions by refraining from the imposition of new measures and eliminating existing ones.

Some factors previously boosting trade growth may have waned

However, some changes in the relationship between trade growth and WGP growth may be structural. World trade can grow faster than WGP for a sustained period only if the prices of international goods and services continue to decline relative to the prices of domestic goods and services. These relative price declines can occur through such factors as new trade agreements to reduce tariffs and other trade barriers, or technological innovations to lower the costs of international transportation. The strong trade growth relative to WGP (a ratio of 2:1) in the 1990s and 2000s was indeed supported by these factors. For example, the achievements of the Uruguay Round of multilateral trade negotiations in the General Agreement on Tariffs and Trade (GATT); the economic integration of the economies in transition, China and other developing economies into the global economy, which removed and reduced barriers to international trade and investment, as exemplified in the process of China's accession to the World Trade Organization (WTO); the increased trade and monetary integration in the European Union (EU), especially the adoption of the euro for a growing number of countries in the region; the reduction of transportation costs by the revolution in information and communication technology and other technologies; and the formation and increasing expansion of global value chains, which distributed various stages of production to different countries, have all significantly promoted international trade. This led to a much faster growth of trade flows in many countries relative to the growth of their GDP and, at the global level, to the growth of world trade at twice the rate of WGP.

---

1   World Trade Organization, "Report on G-20 Trade Measures (mid-May 2014 to mid-October 2014)", 5 November 2014.

Some of these key factors driving the growth of world trade before the global financial crisis may have run their course. The WTO Doha Round of multilateral trade negotiations, for example, has made little progress in the past fourteen years, failing to provide new impetus to trade growth. Some may argue that the Doha Round has been at an impasse since 2001, but world trade still registered high growth in the years before the financial crisis of 2008. This is because world trade in the run-up to the crisis continued to benefit from the lagged effects of the trade liberalization of the earlier years. For example, although China's accession to the WTO occurred in 2001, China had a grace period of five years to gradually remove or lower a large number of trade barriers. By now, the lagged benefits from the earlier trade agreements before the Doha Round may have tapered off. The proliferation of various regional trade agreements (RTAs) may generate some new trade flows in some regions, but the overall effects of RTAs on world trade in the long run are not certain and cannot replace the role of the multilateral trading system (see the section on trade policy).

The integration process of the economies in transition and China into the global economy, after accelerating in the 1990s and 2000s, may also have reached a steady state. For instance, after two decades of rapid growth in its exports, at an annual rate of above 20 per cent, China's share in total world trade has increased from a small fraction to about 12 per cent, in line with its share of GDP in WGP. With its wages increasing markedly, its process of transferring labour from the agricultural sector to the manufacturing sector diminishing, and its restructuring towards the services sector, as well as the rising environmental costs associated with industrialization, China's growth in exports is not expected to return to a double-digit pace. On the positive side, the rise of the African economies can provide a renewed impetus to world trade in the next decades, but it will take some time to see the results on a large scale, as the region's share in world trade is still small, at about 3 per cent.

In short, growth of world trade is projected to pick up some momentum from the subdued pace of the past few years in the aftermath of the financial crisis, but the dynamism of the two decades before the crisis may not return soon.

Regional trends

Developed countries are expected to see some improvements in trade flows, with export growth rising from 3.5 per cent in 2014 to 4.4 per cent in 2015. Import growth will also progress at a similar rate through 2016. Trade growth in the United States of America has been relatively weak, although export and import growth has still been above GDP growth. Trade grew by 2.7 per cent in 2014, and a substantial strengthening of trade is expected over the forecast period, with exports growing by 5.3 per cent in 2015 with some slowdown in 2016 to 4.8 per cent as dollar strength cuts into trading partners' purchases. This will be driven by increased foreign demand for capital goods and industrial supplies. In addition, there have been two other developments affecting trade in the United States—significant increases in domestic oil production and a relatively rapid appreciation of the dollar vis-à-vis other currencies. The degree to which the rising dollar will have an impact on export growth remains to be seen; it will depend on the level at which exchange rates stabilize as well as the situation among the trading partners. Import volume growth is expected to rise in a similar pattern as export growth.

Despite the fragile situation in Western Europe, exports and imports are estimated to have grown by 3.2 per cent in 2014, relatively high compared to GDP growth. The currency dynamics have played a role, as the appreciation of the euro in 2013 dampened exports;

Developed countries see some improvement in trade...

however, its depreciation in the latter half of 2014, and continuing on into the forecast period, is expected to provide a support to exports. Over the forecast period, both export and import growth are expected to improve for the new EU members along with growth prospects for the rest of the EU, with export growth expected to rise from 4.8 per cent in 2014 to 5.1 per cent in 2015 and 5.4 per cent in 2016. Imports are expected to grow similarly, by 5.2 and 5.8 per cent in 2015 and 2016, respectively. As highlighted in chapter I, the geopolitical tension around Ukraine has also impacted trade in a number of countries in the region and could further dampen trade prospects if there is a significant flare-up or further tightening of sanctions. The EU as a whole is expected to see export growth rise from 3.3 per cent in 2014 to 4.4 per cent in 2015 and 4.7 per cent in 2016, with a similar upward trend expected for imports.

...although, intra-EU trade remains sluggish

An interesting feature of the EU region (EU-28) has been the changes in trends with regards to intra- versus extra-EU trade. For most of the past decade, including the crisis period, intra- and extra-EU exports have followed a very similar pattern (figure II.2). However, since mid-2011, intra-EU exports have remained roughly flat, whereas extra-EU exports have risen by more than 7 per cent. More recently, beginning between the fourth quarter of 2012 and the first quarter of 2013, extra-EU imports were flat on average and intra-EU imports increased, albeit from a low level. Overall, the low growth in the euro area has continued to put a damper on intraregional trade, although this may pick up in the forecast period as some modest improvements in euro area growth are expected.

In developed Asia and Oceania, exports have increased relatively rapidly, up from 2.8 per cent in 2013 to 5.0 per cent in 2014. Japanese export growth was roughly the same between 2013 and 2014, despite the substantial depreciation of the yen vis-à-vis the United States dollar. This has resulted in a continuing trade deficit, as imports have remained relatively strong over the same period, although with considerable volatility due to changes in sales taxes. Australian export growth remains relatively strong, although lower than in pre-

Figure II.2
European Union trade volume: intra- and extra-EU trade, 2005 Q1–2014 Q2

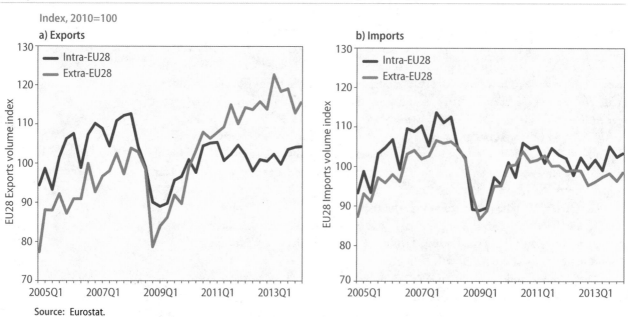

Source: Eurostat.

vious years as minerals prices have fallen and exports to China have tempered. These trends are expected to continue into 2015, further dampening Australian exports. The region as a whole is expected to see some weakness in 2015, with export growth falling to 2.8 per cent, with some improvement in 2016 to 4.1 per cent. Import growth is expected to decelerate from its 2014 high of 4.4 per cent to 3.7 per cent in 2015 and 1.8 per cent in 2016.

Export trends for the Commonwealth of Independent States (CIS) have been heavily affected by the flattening or contraction in oil output in the CIS energy exporters and the ongoing conflict in Ukraine. A plateau in oil production has curbed export growth of the Russian Federation, while exports plummeted sharply in Ukraine. The overall weakness of the economy of the Russian Federation has slowed export growth in other CIS countries. Exports from the region in 2014 are estimated to be at about the same level as 2013 and are expected to rise somewhat over the forecast period, by 0.6 per cent in 2015 and 1.7 per cent in 2016. The depreciation of the Russian currency and the ban by the Russian Federation on food imports from the Organization for Economic Cooperation and Development (OECD) countries have led to a contraction in imports; devaluations in Kazakhstan and Ukraine and lower remittances in smaller CIS economies have also reduced import growth in the region. Imports in the CIS are estimated to fall by 3.4 per cent in 2014 and improve slowly over the forecast period, rising by only 0.2 and 1.1 per cent in 2015 and 2016, respectively. Despite the slow growth in the EU, South-Eastern Europe is expected to see continued export expansion, albeit with some volatility. Exports are estimated to grow by 6.5 per cent in 2014, rising to 7.4 per cent in 2015 and then receding slightly to 5.3 per cent in 2016. Import growth is expected to strengthen in the forecast period, rising from 6.0 per cent in 2014 to 6.8 per cent in 2015 and 7.0 per cent in 2016.

CIS trade is weighed down by conditions in the Russian Federation

Growth of exports from developing countries is expected to increase from 3.9 per cent in 2014 to 4.6 per cent in 2015 and 5.5 per cent in 2016, while growth of imports will expand similarly from 3.8 per cent in 2014 to 5.3 and 6.0 per cent in 2015 and 2016, respectively. Africa's exports continued to be relatively weak in 2014, growing only by 2.0 per cent. This weakness was driven by a variety of factors, including slow growth in North Africa and persistent fragility in Central Africa. Tourism and commodity exports have also been slowed by a number of factors, including the Ebola outbreak, terrorist attacks and domestic and political turmoil. This is expected to reverse somewhat in the forecast period with export growth rising to 4.6 per cent in 2015 and 5.0 per cent in 2016, driven by a reversal in North Africa to positive export growth, continued robust growth in East and Southern Africa and improvements in West Africa. Import growth is expected to continue strengthening after rising to 5.4 per cent in 2014, up to 7.0 per cent by 2016.

Developing countries will see an improvement in trade growth over the forecast period

East Asia experienced relatively moderate export growth in 2014, albeit with significant divergence among countries. Amid strong demand for electrical and electronic goods, manufactures exporters, such as Malaysia, the Philippines and Viet Nam, continued to perform significantly better than commodity exporters like Indonesia. Exports increased moderately in China, the Republic of Korea, Singapore and Taiwan Province of China, but were virtually flat in Thailand and contracted slightly in Indonesia. In Indonesia, the decline can be attributed not only to weak international commodity prices, but also to new regulations banning unprocessed mineral shipments. In Thailand, the stagnation mainly reflects the impact of the political turmoil in the first half of 2014 and a shift in global demand away from hard discs. Overall, the region is estimated to have seen 4.0 per cent growth in exports in 2014. This will improve in the forecast period to 4.8 per cent in 2015 and 5.4 per cent in 2016 as global demand picks up. This pace is, however, still well below pre-crisis trends.

Import growth has been slightly weaker, at only 3.5 per cent in 2014, although a gradual recovery to 4.9 per cent in 2015 and 5.5 per cent in 2016 is expected.

South Asia shows relatively strong export growth

Most South Asian economies, including Bangladesh, India, the Islamic Republic of Iran and Sri Lanka, recorded relatively strong export growth in 2014. Garment shipments—the main export good in Bangladesh, Pakistan and Sri Lanka—continued to expand at a solid pace amid robust demand from developed economies. Several countries also benefited from the marked depreciation of their currencies in 2013 and from strong growth in tourism revenues. The region as a whole is estimated to have seen export growth of 8.6 per cent in 2014. The prospects for exports remain favourable, with average growth projected at 8.5 per cent in 2015 and 9.1 per cent in 2016. On the import side, South Asia's economies generally benefited from the significant decline in global commodity prices, notably fuel prices, in the past year. Moreover, some country-specific measures, such as an import duty on gold and silver in India, helped curb total import spending. Import growth is estimated at about 4.0 per cent in 2014, but is expected to strengthen over the forecast period to 6.1 per cent in 2015 and 7.6 per cent in 2016.

In Western Asia, the major oil exporters have seen a slight decrease in oil demand, which, combined with the fall in oil prices, has lowered export figures for oil exporters such as the Cooperation Council for the Arab States of the Gulf (GCC) countries. These trends are expected to continue into the forecast period, with potentially still sharper falls in the value of oil exports from the GCC countries over the next few years, depending on whether oil price trends continue. Conversely, Turkey has benefited from the depreciation of its currency, which has increased the competitiveness of its exports. The depreciation has caused Turkish imports to fall. Exports from Western Asia are estimated to have rebounded slightly from low growth in 2013 to growth of 3.0 per cent in 2014, but this remains below pre-crisis trends. Export growth is expected to grow at the same pace in 2015 and then increase to 5.3 per cent in 2016. Despite the falling oil prices, import volumes have remained strong in the region, growing by 4.9 per cent in 2014, and are expected to rise by 6.6 per cent in 2015 and 7.4 per cent in 2016, driven by large-scale infrastructure projects.

The trade picture for Latin America is mixed, with some improvement expected

Expectations regarding trade for Latin America and the Caribbean are mixed. Exports of Mexico and Central America are estimated to have increased by 4.7 per cent in 2014, and are expected to maintain a similar pace of 4.1 per cent in 2015 and 4.7 per cent in 2016. Import growth has remained relatively strong after a dip in 2013 and is expected to stay above 5.0 per cent between 2014 and 2016, driven in part by strong domestic demand and investment. By contrast, slow growth in Europe and the growth moderation in China continue to weigh on exports of South America. Some improvement in exports from South America is expected over the forecast period, with 2.8 per cent growth expected in 2015 and 3.5 per cent in 2016. After slowing down in 2014, owing to subdued investment and household consumption, imports to South America are expected to rise gradually over the forecast period to 3.2 per cent in 2015 and 4.8 per cent in 2016.

Trade decomposition

Many of the shifts in trade patterns that were observed over the past few decades continued in 2014, with developing countries exporting an increasing share of world trade by value, particularly manufactured goods. The destination of exports points to a more pronounced shift, as developing countries export a higher share to other developing countries than in the past, with a comparable fall in developed-country exports to developing countries (figure II.3). By contrast, the shift in exports to developed countries has been considerably lower, and developed countries still export most of their goods to other developed countries. Much of the rise in developing countries' share of world exports is due to East Asia's rapidly increasing share of global manufacturing exports, which has risen from one fifth in 1995 to over one third in 2013 (figure II.4). The expansion of China's world trade profile has been a significant driving force in this rise, with a more than fivefold increase in the country's share of global manufacturing exports, to about 17.3 per cent in 2013. A significant portion of the shift in manufactured goods trade shares has come at the expense of the United States,

Figure II.3
Regional shares of exports to developing and developed countries and economies in transition, 1995–2013

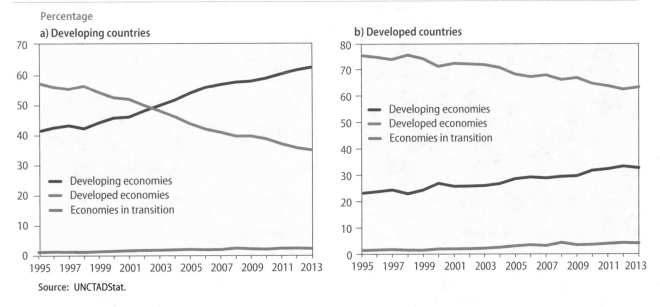

Source: UNCTADStat.

Figure II.4
Regional share in global manufacturing exports

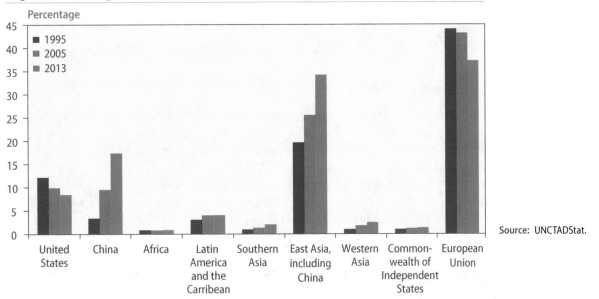

Source: UNCTADStat.

whose share fell by almost 4 percentage points. The EU is still the leading global manufacturing exporter, but its share also decreased, from 44.0 per cent in 1995 to 37.2 in 2013. If current trends persist, East Asia will take over as the largest exporter of manufactures by value in the forecast period.

Within the manufacturing sector there have been some significant changes, particularly as global value chains have expanded across the globe. Along with its overall increase in manufacturing exports, East Asia has seen its share of electronics exports rise from less than 20 per cent in 1995 to about 50 per cent in 2013. Mirroring this upward trend in East Asia, major developed-country electronics exporters, such as Japan, the United States and some European countries, have seen their shares diminish. There have been two parallel developments in this process. Some East Asian economies such as the Republic of Korea and Taiwan Province of China have seen their exports of intermediate goods to other countries (mainly in the region) rise, along with increases in the intermediate goods embedded in their own exports. China, on the other hand, continues to rely to a much greater degree on imported inputs for its exports with limited input into other country's production processes. Meanwhile, the Philippines has seen its exports increasingly contribute to value chains in other countries, while absorbing a decreasing fraction of inputs from other countries in their own exports.

Trends for exports of primary products are somewhat different, influenced to some degree by changes in commodity prices over the past years. Overall, there has been a significant decline in the EU share in primary product exports, from 32 per cent in 1995 to about 22 per cent in 2013. This decline has been seen across almost all types of commodities, with only a few exceptions, such as tobacco, some types of crude materials, and animal oils and fats. In particular, there have been noticeable declines in the EU export shares in products such as meat, sugar, dairy products, beverages and crude fertilizers. However, the region continues to provide a significant portion of the world's exports in many of those areas. At the same time, some regions have increased their market shares of primary commodities, with the biggest increase coming from Western Asia—although this was only by a little more than 8 per cent over the same period, particularly in fuels. For fuels in particular, the CIS has seen an increase from 1995 to 2013 by 4.5 percentage points to almost 15 per cent of world fuel exports. The United States has seen a relatively large increase in its share of fuel exports as well, by 55 per cent between 1995 and 2013. This increase still only puts United States' fuel exports slightly above 4 per cent of the world total, but this is high enough to rank in the top five world fuel exporters.

Trade in services

World services exports have continued to increase in recent years, providing some support to the sluggish performance of global trade. According to the most recent data, global exports of services increased by 5.5 per cent in 2013 and 7.0 per cent in the first quarter of 2014, at current prices. As a result, services exports reached $4.7 trillion in nominal value in 2013, about 20 per cent of total exports. The upward trend in services exports has been driven by developing countries, particularly in Asia and Latin America, as well as economies in transition (figure II.5). In addition, least developed countries (LDCs) have exhibited a remarkably fast expansion, although starting from a low initial level. As a result, between 2000 and 2013, the share of developing countries in world services exports rose from 23 per cent to 30 per cent, particularly in construction and computer and information services (figure II.6).

Trade in services is highly correlated with foreign direct investment (FDI). Over 70 per cent of world FDI outflows between 2010 and 2012 were related to services activities. Developing countries' share in global FDI outflows into services is still low at 17.0 per cent, but this represents a remarkable increase from the early 1990s when it was only 0.6 per cent. Services trade also requires cross-border movement of people supplying services in export markets, particularly the provision of professional and business services, and thus has a strong linkage to the growth in global remittance flows.

Figure II.5
Evolution of services exports by region, 2005–2013

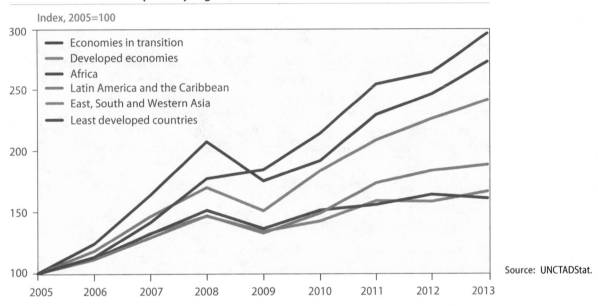

Source: UNCTADStat.

Figure II.6
Developing economies: share in world services exports by sector, 2000 and 2013

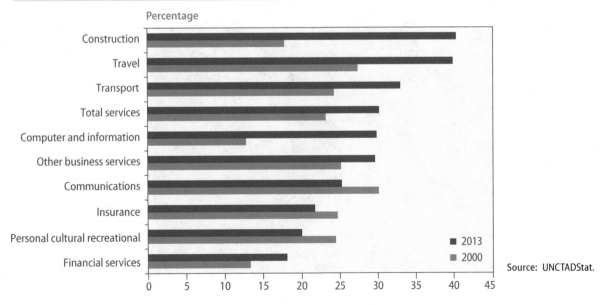

Source: UNCTADStat.

Between 2008 and 2013, the most dynamic services trade sectors in developing countries were computer and information services (figure II.7), posting an annual average growth in exports of these services by 13.0 per cent. Other fast-growing services trade sectors for developing countries were insurance services, followed by travel services and financial services. Communication services, however, have not yet recovered their pre-crisis level. Meanwhile, LDCs posted the highest increase in computer and information services, insurance services and, in particular, construction. However, these sectors together represented just 7.0 per cent of total services exports for LDCs in 2013.

Primary commodity markets

Prices of major commodity groups declined in 2014, with the exception of tropical beverages

Non-oil commodity markets strengthened during the first quarter of 2014, led by strong food and tropical beverages prices, but eased thereafter. As a result, the United Nations Conference on Trade and Development (UNCTAD) Non-oil Nominal Commodity Price Index[2] increased from 245 points in January to 252 points in March 2014, and decreased afterwards by 6 per cent to reach 236 points in September (figure II.8). The average value of the index over the period of January–September was down about 6 per cent compared to its equivalent value in 2013, but it remained high relative to its long-term trend. Compared to 2013, price trends of major commodity groups registered a decline, with the exception of tropical beverages.

Figure II.7
Exports of services by sub-category, 2008–2013

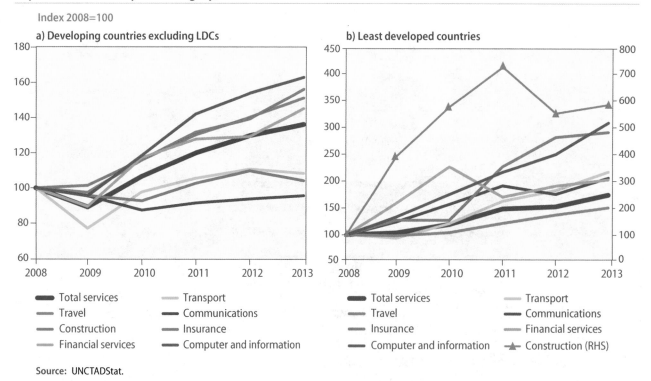

Source: UNCTADStat.

---

2   The UNCTAD Non-oil Nominal Commodity Price Index covers these subgroups of commodities: food, tropical beverages, vegetable oilseeds and oils, agricultural raw materials, and minerals, ores and metals.

Box II.1
Trends in international tourism

Demand for international tourism remains robust

Despite a global economy in low gear, international tourist arrivals (overnight visitors) increased by 5 per cent worldwide in 2013, reaching a record of 1.1 billion. This upward trend continued in the first half of 2014, when international arrivals grew close to 5 per cent compared to the same period in 2013, with the Americas recording the highest growth (6 per cent), followed by Asia and the Pacific and Europe (5 per cent). Thus, global results are in line with the World Tourism Organization (UNWTO) forecast of 4.0 to 4.5 per cent for 2014 and above the long-term forecast of 3.8 per cent for the period 2010 to 2020.

The positive conditions of the tourism sector are also reflected in the confidence index as measured through the UNWTO Panel of Experts. Since 2013, the confidence index has increased to a level only reached in 2007, previous to the financial crisis. However, the most recent four-month survey shows a slight decline in confidence, largely due to the current geopolitical and health risks across the world, including the Ukraine crisis, the conflicts in the Syria Arab Republic and Iraq, and the Ebola outbreak in West African countries.[a]

Export earnings from international tourism reach $1.4 trillion

Total export earnings generated by international tourism reached $1,409 billion in 2013. Receipts earned by destinations from international visitors—as recorded in the Balance of Payments Travel credit—grew by 5 per cent in real terms to reach $1,195 billion, while an additional $214 billion was earned by international passenger transport (rendered to non-residents).

International tourism (travel and passenger transport) accounts for 30 per cent of the world's exports of services and 6 per cent of total exports, a contribution that is similar for developed and emerging economies. For the group of developed economies, tourism generated $924 billion in exports in 2013 (figure II.1.1); as an export category it ranked fourth after chemicals (including pharmaceuticals), fuels and automotive products, but ahead of food. For emerging economies, tourism generated $485 billion in exports in 2013, and it ranked fourth after fuels, food, and clothing and textiles. However, tourism is the first export earner in many emerging economies, including several least developed countries such as

Figure II.1.1
Exports earnings from international tourism and other export categories, 1995–2013

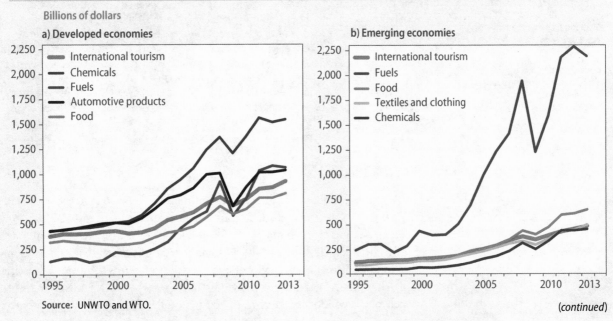

Source: UNWTO and WTO.

(continued)

Box II.1 (*continued*)

Burkina Faso, Gambia, Haiti, Madagascar, Nepal, Rwanda and the United Republic of Tanzania. Furthermore, although fuel is the largest export category worldwide, earnings are heavily concentrated in a few large oil, gas and coal exporters. By contrast, many countries benefit from tourism, which also tends to generate more employment. Additionally, it is interesting to note that during the 2009 economic downturn, international tourism was more resilient than other trade categories, decreasing only by 5 per cent, compared to overall exports declining by 11 per cent.

Tourism in small island developing States

Tourism is a major export and source of foreign revenue, particularly for islands. Small island developing States (SIDS) are a group of 57 countries and territories which share common geographic and economic challenges. In 2013, SIDS welcomed 41 million international tourist arrivals (61 tourists per every 100 residents), plus at least 18 million cruise arrivals (not all countries report). Revenues from international tourism in destinations reached $54 billion, plus an estimated $8 billion in passenger transport, bringing the overall contribution to exports to $62 billion, which represents 9 per cent of SIDS total goods and services exports. Furthermore, tourism accounts for more than half of exports in 12 out of 43 SIDS with data available, and it is the top export category for 23 out of 30 SIDS that provide a breakdown by export category.[b] Islands where tourism is a major export earner include Aruba, Bahamas, Barbados, Bermuda, Cabo Verde, Dominican Republic, Fiji, French Polynesia, Haiti, Jamaica, Kiribati, Maldives, Mauritius, Sao Tome and Principe, Seychelles and Tonga.

The United Nations declared 2014 as the International Year of Small Island Developing States, with Samoa hosting the Third United Nations Conference on SIDS in September 2014.[c] The Samoa Accelerated Modalities of Action Pathway presented a basis for action in various priority areas for the sustainable development of SIDS through durable partnerships and capacity-building. The document recognized the role of tourism in sustainable development and as a significant driver of economic growth and decent job creation.

Travel facilitation and connectivity

Air connectivity and travel facilitation are key factors in the successful development of sustainable tourism. Implementing adequate policies aimed at openness and easy access can boost tourism growth as well as promote trade and investment, infrastructure development, ease of doing business and social, educational and cultural exchanges. In fact, the G20 Leaders' Summit in 2012 recognized the role of travel and tourism as a vehicle for development and economic growth, and committed to work towards developing travel facilitation initiatives in support of job creation and poverty reduction.

For instance, many destinations can gain by revising and improving visa procedures. Visas can provide essential functions with regard to security, immigration control, limitation of duration of stay and activities, and the application of measures of reciprocity. However, too restrictive a policy can act as a constraint. The challenge is finding a beneficial balance. In recent years, UNWTO has been working closely with partners and stakeholders to move this agenda forward.[d] A great deal of progress has been made towards visa facilitation, especially the multilateral agreements that mutually exempt all or certain categories of travellers from the visa requirement. Between 2010 and 2012, over 40 countries made significant changes to their visa policies, facilitating travel from "visa required" to "visa on arrival", "eVisa" or "no visa", according to UNWTO research.

a See *UNWTO Tourism Highlights 2014 edition*, available from http://mkt.unwto.org/highlights and UNWTO World Tourism Barometer, available from http://mkt.unwto.org/barometer.

b *Tourism in Small Island Developing States (SIDS), Building a more sustainable future for the people of Islands*, available from www.wtoelibrary.org/content/gx426g.

c For Conference resources and documents, see www.sids2014.org.

d See "Facilitation of tourist travel", available from http://rcm.unwto.org/content/facilitation-tourist-travel.

Source: UNWTO.

Food and agricultural commodities

Since early 2014, prices of food and agricultural commodities have been trending in different directions (figure II.9). Prices of food, grains in particular, rose in early 2014, owing to dry and freezing weather in the main agrifood producing countries, such as the United States, and conflict between Ukraine and the Russian Federation. Thereafter, thanks to improved weather conditions that boosted global output, prices of grains tumbled. For example, the price of yellow maize n° 3 grade increased by 10 per cent between January and April 2014 to $231 per ton. Then it dropped by nearly 22 per cent to $180 per ton in September 2014, the lowest level since August 2010. The benchmark Thai rice price remained relatively

Figure II.8
Price indices of selected groups of commodities, January 2009–September 2014

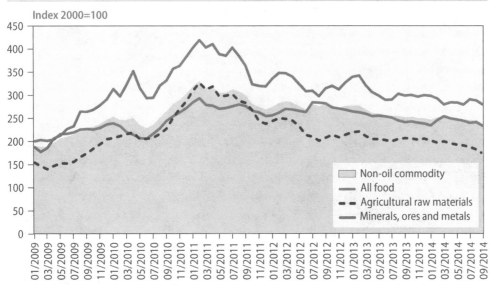

Index 2000=100

low compared to the past few years, albeit with some fluctuations, owing to comfortable stocks carrying over from the previous seasons and the releases from Thai government stockpiles. The price averaged $428 per ton over the period of January-September 2014, 21 per cent lower than the price for the equivalent period in 2013. In contrast, sugar prices increased by 15 per cent from January to March 2014 to 18 cents per pound, following adverse weather in Brazil, a big sugar producer, and concerns over the El Niño phenomenon. Afterwards, sugar prices decreased owing to large inventories and, in September, averaged 16 cents per pound. Beef prices strengthened over the first nine months of 2014, amid a tight supply induced by drought and high feed costs in the United States that weighed on global red meat production.

In vegetable oilseed and oil markets, prices generally eased, but with some short-term fluctuations. The UNCTAD Vegetable Oilseeds and Oils Price Index declined by 17 per cent beginning in January to average 224 points in September 2014. This downward trend was driven by drops in prices for soybeans, soybean oil and palm oil, which decreased by 24, 10 and 18 per cent, respectively, owing mainly to good crop conditions. By the next crop season, comfortable world inventories and a good outlook for vegetable oilseed and oil production should keep downward pressure on prices.

The prices for tropical beverages increased in 2014 after a steady decline beginning in 2011. The UNCTAD Tropical Beverages Price Index rose by 29 per cent between January and September 2014 to 221 points, led mainly by strong coffee and cocoa prices. Over this period, the coffee composite indicator index increased by nearly 46 per cent. Cocoa prices gained 14 per cent over the same period owing to strong demand from the chocolate manufacturing industry. These international price increments are often not passed onto small farmers who dominate the production of coffee, cocoa and other agricultural commodities in a number of producing countries (box II.2).

In raw agricultural commodity markets, prices generally trended down over the first nine months of 2014, amid subdued economic activity of major industrial economies. In September, the UNCTAD Agricultural Raw Materials Price Index was 14 per cent lower

**Strong cocoa and coffee
prices drove increases of
tropical beverage prices**

Figure II.9
Price indices of selected food and agricultural commodity groups, January 2009–September 2014

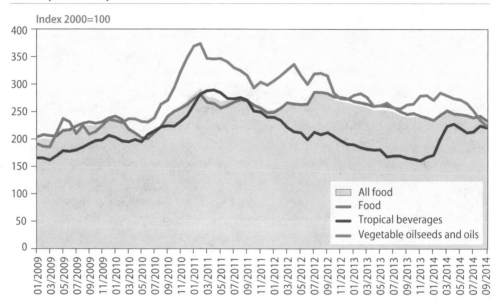

Index 2000=100

Source: UNCTAD secretariat, based on data from UNCTADStat.

than its value in January. The price of natural rubber (n° 3 RSS) fell by 29 per cent over the period, owing to oversupply and rising stocks. For cotton, the relatively high prices during the first half of 2014 were followed by a significant price drop in the third quarter. In September 2014, the Cotton Outlook Index A fell to 73 cents per pound, the lowest level since December 2009. Record-high global cotton stocks, a good crop outlook in the United States—the world's biggest cotton exporter—and a lower expected import quota by China in 2015 weighed heavily on cotton prices. In the outlook period, international prices for most agricultural commodities should moderate further, particularly if current crop conditions continue. However, weather concerns, such as the effects of the El Niño phenomenon, are likely to be the major upside risk factor.

Minerals, ores and metals

Downward pressures on prices of minerals, metals and ores continue

The prices of minerals, ores and metals have trended downward from their peak in 2011, with some short-term price fluctuations. During the first nine months of 2014, the UNCTAD Minerals, Ores and Metals Price Index averaged 285 points, compared with 309 points during the same period in 2013. However, this general trend disguises the divergent performance of individual minerals, ores and metals. For instance, while the iron ore market was bearish, nickel and zinc markets were characterized by a strong price recovery from 2013 (figure II.10).

The market for nickel was characterized by oversupply and sliding prices in 2013. However, the market dynamics have changed notably, following the enforcement of an export ban of unprocessed ores in January 2014 by Indonesia, the world's leading nickel mining country. Concerns over a supply shortage coupled with speculative buying by

Box II.2
Small farmers and commodity prices: cocoa and coffee producer prices

Small farmers are important actors in agricultural global value chains as they produce a large share of traded agricultural commodities. In particular, they dominate the production of tropical beverages as they account for more than 80 per cent of cocoa and about 70 per cent of coffee traded on global markets. Small farmers are price-takers and are atomized, and their incomes—which tend to fluctuate significantly—are largely determined by domestic and external factors beyond their control. These include domestic trade policy, price volatility on international markets and many others. Furthermore, many small farmers do not receive an adequate return on their activities. According to data from the period 2006 to 2011 from the International Cocoa Organization (ICCO), the average share of cocoa producer prices in international prices varied from 50 per cent in Côte d'Ivoire to 72 per cent in Cameroon and to 89 per cent in Ecuador. For coffee, producers in Viet Nam obtained 82 per cent of the international price, while an Ethiopian coffee producer received only 61 per cent. High taxation of the domestic cocoa sector in Côte d'Ivoire, currently at about 22 per cent of exports, has contributed to reducing the price share accruing to farmers. In contrast, relatively higher cocoa producer prices are noted for Cameroon, where domestic taxes have been eliminated and export levies reduced to as low as five cents per kilogram. In Ethiopia, the relatively low price received by coffee producers is associated with factors including relatively high marketing and transaction costs, collusion of buyers, and high concentration of exporters.

Small farmers in low-income developing countries are also affected by increasing market concentration in the agricultural food industry at the global level. For some products, a small number of multinational companies control a large share of the global market. For example, the three largest cocoa multinational companies buy about 50 to 60 per cent of world cocoa production, and this oligopolistic power could erode the limited negotiation room left for small farmers, weakening even further their ability to derive fair benefits from international trade.

Several policies and actions can help small farmers to address some of these challenges. For example, strengthening farmers' associations would increase their bargaining power by allowing them to deliver in bulk, facilitating quality control, and helping to meet traceability requirements. Negotiating contract farming on behalf of small farmers, whereby transnational corporations source their inputs directly from small farmers, could help to overcome the problems related to having many intermediaries, which leads to higher producer prices. This is the essence of the newly established Public-Private Partnership between Unilever and the International Fund for Agricultural Development. Small farmers can also take advantage of the expanding niche markets in organic products and thus benefit from price premiums these markets offer. For instance, there is high demand for organic cocoa beans driven by food safety and environmental concerns, but supply represents only 0.5 per cent of total cocoa production. This segment offers sizable opportunities.

In addition, there is a need to introduce and enforce competition laws in producer and consumer countries in order to reduce imbalances in bargaining power between sellers and buyers. Enforcement is particularly important at the international level to prevent excessive market power that might result from mergers or acquisitions. Moreover, for countries such as Côte d'Ivoire, lowering domestic taxes could help to increase the share of the international price paid to small farmers. Furthermore, as the case of the Cocoa Board (Cocobod) in Ghana has shown, Governments could provide well-tailored extension services and sponsor institutions that offer subsidized training and credit to small farmers in order to increase their efficiency and competitiveness. The experience of Equity Bank Kenya, with its provision of credit and advisory services to millions of small farmers, also illustrates that even the private sector can make a profit while helping small farmers to transform their activities into sustainable small businesses. Finally, small farmers in low-income developing countries would benefit from domestic policies aimed at increasing local value retention along commodities value chains. For example, thanks to national policy reforms and private sector investments, cocoa has increasingly been processed in countries such as Brazil, Côte d'Ivoire, Ghana and Indonesia.[a] These experiences offer small farmers the opportunity to be an integral part of domestic value chains.

a According to ICCO, origin grindings for cocoa accounted for about 44 per cent in world total grindings in the 2012/2013 crop season, an increase from about 32 per cent in 2000/2001.
Source: UNCTAD.

Figure II.10
Price indices of selected minerals, ores and metals, January 2009–September 2014

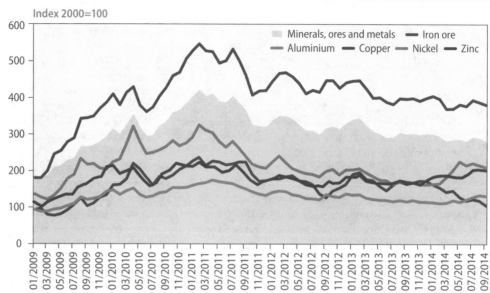

Index 2000=100

Legend: Minerals, ores and metals · Iron ore · Aluminium · Copper · Nickel · Zinc

Source: UNCTAD secretariat, based on data from UNCTADStat.

financial investors have led to the surge of nickel prices. In May 2014, the London Metal Exchange (LME) nickel price rose to a 27-month high of $19,434 a ton, an increase of 38 per cent compared to the price in January 2014. Although prices trended downward in the following months, the average price of nickel during the first three quarters of 2014 was 12 per cent above the price in the same period of 2013. The zinc market rallied in the first nine months of 2014, and the average price rose by 12 per cent compared to the January–September average in 2013. In August 2014, the LME zinc price surged to a three-year high of $2,329 per ton. Stronger demand, driven partly by the growth of automobile production combined with expected tighter supply and decreasing stocks, underpinned the price recovery.

The performance of the copper market was lacklustre in the first three quarters of 2014. Prices averaged $6,940 per ton, down from $7,383 in the same period of 2013, translating into a 6.4 per cent decline. In March 2014, the LME copper price fell to $6,666, the lowest level since July 2010. Rising mine production and concerns over demand prospects from China contributed significantly to the price decline. Furthermore, China's first corporate bond default in March 2014, and a probe into possible base metals financing fraud, increased market uncertainties about China's future copper demand. The prices of iron ore registered a sharp decline of 36 per cent in the first nine months of 2014. The price plunge was mainly due to oversupply by the world's major mining groups and weakening growth in steel production in China, where the subdued property market has suppressed the demand for steel.

In 2015, barring unexpected supply disruptions, the price trends of base metals and ores will be largely determined by the demand from major consuming countries, especially China. The country's economic restructuring from investment towards consumption is likely to support the prices of metals, which are widely used in consumer goods such as zinc, tin and lead, and put pressure on the prices of copper and iron ore.

Oil market prices

In 2014, the Brent oil price declined considerably during the second half of the year, bringing the annual average price down to $102 per barrel (pb), slightly lower than the previous forecast.[3] Lower prices mainly reflected the gap between oil demand growth and oil supply growth (figure II.11), which is expected to continue in 2015. As a result, the average Brent oil price in 2015 is expected to decline to $92 pb, significantly lower than in recent years. In 2016, as the global economy is expected to improve, oil demand growth will increase and drive prices up to an average of $96 pb.

Oil demand growth has been slowing throughout 2014, on the back of sluggish economic activity in several key economies, including Japan and Western Europe. In addition, weaker-than-expected GDP growth in China has also weighed on oil demand. As a result, growth in oil demand was at its lowest level in two and a half years during the second quarter of 2014. According to the International Energy Agency, global oil demand is expected to have grown by 0.6 million barrels per day (bpd) in 2014[4], bringing total demand up to 92.4 million bpd, lower than originally anticipated. In 2015–2016, although the United States is expected to partially offset weaker demand from other developed economies, global demand growth for crude oil should continue at a moderate pace, in line with the overall demand for commodities. Oil demand growth in 2015 is not expected to exceed 1.1 million bpd, which will bring total demand up to 93.5 million bpd.

Conversely, oil supply has seen strong growth, both from Organization of the Petroleum Exporting Countries (OPEC) and non-OPEC members, reaching 92.8 million bpd in the second quarter of 2014, 1.2 million bpd higher than demand during the same quarter. Oil output from OPEC members has been relatively steady, despite conflicts in Iraq, which produces more than 3 million bpd and became a major pillar of global supply. Against the

Oil demand growth slowed down throughout 2014 and will continue at a moderate pace in 2015

Despite the military conflict in Iraq, there is strong growth in global oil supply

Figure II.11
World oil demand and supply, 2004–2014

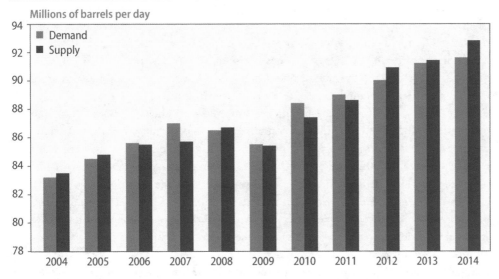

Millions of barrels per day

■ Demand
■ Supply

Source: International Energy Agency.
Note: Data for 2014 are as of the second quarter.

---

3   See United Nations, "World economic situation and prospects as of mid-2014" (E/2014/70).

4   Based on September's Oil Market Report.

backdrop of political and military tensions in Iraq, investors had originally worried about supply disruptions and oil prices shot up to a high of $115 pb in June (figure II.12). However, only a small portion of Iraq's oil output had been threatened, as conflicts were taking place in northern parts of the country. Concerns about disruptions were short-lived and in July 2014 prices started to resume their downward trend, reinforced by the expectations that global oil supply would remain stable throughout the year and the forecast period. Another positive sign has been the recovery in Libya's oil output, which offset losses from other OPEC members. As a whole, OPEC crude oil production (excluding natural gas) is estimated to have exceeded 30 million bpd in 2014. At the same time, supply from developed economies, in particular from the United States, has also been growing strongly and is estimated to have expanded by 1.5 million bpd in 2014, reaching 19.5 million bpd.

Throughout the forecast period, oil supply is expected to remain stable from both OPEC and non-OPEC sources. For OPEC members, several positive prospects are expected to reinforce supply stability. Oil production and exports from the Islamic Republic of Iran could edge up in 2015, beyond the current one million bpd, if an agreement over nuclear negotiations is reached between the Islamic Republic of Iran and members of the Security Council. At the same time, risks of supply disruption have edged down in Iraq.

Global supply will remain robust

Despite the fact that demand growth is expected to remain slow, OPEC members are not expected to trim oil production to support Brent prices throughout the forecast period. In August 2014, Saudi Arabia cut its oil output by 330,000 bpd in response to lower demand from its customers. However, as recently announced by Saudi Arabia, further cuts from OPEC members are not expected during the forecast period. Oil supply from developed economies is also expected to remain strong, in particular from Canada and the United States, and is set to expand by 0.9 million bpd in 2015.

Oil prices are expected to decline faster than originally anticipated

Against this backdrop, oil prices are estimated to have declined to an average of $102 pb in 2014. Supply concerns eased, demand remained tepid, and, in July, hedge funds considerably reduced their net long exposure to Intercontinental Exchange Brent to the lowest since January 2013. As a result, the Brent crude oil price decreased by almost 5 per cent in August compared to July. In September and October, oil prices deepened their slide (figure II.12), settling below $90 pb, especially after weak industrial and retail data in China was released and output growth for major EU economies was revised downward. The appreciation of the United States dollar has also reinforced the downward trend of the Brent oil price. The stronger dollar weighs on oil markets as it makes commodities denominated in United States dollars more expensive for countries holding other currencies.

In 2015, the average crude oil price is expected to decline by about 10 per cent to $92 pb from $102 pb in 2014. This forecast is based on the assumption that OPEC countries will not cut production to support oil prices and that global oil demand growth will continue to be weak. In 2016, the Brent oil price is expected to recover moderately to $96 pb, provided that global demand growth accelerates gradually while oil output remains stable.

Weaker growth in oil demand could drive prices even lower than forecast

Nevertheless, there are important risks to this forecast. On the downside, growth in oil demand could be weaker, particularly from China, Japan and Western Europe, which would drive prices lower than forecast. On the upside, if OPEC members decide to cut oil production, oil prices could rebound faster than anticipated. At the same time, if the conflict in Iraq escalates, supply disruptions could be a major concern, which would lift the Brent price above the projected price. In addition, current reciprocal sanctions between the Russian Federation and leading OECD countries are raising more concerns about possible consequences for the Russian Federation's oil production and exports.

Figure II.12
Europe Brent spot price FOB, January 2013–October 2014

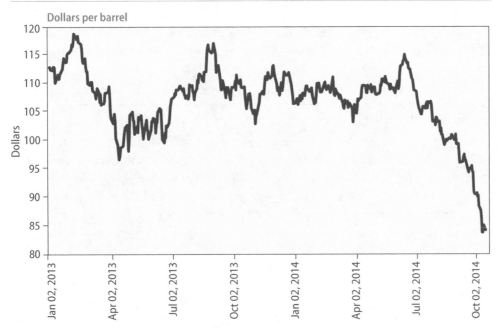

Source: United States Energy Information Administration.

Trade policy developments

Multilateral trade negotiations

The Doha Round was launched in 2001 and the original intention was to conclude the round by 2004.[5] However, recurrent setbacks and the prevalence of alternative negotiating forums, such as regional and plurilateral processes, was increasingly perceived as affecting the credibility of the Multilateral Trade System (MTS) and significantly raised the stakes of the Ninth WTO Ministerial Conference (MC9) in December 2013. Of concern in the run-up to MC9 therefore was the need to find concrete deliverables, focusing on a limited number of issues to enable a subsequent conclusion of the entire Doha Round.

The Doha Round has made little progress in the last decade

The MC9 resulted in adoption the Bali Ministerial Declaration and a set of decisions known as the Bali Package. The package includes: (i) the Trade Facilitation Agreement (TFA); (ii) the five decisions on agriculture regarding (a) the definition of general services, (b) public stockholding for food security purposes, (c) tariff-rate quota administration, (d) export competition, and (e) cotton; and (iii) four decisions on development-related issues, namely (a) preferential rules of origin (RoO), (b) operationalization of the LDC services waiver, (c) duty-free and quota-free (DFQF) market access for LDCs, and (d) a monitoring mechanism on special and differential treatment (SDT). These texts were negotiated as a package, thus the balance of ambitions and interests within and across the issues was a key stumbling block. The package was generally considered as a major achievement. However,

The Doha Round faces new uncertainties as the WTO failed to adopt a legal protocol to implement the TFA

---

5   United Nations, "Report of the Secretary-General on international trade and development" (A/69/179); UNCTAD, "Towards an enabling multilateral trading system for inclusive and sustainable development" (TD/B/C.I/MEM.5/5).

the recent failure at the WTO General Council in July 2014 to adopt a legal protocol necessary to implement the TFA— due to differences among WTO members regarding the linkage between the TFA and post-Bali negotiations on public stockholding for food security purposes—generated significant uncertainty over the prospects for the Bali Package implementation and the entire Doha Round.

Trade facilitation

Onerous and complex customs and transport procedures constitute a substantial part of trade transaction costs, and reducing them through trade facilitation measures is important in boosting trade worldwide. As a result, trade facilitation is expected to generate important welfare gains, particularly for developing countries. Furthermore, many of the specific trade facilitation measures covered by the TFA have proven to have a high return on investment, as they help to reduce costs and increase revenue collection. The reforms also usually have a direct effect on development by improving inter-agency collaboration, investing in human and institutional capacity-building, enhancing good governance and helping the informal sector to participate in the formal economy and international trade. The TFA was the first binding multilateral agreement negotiated since the Uruguay Round and addresses some 37 substantive import, export and transit procedures. It seeks to clarify and improve existing GATT disciplines on customs procedures relating to Article V (freedom of transit), Article VIII (fees and formalities) and Article X (publication and administration of trade regulations).

There is a persistent difference in members' perceptions regarding the linkage between the TFA and other areas of negotiations

While recognizing the economic case of trade facilitation, developing countries, particularly LDCs lacking institutional capacities, were concerned over adjustment costs they would have to bear, as implementation of some measures (e.g., single window procedures) were found to be relatively complex or costly, while other measures were feared to be difficult to eliminate (e.g., mandatory use of customs brokers). It is in recognition of such concerns that the TFA incorporated an unprecedented form of special and differential treatment for developing countries, which formally establishes a linkage between their implementation capacity, provision of capacity-building support and the timing and level of commitments. Accordingly, implementation of various commitments was modulated into three categories of modalities: (i) immediate implementation upon entry into force of the TFA (for a least developed country member within one year after entry into force); (ii) implementation subject to predetermined transition periods; and (iii) implementation subject to the provision of capacity-building support and capacity acquisition. Following MC9, each developing country was to designate for itself those commitments they would be implementing under each category. Since timely and effective provision of capacity-building support was a major cause for concern for many countries, recent efforts have led to the creation of a WTO facility on trade facilitation as a potential source of funding as a last resort while concern continues to exist over the appropriate level of funding. Other international organizations, including UNCTAD, have created additional technical support facilities and reaffirmed their support to assist in implementing the TFA.

Following MC9, WTO members had until 31 July 2014 to adopt a protocol to amend the WTO agreement to incorporate the TFA in its legal architecture on a definitive basis. The proposed protocol would then be open for acceptance until 31 July 2015. It was not adopted, however, owing to persistent difference in members' perceptions regarding the TFA linkage with other areas of negotiations.

Agriculture

Against the backdrop of rising and volatile food prices, many food-insecure countries had introduced public stockholding programmes, such as the procurement of wheat and rice at subsidized, administered (i.e., higher-than-market) prices from low-income farmers as implemented in India. The original proposal on food security was aimed at exempting such price support from the scope of the Aggregate Measure of Support, so that such support is exempt from any quantitative limits. In the absence of agreement on a permanent solution, an interim solution was found at MC9 in the form of a "peace clause", i.e., an exemption from legal challenge under dispute settlement procedures. The interim nature of the peace clause was the key stumbling block in the negotiations. It was agreed at Bali that WTO members were to engage in negotiations to find a permanent solution for adoption by 2017. This work remains at a preliminary stage with a few new proposals submitted by different groupings (e.g., the United States, G-33) with the proponents of reform reemphasizing their original proposals to introduce formal changes in relevant WTO provisions, while the food-insecure countries are underlining the need to evaluate countries' experiences on food security issues and policies.

Development issues

While delivering on LDC issues constituted the central elements of development issues, the Bali outcomes in these areas are relatively modest. DFQF market access is an agreed international development target already contained in Millennium Development Goal 8, as further reaffirmed in the United Nations Istanbul Programme of Action for LDCs, which set the target of doubling the share of LDC exports by 2020. The Bali outcome urged, but did not require, expeditious improvement of DFQF coverage by 2015 for those countries that had not provided DFQF treatment for 97 per cent of tariff lines. The outcome on preferential RoO takes the form of non-binding guidelines for making RoO simpler and more transparent. Besides, the importance of continued technical assistance to address the development aspects of cotton was reaffirmed, and a Monitoring Mechanism on SDT to monitor the implementation of existing SDT provisions was established.

Issues related to LDCs make modest progress

Concerning the operationalization of the LDC services waiver, the Bali Package provided a road map for the implementation of preferential market access for LDC services and services suppliers to be covered by the waiver. The waiver is aimed at allowing non-LDCs to deviate from General Agreement on Trade in Services (GATS) Most Favoured Nation (MFN) obligations to provide services preferences in relation to market access restrictions (but not national treatment, the inclusion of which is subject to approval). Although the waiver was adopted in 2011, no WTO member has introduced services preferences for LDCs. The proposed road map rests largely on the formulation by LDCs of a collective request identifying the sectors and modes of their export interest. On that basis, the Council for Trade in Services was expected to convene a high-level meeting within six months, so that developed and developing countries in a position to do so could pledge to implement the provision of services preferences for LDCs. This implied that the onus was on LDCs to identify existing market access barriers affecting their exports and request their elimination on a preferential basis to facilitate their exports. In July 2014, the LDC group submitted such a collective request. The convening of the high-level meeting has now been placed on the agenda of the Council for Trade in Services.

The way forward

The inability of WTO members to implement the TFA has created new uncertainties over the prospects for the post-Bali work on the Doha Round. At Bali, it was already recognized that the package, although important, was not a substitute for the overall Doha Round. As a way forward, WTO members were to prepare a clearly defined work programme on the remaining issues of the Doha Round by the end of 2014. These programme guidelines were to prioritize those issues where legally binding outcomes were not achieved at MC9 as well as all other Doha issues central to concluding the Round, while also fully exploring different negotiating approaches, presumably including plurilateral or sectoral approaches. Discussions to date have pointed to some key principles: (i) the need for a balanced approach to agriculture, non-agricultural market access (NAMA) and services; (ii) the centrality of the development dimension; and, (iii) the need to focus on "doables". Views differ on whether to use the draft modality texts on agriculture and NAMA of 2008 as the basis of future work.

In this process of defining a balanced package for the post-Bali work, it is important that it reflects new trade and policy developments affecting various negotiating areas. For instance, the environment surrounding agricultural negotiations has evolved significantly since 2008. Higher commodity prices have sharpened food security and rural livelihood concerns, and prompted many net-food importing countries to seek to secure domestic food supply through several policy interventions, including production support, public stockholding, international purchases and border protection against import surges. High prices, and national policy reforms, have led to a substantial reduction in the use of trade-distorting support and export subsidies in major subsidizing countries. This in some cases entailed so-called box shifting—the conversion of trade-distorting support, such as price support (amber box), into non- or minimally trade-distorting support, such as direct payment to farmers (green box). However, the resulting concentration of agricultural subsidies in the green box category has raised concern over potentially trade-distorting effects of such support.

The relative incidence of non-tariff measures (NTMs), such as sanitary and phytosanitary (SPS) measures and technical standards, in affecting developing countries' exports has increased over the years. In agriculture, the average restrictiveness of NTMs is about 20 per cent, more than twice the average tariff of 7 per cent. The costs of compliance are disproportionately high for low-income countries as many lack the capacities required to comply. On the other hand, while average industrial tariffs declined in the 2000s, tariff protection remains important in manufacturing sectors, as many countries seek to support manufacturing capacities and job creation, particularly in labour-intensive consumer industries.

Plurilateral trade agreements

The composition of the post-Bali work programme is likely to be influenced by parallel plurilateral and regional processes. In July 2014, 14 countries representing 86 per cent of global trade in environmental goods launched plurilateral negotiations for an environmental goods agreement. The agreement is argued to promote green growth and sustainable development while providing impetus for the Round's conclusion. The negotiations are open to all WTO members and the results would be extended on an MFN basis. These would be built on efforts to reduce import tariffs to below 5 per cent by 2015 on a list of 54 environmental goods as identified by the Asia-Pacific Economic Cooperation countries in 2012. Environmental goods include wind turbines, air quality monitors and solar panels.

The negotiations would first aim at eliminating tariffs, and subsequently address NTMs affecting the products and environmental services.

Another important plurilateral initiative is the negotiations for a trade in services agreement (TISA) involving 23 WTO members, representing 70 per cent of global services trade. The negotiations aim for a comprehensive and ambitious services liberalization by capturing autonomous and preferential liberalization, and seeking to adopt horizontal application of national treatment to all sectors and modes of supply. The TISA is expected to build upon the GATS approach to promote subsequent multilateralization and participation of new members. Automatic multilateralization of the results based on the MFN principle will be temporarily pushed back as long as there is no critical mass of countries joining TISA, implying that the future TISA would be a preferential agreement to be covered under GATS Article V. Plurilateral discussions also continue, while currently pending, on expanding the product and country coverage of the existing WTO Agreement on Information Technology. The revised Agreement on Government Procurement, concluded in 2012, became effective in April 2014. Whether plurilateral approaches—together with their systemic implications—are useful in bringing forward the Doha Round negotiations warrants careful reflection.

Evolving regional trade agreements

The most significant challenge to the multilateral trade system is the increased prevalence of RTAs. As of June 2014, some 585 notifications were made to the WTO, of which 379 were in force. Each developed country had preferential access to an average of 23 countries in 2012, and about 60 per cent of their trade is covered by some RTAs.[6] Twenty-first century RTAs qualitatively differ from previous RTAs in their scope, composition and depth. They are oriented towards a deeper and more comprehensive integration with a strong regulatory focus on providing a viable platform for regional value chains by ensuring a duty-free and non-tariff-barrier free trading environment. This integration of RTAs with regulatory systems will render them more compatible and transparent. In addition to full market opening, they now encompass a range of behind-the-border regulatory measures including investment, competition policy, capital movement, intellectual property rights and government procurement.

The emergence of "mega-RTAs" represents a major shift in trade relationships, over which many developing countries have no control. The Trans-Pacific Partnership Agreement (TPP), Trans-Atlantic Trade and Investment Partnership Agreement (TTIP) and Regional Comprehensive Economic Partnership Agreement (RCEP), would all create giant economic zones covering substantial proportions of world trade in goods and services (Table II.1). These mega-RTAs are qualitatively different from previous RTAs in their size, depth and systemic consequences and generally draw on a template developed by major players. By inducing deeper liberalization and high-standard, cutting-edge regulatory harmonization that covers an increasing share of world trade, they could affect incentives for multilateralism, and could further erode the primacy of the MTS, which is built upon the non-discrimination principle. This would have significant implications for countries' incentives to negotiate MFN liberalization at the global level, while some issues with systemic implications, most notably domestic agricultural support, would continue to be most efficiently

RTAs cannot replace the role of the multilateral trade system

6   UNCTAD, *Key Statistics and Trends in Trade Policy* (UNCTAD/DITC/TAB/2013/2).

Table II.1
Comparison of "mega-RTAs"

Regional trade agreement	Members	Percentage share in world exports	Intra-group exports as a percentage of global exports	Intra-group imports as a percentage of global imports	Combined GDP as a percentage of world GDP	Bilateral agreements among parties
Pacific Alliance	4	2.7	3.9	4.5	2.8	6
RCEP	16	27.3	42	47.4	29.5	23
TISA	23	70.3	na	na	67.3	
TPP	12	26	46.3	38.3	38.9	25
Tripartite FTA	26	1.7	11.9	12.9	1.6	4
TTIP	2	43.9	17.3	14.3	45.4	0

Source: UNCTADStat and WTO.
Note: EU is counted as one entity. Trade and GDP figures are for 2012.

negotiated at the multilateral level. By developing cutting-edge disciplines, it is often argued that mega-RTAs would set a new template for future trade and investment cooperation.

For instance, emerging mega-RTAs would shift their focus towards regulatory harmonization to reduce divergence in national standards affecting trade. Regulatory harmonization and mutual recognition could remove barriers arising from diverse technical standards, and license and qualification requirements on services and services suppliers. Such regulatory cooperation would be more feasible under RTAs. Some new proposed disciplines under mega-RTAs (e.g., TTIP) include regulatory coherence, whereby each member is required to have an institutional mechanism at the central government level to facilitate central coordination and review of newly covered regulatory measures. This may include conducting impact assessments of a proposed regulatory measure in the light of its objective and efficiency. This could constrain the ability of regulatory authorities. For a third country adopting lower standards, this could represent upward harmonization of regional standards and might have adverse effects on exporting in regional markets in developing countries.

> Mega-RTAs would shift their focus towards regulatory harmonization to reduce divergence in national standards

Recent mega-RTA negotiations (e.g., TPP) have also sought to address the potentially anti-competitive effect of state-owned enterprises (SOEs) that tend to receive some preferential treatment including preferential finance.[7] Some regional disciplines have sought to establish competitive neutrality between SOEs and private companies by eliminating such structural advantages. At the same time, some developing countries have stressed the importance of SOEs in delivering public policy goals. Concern over possible limitation of regulatory autonomy also arose in relation to the Investor-State dispute settlement (ISDS) mechanism increasingly incorporated in RTAs. The ISDS is seen to confer greater rights to foreign investors and lead to "regulatory chill" as regulators might refrain from taking certain regulatory actions (e.g., environmental regulations) for fear of legal challenge under ISDS. Non-trade concerns and geopolitics (linked with the compatibility issues with other RTAs) sometimes play important roles, either as stimulants or obstacles to RTAs. Concerns about infringement of sovereignty and giving unfair privileges to transnational corporations, for instance, have led to objections to RTA clauses allowing ISDS before arbitral tribunals; this would, for example, prevent German ratification of the EU-Canada RTA or acceptance of ISDS in the TTIP.[8]

---

7   See, for instance, http://www.ustr.gov/tpp.

8   Stefan Wagstyl, "Germany expresses concerns about US and Canada trade deals", *Financial Times*, 25 September 2014.

From a development perspective, mega-RTAs—and the twenty-first century RTAs more generally—might represent a risk for weaker and more vulnerable developing countries as they can simply be left out. When these countries do take part, locking in existing preferential market access conditions under unilateral preferential arrangements is often a key motivation (e.g., in the context of economic partnership agreements between the African, Caribbean and Pacific Group of States and the EU). Larger and more competitive developing countries face challenges in effectively securing improved market access, as RTAs often preserve high tariffs on import-sensitive products that attracted high protection on a MFN basis, including dairy, sugar and apparel. In contrast, ensuring an adequate content, pace and sequence of their own liberalization is a key concern of developing countries, as the effect of reciprocal tariff elimination would be greater for them, given economic asymmetries. Furthermore, with their stronger behind-the-border disciplines that are "WTO+" or "WTO-X", RTAs may constrain countries' policy space to implement proactive trade and industrial policies for development purposes. It is therefore important that market-opening objectives are critically balanced with the flexibility to design and implement measures to build essential productive capacities and move up the value ladder[9].

The level of services commitments is illustrative of the significance of RTAs in inducing effective liberalization, particularly in developing countries. Trade in services has become a major feature of RTAs, particularly North-South RTAs. Research based on a WTO dataset on services commitments suggest that for developed countries, RTA commitments represent only limited improvements from their GATS commitments because these countries generally register a higher level of GATS commitments than developing countries.[10] In contrast, for developing countries, the level of RTA commitments is markedly higher than GATS commitments in all sectors, due in part to the fact that developing countries' initial GATS commitments are relatively low. This may also be explained by the asymmetric bargaining structure of North-South RTAs.

Consolidation and expansion of South-South regional integration initiatives are increasingly pursued to create a platform to support developing countries' integration into regional value chains, and to foster economies of scale, diversification and technology upgrading. In Africa, efforts are directed at boosting intra-African trade by fast-tracking the establishment of a continental pan-African free trade agreement by 2017, building upon the existing tripartite free trade agreement initiative among the East African Community, the Common Market for Eastern and Southern Africa and the Southern African Development Community. In Asia, the Association of Southeast Asian Nations (ASEAN) is headed towards the formation of the ASEAN Free Trade Area in 2015 to support the creation of the ASEAN Economic Community in 2020. In Latin America, new initiatives have emerged such as the Pacific Alliance, alongside the traditional arrangements of the Andean Community and the Common Market of the South (MERCOSUR). A dialogue between MERCOSUR and the Pacific Alliance has been initiated. Many South-South RTAs have also acted as platforms for the development of productive capacity, regional transport and infrastructure networks, and connectivity. Such cooperative initiatives, along with liberalization, have proved to be essential components of "developmental regionalism".

Vulnerable countries face the risk of being excluded from large RTAs

South-South regional integration initiatives continue on the rise

---

9   UNCTAD, *Trade and Development Report 2014: Global Governance and Policy Space for Development* (United Nations publication, Sales No. E.14.II.D.4).

10   UNCTAD, "Services, development and trade: the regulatory and institutional dimension" (TD/B/C.I/MEM.4/5; "Impact of access to financial services, including by highlighting remittances on development: economic empowerment of women and youth" (TD/B/C.I/EM.6/2).

Further coherence is
needed between the MTS
and the RTAs

The quantitative expansion, proliferation and qualitative deepening of RTAs highlight the need for coherence between the MTS and RTAs. It is important to secure convergence between the multilateral and regional processes to ensure an optimal mixture of both arrangements, as well as coherence among regional processes, so that they can, in their totality, create an enabling environment for sustainable development. There is also the need for strong multilateral oversight and effective disciplines, including setting minimum standards for regional regulatory provisions. Developmental coherence is required so that SDT and policy space available under the MTS is not overridden by RTAs. RTAs could also promote broader cooperation.

As of 2013, almost half of world trade took place between countries that had signed RTAs, with almost one third regulated under deep trade agreements. While most developing countries' trade still occurs outside the coverage of RTA rules, there are notable exceptions among some countries of South-East Asia, Southern Africa and Latin America. However, the percentage of global trade taking place under RTAs has not kept pace with the increase in numbers of RTAs, partly because the bulk of world trade still remains between countries or regions that have not yet concluded any RTAs with one another (i.e., China, Japan, the EU and the United States).

Future direction at the multilateral level

Non-negotiating
functions of the WTO
are fundamental to
the transparency,
predictability and
stability of
international trade

While much attention is given to the prolonged Doha Round negotiations, the WTO non-negotiating functions are fundamental to the transparency, predictability and stability of international trade. Existing WTO rules and disciplines serve as the guardian against protectionism and discrimination. In the aftermath of the global economic crisis, the surge in protectionism was much feared but was relatively well contained, thanks essentially to countries' adherence to WTO norms and self-restraints. Such legal foundation of the MTS needs upholding; restrictive measures may disrupt trade. A recent WTO report finds that G20 members put 93 new trade-restrictive measures in place between mid-May and mid-October of 2014, over half of which are trade remedy actions.[11] While trade affected by these measures remains marginal, nonetheless it remains of concern that 962 of a total of 1,244 trade-restrictive measures taken since the global crisis remain in place. These measures are estimated to cover $757 billion or 4.1 per cent of world imports, about 5.3 per cent of the value of G20 imports.

It is also generally believed that the WTO dispute settlement mechanism (DSM) continues to function well as countries continue to use the system. A total of twelve panels were established in 2013, a ten-year high. This not only indicates unaffected legitimacy enjoyed by the DSM, but also rising tensions in trade relations. Recent disputes have increasingly addressed measures reflecting global concerns at the interface of trade and neighbouring public policy areas. These concerns include: health-related packaging regulations on tobacco; measures promoting renewable energy (wind and solar power technology), including through domestic content requirements; sustainable exploitation of natural resources (raw materials and rare earths); and animal welfare (seals, dolphins). Traditional disputes continue to be raised, including those on anti-dumping and subsidies.

The centrality of the MTS is also evidenced by the fact that the MTS continues to be headed towards universality as it attracts new members. Thirty-two countries have acceded

---

11   World Trade Organization, "Report on G-20 Trade Measures", op. cit.

since 1995, bringing WTO membership to 160, with Yemen being the most recent member. Seychelles' accession is expected by end-2014. These countries have embarked on substantial policy reforms to make their trade regime WTO-compatible. Negotiating balanced terms of accession consistent with their development needs has been a major challenge.

The MTS could be seen as having the characteristic of a public good; however, its relevance and credibility are facing challenges, owing to difficulties encountered in delivering negotiated outcomes in the Doha Round. Strengthening the MTS architecture to better respond to changing economic realities and global challenges would also help address these difficulties. Various twenty-first century trade issues have also been proposed by different analysts as the future agenda for the MTS.[12] For instance, the increased prevalence of trade within global value chains (GVCs) is said to have called for shifting focus of trade liberalization approaches in favour of deeper liberalization, addressing the "trade-investment-services-know-how nexus" by adopting a whole supply chain perspective, and addressing (on a cluster-by-cluster basis) tariff and non-tariff regulatory barriers that increase trade costs throughout GVCs. This argument needs to be weighed against the fact that tariff protection remains prevalent, even in countries integrated in GVCs, and that tariff and industrial policy intervention continue to be used in developing countries to build productive capacity, trigger structural transformation and promote upgrading within GVCs.[13]

Global value chains are promoting different approaches towards trade liberalization

Another stream of ideas is to update the "WTO rule book" to better reflect the increased interaction of trade with broader public policies, as such interactions have emerged as new sources of trade disputes. WTO members' prioritizing of trade facilitation and the food security agenda in the Bali package already reflects the changing policy focus to promote trade in GVCs and address interaction between trade and food security. Other suggested agenda items include the relationship between trade and climate change and green growth (e.g., border tax adjustment, local content subsidies, trade-related investment measures and government procurement for renewable energy). Similar to food prices, high energy prices have heightened the concern over access to energy and raw materials (e.g., renewable and fossil fuel subsidies, and export restrictions).

The manner in which the Doha Round has evolved over the past thirteen years indicates the importance of strengthening the negotiating function of the WTO in the future. In retrospect, a large negotiating agenda going beyond the two built-in agendas of agriculture and services may be seen as having contributed to slow progress throughout negotiations. The appropriate level of contributions to be made by developed and developing countries, in terms of issues such as liberalization commitments, became a persistent stumbling block, leading some commentators to question the validity of the current design of SDT. Some institutional factors were also found not to be amenable to efficient negotiations, such as consensus-based decision-making, large and diverse membership, the single undertaking principle, a lack of leadership and weakened business interest. Careful reflection is warranted on how best to strengthen the negotiating function in the presence of parallel plurilateral and regional negotiating processes.

The negotiating function of the WTO should be strengthened

---

12   See World Trade Organization, "The future of trade: the challenges of convergence", Report of the Panel on Defining the Future of Trade convened by WTO Director-General Pascal Lamy, 24 April 2013, Geneva.

13   UNCTAD, *Trade and Development Report 2014*, op. cit.

Trends and implications at the national trade policy level

Policymakers face the challenge of an uncertain global trade system

National trade policymaking should be undertaken within the framework of applicable international rules. However, this is becoming increasingly difficult since both the MTS and RTAs are moving towards ever-greater uncertainty and fragmentation. Heightened attention needs to be paid to: national trade policymaking that is consistent with broader national development objectives and strengthened productive capacities; ensuring coherence of RTAs with the multilateral trading system; and the collection, analysis and dissemination of data on trade and its socioeconomic and developmental impact.

All of this would suggest that developing-country policymakers, whether or not their countries are party to major RTAs, should strive to maximize their information and analysis of these factors in order to determine appropriate responses at the national, regional and multilateral levels. For instance, in determining the potential trade creation or diversion effects of RTAs, consideration must be given to the volumes and structures of trade between individual parties and non-parties to RTAs, similarity of products traded, and prevailing trade regimes (including preferences granted). Policymakers must also pay special attention to the collection and analysis of data about non-tariff measures (such as technical barriers to trade), SPS measures, quantity and price controls, and contingency protection or restrictive RoO, given the prevalence and impact of such measures in international trade and their implications for economic development and public health, food security and environmental objectives.

At the same time, to strengthen the ability to cope with whatever international frameworks (or lack thereof) eventually emerge, further efforts should also be undertaken by developing countries and economies in transition to develop their productive capacity and promote structural economic transformation (including diversification) and trade competitiveness. This would facilitate conformity with any higher and/or harmonized standards agreed upon under RTAs. Trade and other economic or social objectives, such as health, food security or sustainability, should be organically linked within the internationally agreed development goals under the post-2015 development agenda. In this regard, special priority should be provided to trade in agriculture, which may generate significant impetus for economic growth, enhanced food security, poverty reduction and sustainable development.

Last but not least, the concurrence of two multilateral negotiation processes—the post-2015 development agenda and the WTO Doha Round—could still present a unique opportunity to strengthen global policy coherence, thereby linking international trade to inclusive and sustainable growth.

Chapter III
International finance for sustainable development

In 2015, the international community will adopt a new development agenda, aiming to end poverty and promote sustainable development globally and in every nation. Since the launch of the United Nations World Commission on Environment and Development report, "Our Common Future",[1] twenty-five years ago, the global community has significantly advanced its understanding of the interlinkages between the economic, social and environmental dimensions of sustainable development, while the rapid pace of technological progress and economic globalization has dramatically reshaped the real economy. At the same time, since the United Nations adopted the Monterrey Consensus on Financing for Development in 2002, the global financial system has become much more complex; however, the mechanisms for managing finance at both domestic and international levels have not kept pace with this increased complexity or the imperatives of sustainable development.

The realization of an ambitious and transformative post-2015 sustainable development agenda will require a comprehensive and enabling financing framework. Despite some significant changes in the frameworks for international finance, channelling savings to investments in sustainable development remains a formidable challenge, further exacerbated by the financial crisis in 2008. In intermediating credit to productive investment, the international financial system needs to ensure that resources are efficiently, equitably and sustainably allocated to sustainable development, thereby facilitating progress across its three dimensions in a balanced and integrated way, while, at the same time, minimizing the risk of financial instability and crises.

A transformative post-2015 sustainable development agenda will require an enabling financing framework

Current financing and investment patterns are inadequate in achieving significant sustainable development outcomes. Private international capital flows are not only often volatile, they are also insufficient in volume and maturity to fund sustainable development—an endeavour which typically requires long-term investment. At the same time, public financial flows (i.e., official development assistance (ODA) and concessional lending from public institutions) to realize the sustainable development goals remain deficient. Efforts to raise public resources through taxation are stymied by financial engineering, tax loopholes and accounting practices. The absence of an international system for debt restructuring contributes to greater uncertainty, and possibly higher costs, for countries seeking to raise additional resources in the sovereign bond market (box III.1). Financial sector regulations have not yet fully mitigated the risks exposed by the 2008 financial crisis. Finally, the governance reforms of the international financial architecture continue to lag behind changes in global economic and financial structures.

---

1   United Nations, "Our Common Future", Report of the World Commission on Environment and Development (A/42/427).

Box III.1

Argentina and the sovereign debt litigation: implications for future debt restructuring

In recent years, almost 50 per cent of sovereign defaults[a] involved legal disputes abroad—compared to just 5 per cent in the 1980s—and 75 per cent of these litigations involved distressed debt funds, also known as vulture funds that typically oppose orderly debt restructuring as holdout creditors. Recent developments in the legal dispute between NML Capital Ltd.[b] and Argentina have set a legal precedent with grave consequences for the future of sovereign debt restructuring. The judgement of the United States court not only upheld the commercial and speculative interest of a hold-out creditor, it also undermined the notion of sovereign immunity and adversely affected third parties, including those bondholders who accepted the debt restructuring and payment settlement system.

Argentina defaulted on most of its external debt in December 2001 and managed the debt crisis with two rounds of debt swaps in 2005 and 2010. The Congress of Argentina passed the Lock Law in 2005, which prohibited the Government from reopening the swap or making any future offer on better terms. In addition, the debt swap agreement included a Right upon Future Offers (RUFO) clause, which established that if Argentina offered better terms to the creditors refusing the swap (the so-called hold-outs) in the future, these terms should be extended to those who did accept the debt restructuring (the so-called hold-ins or exchange-bond holders).[c] These ensured that exchange-bond holders would not lose out on any better deal in the future and motivated 92.4 per cent of the bond holders to accept the restructuring deal and sizeable discounts on the face value of the bonds. However, the lack of a legal basis to bind in hold-out creditors prevented Argentina from bringing a closure to the 2001 debt default and led to "the sovereign debt trial of the century".

While Argentina regularly serviced its restructured debt since 2005 and managed to reduce its external debt stock from 153.8 per cent in 2002 to 26.2 per cent of its gross national income (GNI) in 2012, the NML litigation and judgement of the United States court forced Argentina into selective or restricted default, as of 31 July 2014. The Southern District Court of New York invoked a broad interpretation of the so-called *pari passu* clause, which required Argentina not only to treat all bond holders equally but also to make rateable payments in full, in terms of what it owed to the hold-outs, equivalent to $1.33 billion. The United States court ruling became enforceable, as Argentina issued the bonds held by NML under New York state law and agreed to make payments to the bond holders through its trustee, the Bank of New York—a legal entity incorporated under New York commercial law. Accordingly, the courts prohibited the Bank of New York from making any payment to exchange-bond holders until the hold-outs received their rateable payments in full.

Furthermore, the court allowed the hold-out creditors to seek information on Argentine assets worldwide, including those of Argentine officials. Such a ruling, if accepted by other jurisdictions, would not only further infringe Argentina's sovereign immunity, but would also have significant impact on the international financial system, as it would force third-party financial institutions to provide confidential information on the sovereign borrower's global financial transactions to the creditors.[d]

Argentina maintains that it has not defaulted, not only because it was willing to pay, but because it is actually paying.[e] For future payments, Argentina is seeking to replace the foreign banks that have blocked (or may block) its payments with a nationally based mechanism led by the Banco de la Nación Argentina. It is also offering a new debt swap to the holders of restructured bonds, maintaining all terms unchanged, but offering Buenos Aires or Paris as alternative jurisdictions for dispute resolution. Furthermore, Argentina argued that it could not make the full payment to hold-out creditors on the grounds that the payment would violate the RUFO clause in the restructured debt. It is estimated that if the RUFO clause is triggered, Argentina may be required to pay its exchange-bond holders anything from $120 billion to $500 billion.

Critics of the ruling believe that not only is the ruling unfair, since the interpretation of the *pari passu* clause is extremely debatable, but also the ruling challenges some basic legal principles that affect the third parties not involved in the litigation (the exchange-bond holders) and extends the New York court's ruling to other jurisdictions. The New York court injunction, prohibiting payments of euro-denominated Argentine bonds under English law, is indeed currently being challenged in the British courts.

(continued)

a Julian Schumacher, Christoph Trebesch and Henrik Enderline, "Sovereigns defaults in court", 6 May 2014, available from http://papers.ssrn.com/sol3/papers.cfm?abstract_id=2189997.

b A distressed debt fund and a subsidiary of Elliot Management based in the Cayman Island.

c The RUFO clause is valid until 31 December 2014.

d See UNCTAD, "Argentina's 'vulture fund' crisis threatens profound consequences for international financial system", 24 June 2014, available from http://unctad.org/en/pages/newsdetails.aspx?OriginalVersionID=783&Sitemap_x0020_Taxonomy=UNCTAD%20Home.

e The Bank of New York Mellon not only channels payments of bonds issued under New York law, but also euro-denominated restructured bonds issued under English legislation. Moreover, part of the restructured debt is under Argentina's legislation, and so far the United States judge has allowed the financial intermediary for those bonds payments, Citibank, to transfer the payments.

The ruling has huge global and systemic implications, with the potential to derail future debt restructurings by strengthening the hands of hold-out creditors.[f] It provides creditors the incentive to hold-out in a debt restructuring, interferes with the settlement system and further erodes sovereign immunity. The court ruling also incentivizes speculation, as hold-out creditors can push down the prices of a bond and in the process collect hefty payouts in credit default swaps.

In an effort to mitigate the problem, the International Monetary Fund (IMF)[g] and International Capital Markets Association (ICMA)[h] have suggested the inclusion of aggregation clauses in future bond issues. This will provide rules by which bonds in circulation will be aggregated across a series of bond issues, complementing the collective action clauses which provide a majority rule for a single bond issue. This is predicated on the assumption that the volume of bonds required to hold out against a restructuring under the proposed aggregation clauses, would be sufficiently large and will hence create a disincentive to hold out in restructuring. This solution may work for larger economies that have a huge stock of outstanding bonds, but in the case of countries where the volumes are small with few bond issues, it will be very easy for creditors to buy bonds to meet the threshold for a hold out. Moreover, there is a huge existing supply of bonds that could not be covered by the proposed clauses. IMF and ICMA have also proposed the inclusion of a simplified *pari passu* clause to mean equal ranking and not the rateable payment version of *pari passu* applied by the New York court.

There is a need for some kind of legal arrangement to prevent hold-outs from obstructing an orderly debt restructuring. In response to concerns by Member States on the gaps in the existing framework for sovereign debt restructuring, the United Nations General Assembly adopted a resolution on 9 September 2014 entitled "Towards the establishment of a multilateral legal framework for sovereign debt restructuring processes".

Box III.1 (*continued*)

f Brazil, France, Mexico and the United States of America, among others, have filed amicus briefs in New York courts to point out the implications for future debt restructuring.
g IMF, "Strengthening the contractual framework to address collective action problems in sovereign debt restructuring", October 2014, available from http://www.imf.org/external/np/pp/eng/2014/090214.pdf.
h See http://www.icmagroup.org/resources/Sovereign-Debt-Information/.
Source: UN/DESA.

A reorientation of current investment patterns and a stronger complementarity and synergy between public and private investment are sine qua non for sustainable development. The ongoing negotiations on new sustainable development goals and an associated financing framework afford the international community an opportunity to devise a new international financial architecture that is adequate, effective and predictable for achieving sustainable development.

Greater synergies between public and private investments are needed to promote sustainable development

Global imbalances and international reserves accumulation

As discussed in chapter I, global imbalances on the current accounts of major economies have continued to narrow over the past few years, somewhat reflecting a cyclical downturn, weak external demand in deficit countries, and structural changes in a few surplus countries. Global imbalances are projected to remain at a benign level in 2014 and 2015. Nonetheless, many of the structural causes of global imbalances persist, with the potential to undermine long-term economic stability.

The nearly fivefold increase in global foreign-exchange reserves—from $2.1 trillion in 2000 to $12.0 trillion in 2012—can be directly attributed to current-account imbalances in major economies, with emerging and developing countries accounting for an estimated $8.0 trillion of the total reserves.[2] In line with narrowing imbalances, reserve accumulation in emerging markets and developing economies has slowed.

Structural causes of global imbalances persist…

2 IMF, "Currency composition of official foreign exchange reserves (COFER)", available from http://www.imf.org/external/np/sta/cofer/eng/cofer.pdf (accessed 17 November 2014).

... and countries are
accumulating reserves
above recommended levels

Views on the optimal size for countries' international reserves have changed over time. In the 1980s and 1990s, reserves were thought of as insurance against trade shocks, with the rule of thumb suggesting that countries should hold reserves large enough to cover three months of imports. Given that the emerging market crises in the mid-1990s, such as the Mexican "tequila crisis", were triggered by difficulties in refinancing short-term dollar-denominated debt (rather than unexpected trade deficits), the view that reserves should be large enough to meet short-term external debt refinancing needs took hold. This view, however, did not consider that the emerging-market crises of the 1990s were also triggered by reversals in short-term portfolio flows and the unwinding of carry trades. By early 2000, many countries opted for a more comprehensive self-insurance, with adequate reserves to mitigate risks associated with volatile international capital flows and open capital accounts.

Empirical studies suggest that no single factor can explain the reserve accumulation behaviour of all countries at all times,[3] and several factors explain the continued build-up in international reserves. Reserve accumulation can be an outcome of central bank interventions in foreign-exchange markets to smooth exchange-rate volatility or maintain an undervalued currency to support export-led growth strategies. It may also be a strategy associated with the management of excessive capital inflows. As such, reserve accumulation is often correlated with high global liquidity and changes in international investor sentiment. A number of studies, however, find a positive, unexplained residual in more recent years, implying that reserves are higher than what would be predicted by precautionary motives or export-led growth strategies. Further research is required to assess the precautionary needs of individual countries, taking into account the historical trends in capital-account volatility,[4] while international policy coordination can be further strengthened to reduce risks associated with volatile capital flows and enhance financial safety nets.

Reserve accumulation
comes at high
opportunity costs

There are, however, significant costs associated with holding large reserves. First, reserves are typically invested in safe liquid assets, and according to International Monetary Fund (IMF) estimates, the United States Treasury securities and euro-denominated sovereign-backed assets account for 61.0 per cent and 24.5 per cent of global reserves, respectively. The continued accumulation of reserves in safe low-yield assets comes at high opportunity costs, as these could be invested domestically to achieve greater economic, social and environmental outcomes. Second, accumulation of foreign-exchange reserves can increase domestic money supply, which can be inflationary. One way central banks combat this is by sterilizing inflows. However, this has its own costs, since borrowing in local currencies to sterilize inflows usually carries interest costs higher than what central banks can earn on their foreign assets. Furthermore, the large share of developing-country international reserves held in assets abroad implies a net transfer of resources from poorer countries to wealthier ones. A net transfer of financial resources of approximately $970.7 billion from developing to developed countries is estimated in 2014 (figure III.1). This negative net transfer of financial resources for most developing and emerging economies has continued for almost 20 years, with the exception of the least developed countries (LDCs), which con-

---

3   Atish R. Ghosh, Jonathan D. Ostry and Charalambos G. Tsangarides, "Shifting motives: explaining the build-up in official reserves in emerging markets since the 1980s", IMF Working Paper, No. WP/12/34 (January 2012). Washington, D.C..

4   The International Monetary Fund (IMF) has recently adopted a new framework for exploring this further. See IMF, "Assessing reserve adequacy: further considerations", IMF Policy Paper, November 2013.

Figure III.1

Net transfers of financial resources to developing economies and economies in transition, 2002–2014

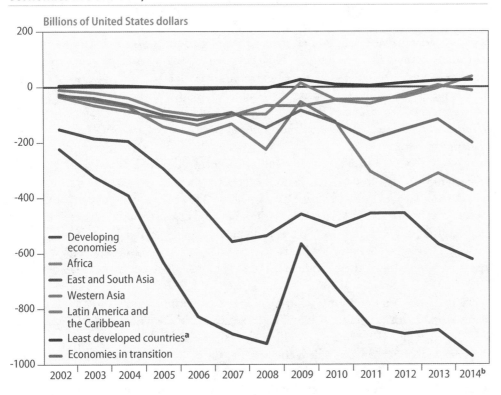

Billions of United States dollars

Legend:
- Developing economies
- Africa
- East and South Asia
- Western Asia
- Latin America and the Caribbean
- Least developed countries[a]
- Economies in transition

Sources: UN/DESA, based on International Monetary Fund World Economic Outlook Database, October 2014 and World Bank, *Migration and Remittances* database.
a Cabo Verde graduated in December 2007 and is therefore excluded from the calculations.
b Partly estimated.

tinue to receive net positive transfers. Finally, excessive reserve accumulation, while sensible at the national level, exacerbates global imbalances and systemic risks worldwide.

There are several proposals at the international level to address global imbalances and the excessive accumulation of foreign reserves in developing countries. A sustained reduction in global imbalances has been an objective of the Group of Twenty (G20) policy coordination. The Commission of Experts of the President of the United Nations General Assembly recommended that the international reserve system make greater use of the IMF Special Drawing Rights (SDRs) as a way to reduce systemic risks associated with global imbalances, and as a low-cost alternative to accumulation of international reserves. However, this idea has not gained sufficient political support in policy discussions.[5]

Absent a political agreement to reduce global imbalances, it has become imperative to effectively address the range of risks embedded in the international financial system in order to reduce the perceived need for self-insurance, and to free up reserves for potential and productive investment in sustainable development. Methods for addressing these risks include: managing risks associated with volatility of cross-border private capital flows; reducing excessive leverage in the financial system; addressing too-big-to-fail institutions; improving coordination of monetary and exchange-rate policies; and ensuring more robust international financial safety nets.

Managing systemic and idiosyncratic risks is an imperative as global imbalances persist

---

5   United Nations, "Report of the Secretary-General on international financial system and development" (A/68/221).

Trends in private capital flows

Private capital flows often
do not reach countries and
sectors that most need
investment for sustainable
development

Attracting stable and long-term private investment for human development and critical infrastructure sectors, including transport, energy, and information and communications technology, is essential for countries pursuing sustainable development. While there is a clear correlation between the level of investment and growth, the quality of investment—particularly its long-term orientation and its potential impact on social and environmental outcomes—matters for sustainable development. International private flows are highly pro-cyclical and portfolio flows, in particular, tend to be highly volatile and ill-suited to support sustainable development priorities (table III.1). Additionally, private capital flows are not necessarily invested in countries most in need and in sectors necessary for sustainable development.

There has been a strong upward trend in international private capital flows to developing countries over the last decade, with net private capital flows to developing countries increasing more than threefold from $155.7 billion in 2005 to $327.7 billion in 2013.[6] Foreign direct investment (FDI) has exhibited the largest increase over the last decade, rising in net terms from $246.4 billion in 2005 to $448 billion in 2013[7] and has also shown greater stability. Outward FDI from developing countries and economies in transition has also increased sharply during this period, reaching $553 billion, or 39 per cent of total outward FDI, in 2013.[8]

Economies in Asia and Latin America have been the largest recipients of FDI

FDI to developing countries, however, has been concentrated in a small number of countries and sectors, largely in Asia and Latin America. Although flows to Africa increased in the last decade, rising from $29 billion in 2005 to an average of $40 billion in the post-crisis years, they remain limited compared to the volume of flows to East and South Asia or Latin America and the Caribbean. In addition, greenfield FDI to developing countries has fallen by more than 50 per cent since the crisis, signalling a potential reduction of the impact of FDI on the real economy or sustainable development. Although the value of announced greenfield projects in LDCs increased by 9 per cent in 2013, it remains significantly below historical levels.

Cross-border banking flows are highly volatile and short-term

Cross border bank flows, an important source of private capital, have demonstrated high volatility in recent years, as a number of international banks—particularly in Europe—remain saddled with financial difficulties, non-performing loans and deleveraging pressures. The stock of total international claims of banks[9] stood at $20.7 trillion in June 2014, down from its peak of $25.1 trillion in March 2008 (figure III.2). The claims vis-à-vis developing countries, as a percentage of total international claims, increased from 10.2 per cent in March 2008 to 18.4 per cent in June 2014 and exceeded the pre-crisis level by September 2010. However, both the share of long-term international claims (those with a duration of one year or longer) and the share of loans flowing to the non-bank private sector declined significantly since 2008. In particular, this has affected financing infrastructure projects in emerging-market and developing countries, a significant portion of which were previously funded by large developed-country banks. There is a concern that

---

6   Calculations by UN/DESA based on the IMF World Economic Outlook database (October 2014) and Balance of Payments Statistics.

7   Ibid.

8   UNCTAD, *World Investment Report 2014: Investing in the SDGs: An Action Plan* (United Nations publication, Sales No. E.14.II.D.1).

9   The consolidated banking statistics of the Bank for International Settlements (BIS) define international claims of BIS reporting banks as the cross-border claims of all reporting foreign banks in all currencies, plus local claims of those banks in foreign currency, but not their local claims in local currencies.

Table III.1

Net financial flows to developing countries and economies in transition, 2005–2014

Billions of dollars

	2005	2006	2007	2008	2009	2010	2011	2012	2013[a]	2014[b]
Developing countries										
Net private capital flows	155.7	251.4	386.6	153.0	440.6	534.7	468.9	175.0	327.7	171.9
Net direct investment	246.4	241.6	342.9	364.9	267.7	352.0	455.2	412.9	448.0	400.3
Net portfolio investment[c]	-55.7	-121.8	-19.6	-61.2	8.2	91.5	57.9	78.6	27.7	73.7
Other net investment[d]	-35.0	131.6	63.3	-150.7	164.8	91.2	-44.2	-316.6	-147.9	-302.1
Net official flows	-66.0	-263.8	-96.6	-132.3	53.8	49.3	-70.6	-21.0	25.5	1.8
Total net flows	89.7	-12.4	290.0	20.7	494.4	584.0	398.3	154.0	353.2	173.7
Change in reserves[e]	-547.3	-670.7	-1056.1	-741.0	-711.7	-884.9	-754.9	-484.2	-631.3	-589.3
Africa										
Net private capital flows	26.0	109.0	11.2	52.1	30.2	-1.2	20.9	60.8	-24.2	23.3
Net direct investment	29.4	25.8	40.8	54.5	47.4	34.8	41.8	35.0	40.0	41.0
Net portfolio investment[c]	1.7	6.9	-2.9	-42.4	-16.4	-0.3	-11.7	3.5	8.9	-0.1
Other net investment[d]	-5.1	76.3	-26.7	40.0	-0.8	-35.7	-9.3	22.3	-73.1	-17.6
Net official flows	-19.6	-143.2	11.7	-37.9	23.1	22.1	10.3	-0.6	91.7	31.5
Total net flows	6.4	-34.2	22.9	14.2	53.3	20.9	31.2	60.2	67.5	54.8
Change in reserves[e]	-63.7	-75.7	-85.8	-75.9	3.3	-22.0	-29.1	-31.3	9.5	23.1
East and South Asia										
Net private capital flows	65.0	56.0	154.1	-28.4	340.5	370.0	321.3	-12.9	253.7	108.3
Net direct investment	128.6	139.9	162.9	155.7	99.6	196.8	264.6	218.2	234.2	207.1
Net portfolio investment[c]	-36.5	-138.9	-45.5	-38.3	28.9	23.0	29.7	-9.1	-79.0	-39.3
Other net investment[d]	-27.2	55.0	36.7	-145.8	212.0	150.3	27.0	-222.0	98.5	-59.5
Net official flows	5.2	-2.1	-42.5	-9.9	9.3	11.4	-49.2	25.2	-2.5	46.9
Total net flows	70.2	53.9	111.6	-38.4	349.8	381.4	272.1	12.4	251.2	155.3
Change in reserves[e]	-344.7	-433.0	-675.2	-490.9	-667.8	-685.2	-505.3	-219.6	-512.6	-524.8
Western Asia										
Net private capital flows	25.1	36.1	112.4	56.9	34.4	49.1	-54.8	-5.0	-37.0	-49.6
Net direct investment	32.1	44.0	46.9	56.7	51.8	35.7	23.1	29.1	24.4	18.3
Net portfolio investment[c]	-5.2	-0.8	-4.9	15.7	-5.8	5.6	-23.4	55.5	42.1	49.5
Other net investment[d]	-1.8	-7.1	70.4	-15.5	-11.6	7.7	-54.5	-89.6	-103.4	-117.4
Net official flows	-21.0	-72.6	-69.6	-89.1	-21.0	-38.8	-55.7	-102.4	-120.4	-141.5
Total net flows	4.1	-36.5	42.8	-32.2	13.4	10.3	-110.5	-107.3	-157.4	-191.1
Change in reserves[e]	-98.5	-107.7	-166.1	-133.0	7.2	-88.2	-110.2	-174.3	-121.8	-76.7
Latin America and the Caribbean										
Net private capital flows	39.6	50.3	109.0	72.4	35.5	116.8	181.5	132.1	135.3	89.9
Net direct investment	56.3	31.9	92.4	98.0	68.9	84.6	125.6	130.6	149.4	133.9
Net portfolio investment[c]	-15.7	11.0	33.8	3.8	1.5	63.2	63.3	28.7	55.8	63.6
Other net investment[d]	-1.0	7.4	-17.2	-29.5	-34.8	-31.1	-7.3	-27.2	-69.9	-107.6
Net official flows	-30.6	-45.9	3.8	4.6	42.4	54.6	23.9	56.7	56.7	64.9
Total net flows	8.9	4.4	112.8	77.0	77.9	171.4	205.5	188.8	192.0	154.7
Change in reserves[e]	-40.4	-54.4	-129.0	-41.3	-54.5	-89.6	-110.2	-58.9	-6.4	-10.9
Economies in transition										
Net private capital flows	36.7	68.0	140.5	-91.2	-43.2	3.0	-42.1	-12.4	29.5	-80.6
Net direct investment	11.5	28.4	34.7	55.4	22.0	12.9	21.0	30.5	8.7	4.6
Net portfolio investment[c]	7.4	5.0	8.4	-22.3	-1.0	12.2	-8.5	-5.9	1.8	-10.9
Other net investment[d]	17.7	34.6	97.4	-124.3	-64.2	-22.0	-54.6	-36.9	19.0	-74.3
Net official flows	-22.1	-31.7	-4.6	-18.3	40.5	-16.1	-18.4	-2.9	-44.2	-8.6
Total net flows	14.7	36.3	135.9	-109.6	-2.7	-13.0	-60.5	-15.3	-14.7	-89.2
Change in reserves[e]	-79.4	-134.6	-170.6	29.5	-10.6	-51.6	-26.6	-25.2	23.4	52.6

Source: UN/DESA, based on IMF World Economic Outlook database, October 2014.

Note: The composition of developing countries above is based on the country classification located in the statistical annex, which differs from the classification used in the World Economic Outlook.

a Preliminary.

b Forecasts.

c Including portfolio debt and equity investment.

d Including short- and long-term bank lending, and possibly including some official flows owing to data limitations.

e Negative values denote increases in reserves.

Figure III.2
International claims of BIS reporting banks vis-à-vis developing countries, 2000–2014 Q2

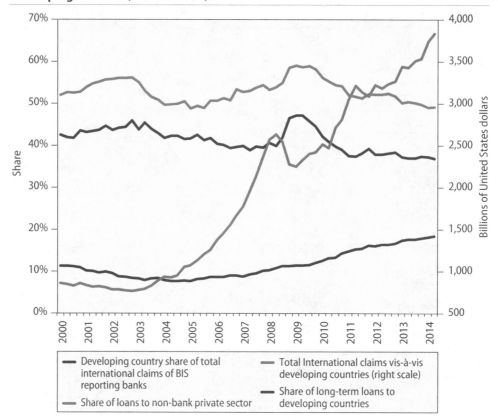

Sources: UN/DESA, based on data from the Bank for International Settlements (BIS).
Note: International claims of BIS reporting banks include cross-border claims of foreign banks in all currrencies plus local claims of foreign banks in foreign currency.

— Developing country share of total international claims of BIS reporting banks

— Total International claims vis-à-vis developing countries (right scale)

— Share of loans to non-bank private sector

— Share of long-term loans to developing countries

the Basel capital adequacy rules will increase the cost of long-term lending from banks, with a potentially negative impact on infrastructure and green investments (see the section on reforming the banking system).

Portfolio investment in emerging markets has evolved, but volatility remains

Portfolio flows have also been highly volatile (box III.2), with aggregate net outflows of as much as $121.8 billion in 2008, contrasting with net inflows of $91.5 billion in 2010 (table III.1).[10] Regionally, East and South Asia experienced net portfolio outflows for the third year in a row in 2014, while Latin America and the Caribbean and Western Asia received large inflows. The nature of portfolio investment in emerging markets has evolved over the past fifteen years, as many local markets have deepened and become more globally integrated. The share of emerging-market bonds and equities in global investors' portfolios has risen sharply over the past decade. This has been driven by the growing importance of emerging markets in the world economy, improvements in the perception of their relative credit risk and credit ratings, and low yields in advanced economies. In particular, as domestic debt markets have grown, foreign investors have increased their purchases of local currency debt, and now play a dominant role in a number of emerging markets. One recent

---

10   A change in methodology for reporting on various elements of the capital account, introduced with the IMF Balance of Payments and International Investment Position Manual, 6th ed. (BPM6) in the last year, means that the date on private portfolio flows is not comparable to data presented in previous editions of the *World Economic Situation and Prospects*.

Box III.2
Managing capital flows to reduce the vulnerabilities of developing countries

Since the late 1970s, global financial cycles—which have featured large capital inflows from developed countries, followed by "sudden stops" or capital outflows—have affected many developing countries. These cycles are driven primarily by developed countries' economic conditions and monetary policy decisions, and often do not necessarily respond to financial needs in developing countries, although a few developing countries continue to finance their current-account deficits with short-term capital flows. Furthermore, in some cases, capital inflows have been too large for the absorption capacity of many of these economies, generating undesired macroeconomic outcomes, such as financial bubbles, excessive consumption credit, currency appreciation, trade deficits and over-indebtedness. This creates financial fragility that frequently leads to financial crises when the tide of foreign capital recedes,[a] while also limiting policy tools available to manage macroeconomic volatility.[b]

Governments need to have at their disposal a suitable set of policies and instruments for managing international capital flows to avoid or reduce disruptive macroeconomic and financial effects. In times of capital inflows, macroeconomic policy measures may include currency market interventions and lower interest rates, if inflation is subdued. Macroprudential measures such as limits on foreign-exchange exposures by financial institutions might be appropriate as well. In times of outflows, foreign reserves, if available, can be used to avoid sharp and excessive currency depreciation.

Following the global financial crisis, a new cycle of capital flows to developing countries started with inflows exceeding pre-crisis levels. To attenuate upward pressures on their currencies, excess liquidity creation and asset bubbles, developing countries such as Brazil, Indonesia, the Republic of Korea and Thailand employed specific capital-account management techniques:[c] Brazil introduced taxes on portfolio inflows and on derivatives (some of which were later removed when flows receded); the Republic of Korea reintroduced a withholding tax on foreign purchases of treasury and central bank bonds; Indonesia adopted a minimum holding period for central bank paper and a limit on short-term borrowing by banks; and Thailand adopted a withholding tax on foreign investors for state bonds. Moreover, these countries used macroprudential domestic financial regulations to influence capital inflows, including reserve requirements on banks' short foreign-exchange positions (Brazil), an increase in reserve requirements on foreign-currency deposits (Indonesia) and ceilings on foreign-exchange positions of banks (the Republic of Korea).[d] Thus, depending on the country in question, these management tools could be price- or quantity-based. While addressing the common challenge of excessive capital inflows, these tools vary across countries depending on the types of flows (and how these flows are channelled internally) and also depending on the institutional capacity to adopt one specific management form or another. Brazil, for instance, has a track record of adopting such techniques countercyclically, benefiting from experience and from having an apparatus in place to achieve greater effectiveness.[e]

During 2009–2010, these measures proved effective in moderating inflows for a period of time. Together with continued interventions in the foreign-exchange markets, upward pressures on exchange rates were reduced. Moreover, these measures provided more room for the macroeconomic policy management necessary to support the policy objectives of stability and sustained growth. For instance, Brazil maintained an expansionary fiscal policy, while Indonesia, the Republic of Korea and Thailand abstained from a more active fiscal policy to counterbalance the inflationary effects of the inflows. These outcomes suggest that the success of capital-account management measures should be evaluated not only by way of looking at what happens with the inflows themselves, but also by the policy space that they can provide to pursue effective growth policies.

Recent empirical literature suggests that capital-account management measures in times of excessive capital inflows can indeed be very useful, especially when applied to debt flows.[f] Iceland's capital management measures during the global financial crisis show that controls on capital outflows can also be a critical tool to stabilize a country's macroeconomic situation in times of a balance of payments crisis.[g] However, unlike developed countries and emerging economies, many developing countries at lower stages of economic development often lack the institutional capacity for effective capital-account management, in which case these countries may be better off maintaining some restrictions on their capital-account transactions.

(continued)

a Andrew G. Haldane, "The big fish, small pond problem", speech delivered at the Annual Conference of the Institute for New Economic Thinking, Bretton Woods, New Hampshire, 9 April 2011; and UNCTAD, *Trade and Development Report 2013: Adjusting to the Changing Dynamics of the World Economy* (United Nations publication, Sales No. E.13.II.D.3).

b United Nations, *World Economic and Social Survey 2010: Retooling Global Development* (United Nations publication, Sales No. E.10.II.C.1).

c IMF, "Recent experiences in managing capital inflows—Cross-cutting themes and possible policy framework", prepared by the Strategy, Policy, and Review Department. Washington, D.C., February 2011.

d UNCTAD, *Trade and Development Report 2014: Global Governance and Policy Space for Development* (United Nations publication, Sales No. E.14.II.D.4).

e Barry Eichengreen, and Andrew Rose, "Capital controls in the 21st century", CEPR Policy Insight, No. 72 (June). London: Centre for Economic Policy Research.

f Adrian Blundell-Wignall, and Caroline Roulet, "Capital controls on inflows, the global financial crisis and economic growth: evidence for emerging economies", *OECD Journal: Financial Market Trends*, vol. 2013/2. Paris.

g Robert H. Wade, "Iceland's boom, bust and capital outflow management", presented at the UNCTAD-GEGI workshop on CAR and global economic governance, 3 October 2013, available from http://unctad.org/en/pages/MeetingDetails.aspx?meetingid=404.

Box III.2 (*continued*)

Governments wishing to apply such policies may face de facto and de jure constraints. De facto restrictions on the capital account refer to pressures from existing and potential lenders and investors. Countries that never adopted such capital management measures before may fear that their adoption for the first time may show weakness in their ability to address their problems with a more conventional set of policies. De jure obstacles stem from multilaterally or bilaterally agreed rules that can forbid or limit a resort to capital-management measures.

Multilateral rules in the IMF Articles of Agreement and in the World Trade Organization General Agreement on Trade in Services do not restrict Governments from managing their capital accounts. There are views that capital-account management measures can be useful in certain circumstances, together with macroeconomic policy and macroprudential measures. However, direct capital-account management may afford many advantages, which can include enhancing the independence of monetary policy and creating space for pro-growth fiscal policy, in addition to reducing the market stigma associated with crisis-driven capital controls, allowing for adaptive development of measures to respond quickly to changes in flow composition, and facilitating the lengthening of maturities in accordance with long-term sustainable development financing needs. Their primary objective should be to prevent crises, not to mitigate their costs.

Bilateral and multilateral agreements can undermine effective capital-account management. In particular, within regional and bilateral trade agreements, countries often pledge to liberalize trade in financial services, which often comes with a commitment to opening up their capital account. Therefore, Governments that aim to maintain macroeconomic stability and wish to better regulate their financial systems should carefully consider the risks in taking on such commitments.

Developing countries should have appropriate capital-account management tools at their disposal. At the same time, the developed countries, where the procyclical capital flows typically originate, would need to better coordinate their monetary, macroprudential and financial sector policies to address the spillover effects of their policies on the developing countries and the global economy. Stronger and more effective international cooperation for managing capital accounts is likely to foster both financial stability and sustainable development.

Source: UNCTAD/DGDS.

study of United States investors found that in their emerging-market bond portfolios, the share of local currency denominated bonds has grown from about 2 per cent in 2001 to about 37 per cent in 2011.[11] Financial deepening and strong macroeconomic fundamentals in these economies, along with higher yields of local currency bonds, largely explain the surge in demand for domestic bonds. There is also evidence that financial deepening in emerging markets and developing countries reduces the sensitivity of domestic financial asset prices to external shocks, but that the participation of foreign investors can increase volatility, financial fragility and contagion.[12]

Emerging-market currencies experienced high volatility with the winding down of quantitative easing

Market concerns regarding the tapering of quantitative easing (QE) by the United States Federal Reserve (Fed) contributed to higher volatility and significant capital outflows from emerging markets during 2013–2014. In 2014, portfolio flows to emerging markets experienced two episodes of "taper tantrums" (i.e., sell-offs by investors in emerging-market securities, driven by the winding down of QE and the forthcoming increases in Fed policy interest rates), with significant depreciations of emerging-market currencies in January and again in September and early October. The currencies of Brazil, South Africa and Turkey were particularly hard hit. Their large current-account deficits are typically financed with

---

11   John Burger, and others, "International investors in local bond markets: indiscriminate flows or discriminating tastes?", November 2013, available from http://macrofinance.nipfp.org.in/PDF/12Pr_Rajeswari_BSWW_EP_First_Draft_Nov2013.pdf (accessed 18 November 2014).

12   IMF, *Global Financial Stability Report: Moving from Liquidity- to Growth-Driven Markets*. Washington, D.C., April 2014.

short-term portfolio flows, and in the case of Brazil and South Africa, falling commodity prices added further pressure (see chapter II).[13] There is significant risk that portfolio flows will reverse as the Fed starts to raise interest rates in 2015 (see chapter I).

Macroprudential measures, capital-account management techniques, and foreign-exchange interventions can reduce the volatility of private flows, and therefore be seen as an essential part of the policy toolkit to manage international capital flows. In addition, given the cross-border spillover effect of monetary policy decisions in the advanced economies, better international and regional coordination of monetary and capital-account policies, and more effective management of global liquidity, are also needed to reduce the risks associated with volatile capital flows.

International public resources for sustainable development

Public finance is essential for providing public goods and services, increasing equity, enhancing macroeconomic stability, and protecting environmental sustainability. Official development assistance (ODA) and other forms of international public finance play an important role in financing development priorities (particularly combating poverty) and increasingly global public goods in many developing countries, particularly in LDCs. Innovative financing mechanisms and South-South Cooperation (SSC) may complement ODA.[14] As part of SSC, the emergence of new public development finance institutions in developing countries presents new opportunities to transform the outlook for international public finance to promote sustainable development.

ODA is growing again and remains important …

Official development assistance

In many critical areas of sustainable development, such as meeting the needs of the poorest or financing national and global public goods, public finance is necessary and cannot be substituted by other sources of finance. Stronger international collaboration on ODA and other forms of international public finance will remain critical to meeting these needs, particularly for those countries with limited capacity to raise public resources domestically. Following the Millennium Summit of the United Nations in 2000 and the 2002 International Conference on Financing for Development in Monterrey, net ODA flows from all member countries of the Organization for Economic Cooperation and Development (OECD) Development Assistance Committee (DAC) increased significantly, from $82.0 billion in 2000 to a high of $134.7 billion in 2013.[15] According to OECD surveys of donors, ODA is likely to increase further in 2014 and stabilize thereafter. Despite the increase in aggregate aid flows, many donors are yet to meet their ODA commitments. Only five OECD/DAC countries—Denmark, Luxembourg, Norway, Sweden and the United Kingdom of Great Britain and Northern Ireland—exceed the target of disbursing 0.7 per

---

13   Jonathan Wheatly, "Investors adapt to 'new normal' as commodity cycle ends", *Financial Times*, 6 October 2014.

14   See for example, Inge Kaul, and Pedro Conceição, eds., *New Public Finance: Responding to Global Challenges*, New York: Oxford University Press.

15   In real terms, 2012 prices. OECD International Development Statistics, available from http://stats.oecd.org/qwids (accessed 17 November 2014).

... but the share of ODA to
LDCs fell in recent years ...

cent of their gross national income (GNI) as ODA. The combined DAC donors' ODA was equivalent to only 0.3 per cent of their total GNI.[16]

The LDCs are the most reliant on international public finance. According to preliminary estimates of OECD/DAC, bilateral net ODA to LDCs increased by 12.3 per cent to reach $30 billion in 2013, but this was mostly owing to the exceptional debt relief for Myanmar.[17] Overall, the share of ODA allocated to LDCs fell in recent years, from 34 per cent in 2010 to 32 per cent in 2012.[18] DAC surveys on its members' forward spending plans indicate that aid flows will increasingly focus on middle-income countries in the medium term, with further declines projected for LDCs and low-income countries, particularly in sub-Saharan Africa.[19] Donors' growing focus on climate financing and the calls for ODA to increasingly leverage private resources are likely to further exacerbate the challenge of channelling sufficient public resources to low-income countries.

... and climate finance is
largely being counted
as ODA

As environmental degradation and climate change have become increasingly urgent issues in international development, climate financing has taken centre stage. In the 2009 Copenhagen Accord of the United Nations Framework Convention on Climate Change (UNFCCC), developed countries agreed to jointly mobilize $100 billion annually by 2020 to address the needs of developing countries.[20] As an initial step, they committed to providing $30 billion in new and additional finance—the so-called fast-start finance—between 2010 and 2012. A preliminary assessment of the fast-start finance finds that $35 billion was mobilized between 2010 and 2012. However, it is estimated that 80 per cent of these resources were also counted as ODA, and disbursed largely through bilateral channels, indicating very little additionality in fast-start financing.[21] Furthermore, fast-start climate financing predominantly targets mitigation efforts, which largely benefits middle-income countries, while financing for adaptation—critical for the most vulnerable, low-income countries—remains inadequate.

A small but rapidly increasing share of ODA is delivered as equity investments and in the form of public-private partnerships to leverage private financing, although less than a third of this type of ODA is currently flowing to low-income countries.[22] Similarly, donor guarantees are increasingly used to facilitate private sector flows to developing countries.

---

16   Ibid.

17   Organization for Economic Cooperation and Development, "Aid to developing countries rebounds in 2013 to reach an all-time high", 8 April 2014, available from http://www.oecd.org/newsroom/aid-to-developing-countries-rebounds-in-2013-to-reach-an-all-time-high.htm (accessed 17 November 2014).

18   Organization for Economic Cooperation and Development, "Targeting ODA towards countries in greatest need", DCD/DAC(2014)20, available from http://www.oecd.org/dac/externalfinancingfor-development/documentupload/DAC%282014%2920.pdf (accessed 17 November 2014).

19   Organization for Economic Cooperation and Development, "Global outlook on aid: results of the 2014 DAC survey on donors' forward spending plans and prospects for improving aid predictability", DCD/DAC(2014)53, available from http://www.oecd.org/officialdocuments/publicdisplaydocumentpdf/?cote=DCD/DAC(2014)53&docLanguage=En (accessed 17 November 2014).

20   United Nations, "Report of the Conference of the Parties on its fifteenth session, held in Copenhagen from 7 to 19 December 2009" (FCCC/CP/2009/11/Add.1).

21   Smita Nakhooda, and others, "Mobilizing international climate finance: lessons from the fast-start period", November 2013, available from http://www.odi.org/sites/odi.org.uk/files/odi-assets/publications-opinion-files/8686.pdf.

22   United Nations, "Mapping of financial flows at the sector level: A UNTT WG contribution in response to a request from the Co-Facilitators for cluster 1", November 2013, available from http://sustainabledevelopment.un.org/content/documents/3352Sector%20mappings.pdf (accessed on 17 November 2014).

Between 2009 and 2011, guarantees mobilized about $15 billion of private sector financing, although they largely bypassed low-income countries. Currently, guarantees are not counted as ODA, but there are discussions on whether and how to include guarantees in a modernized definition of ODA. There are, however, some concerns that these new mechanisms and approaches could divert international public finance away from social needs and poverty reduction programmes that are the central aim of the post-2015 development agenda.[23]

In response to these and other changes in global development finance, and criticism of the existing ODA concept, OECD/DAC is currently reviewing the measurement and monitoring of external development finance, including modernizing the ODA concept. There are proposals to construct an additional, broader measure, known as the total official support for development,[24] which will include "donor effort" (or fiscal impact) of equity and mezzanine financing (hybrid debt and equity) and guarantees by donor-country development institutions. The measure of total official support for development may also include financing at market rates (such as non-concessional loans), financing of the "enablers of development" (such as outlays on peace and security), and private flows mobilized by public sector interventions. While the initial proposals of the DAC secretariat would lead to only modest changes in total recorded ODA flows,[25] this broadened measure of total official support for development is likely to produce significantly larger estimates. There are also discussions that due consideration of the perspectives of the recipient developing countries and an inclusive and transparent process would increase the legitimacy of the reforms in the measurement of ODA. These important discussions could, for example, take place in the context of the upcoming third International Conference on Financing for Development in Addis Ababa, Ethiopia, in July 2015.

Enabling investment through emerging public institutions

As discussed earlier, much of the public sector savings of many developing countries is invested in developed countries through accumulation of international reserves. To reduce the costs and inefficiencies associated with this arrangement, international reserves of developing countries (the surpluses above and beyond what is needed for precautionary purposes) could be invested more effectively in sustainable development. In particular, new and emerging development finance institutions can make use of the surplus resources. The New Development Bank (NDB) of Brazil, the Russian Federation, India, China and South Africa (BRICS), announced in July 2014, and the Asia Infrastructure Investment Bank (AIIB), announced in October 2014, present potential for scaling up financing for sustainable development. As with any new initiatives, these institutions will take time to develop their institutional framework and operational modalities. It will be important, however, to assess their lending models as they are being developed in terms of their governance

New development finance institutions could bolster sustainable development investments

23   Mariana Mirabile, Julia Benn and Cecile Sangare, "Guarantees for development", OECD Development Cooperation Working Papers, No. 11 (September 2013). Paris. Available from http://dx.doi.org/10.1787/5k407lx5b8f8-en (accessed on 17 November 2014).

24   See for example, Organization for Economic Cooperation and Development, "Scoping the new measure of total official support for development", DCD/DAC(2014)35, available from http://www.oecd.org/dac/stats/documentupload/DCD-DACper cent282014per cent2935-ENG.pdf.

25   Organization for Economic Cooperation and Development, "Options for modernising the ODA measure", DCD/DAC(2014)3, available from http://www.oecd.org/dac/externalfinancingfordevelopment/documentupload/ERG%20S1%20Jan%202014%20-%20Options%20for%20Modernising%20the%20ODA%20Measure%20DCD-DAC-2014-3-ENG.pdf.

structures, volume of additional resources, fragmentation of the development finance system, competition among institutions, and incentive structures in order to determine their potential impact on sustainable development finance.

SSC is increasingly viewed as an important complement to ODA and encompasses a diverse range of voluntary intergovernmental cooperation, including technical assistance, project preparation, knowledge-sharing, concessional and non-concessional finance, as well as direct project support. The United Nations estimated SSC at between $16.1 billion and $19.0 billion in 2011 and it is projected to grow as a proportion of global development cooperation.[26]

Sovereign wealth funds could boost investments in sustainable development

A number of countries have established sovereign wealth funds (SWFs) to invest national savings, although only a handful of them have legislative and institutional mandates to invest ethically and for sustainable development.[27] Developing-country-owned SWFs are estimated to have controlled over $4.5 trillion of assets at the end of 2013 (table III.2), representing dramatic growth since 2000.

Regional development banks have also expanded their capital bases and grant contributions to increase their lending volumes and grants in the last decade (figure III.3). Some of these institutions, such as the Corporación Andina de Fomento (Andean Development Corporation) and the European Bank for Reconstruction and Development, have quadrupled their volume of disbursements since 2000.

Additional investment in infrastructure and sustainable development

The African Development Bank has launched the Africa50 Infrastructure Fund, aimed at mobilizing private financing for infrastructure in Africa. Africa50 will focus on national and regional projects in energy, transport, ICT and water sectors.

Over time, lending volumes of development banks could be on par with the World Bank...

The BRICS NDB aims to mobilize resources for infrastructure and sustainable development projects in BRICS countries and other developing economies. Its articles of agreement provide for an authorized capital base of $100 billion, with $50 billion as the subscribed capital and $10 billion as the initial paid-in capital base.[28] The NDB will have equal voting rights for its founding five members. It is estimated that the Bank will have an initial disbursement between $2 billion to $3 billion annually. However, after 10 years, the NDB could disburse $34 billion annually in loans, equity participations, or guarantees with its retained earnings and on the full $100 billion capital base,[29] which would put it roughly on par with the World Bank in terms of loan volume.

---

26   Many Southern partners do not publish data on a yearly basis. As a result, figures on the volume of SSC are estimates based on data collected in preparation for the second international development cooperation report (United Nations, Department of Economic and Social Affairs, forthcoming). Only partial data is available for 2012–2013. Therefore, it is not possible to report the volume of SSC for 2012–2013. It is also recognized in the present report that, due to the specificities of SSC, the reporting of the financial value of such cooperation can only be indicative and cannot capture the actual scale and impact of SSC. See United Nations, "Report of the Secretary-General on trends and progress in international development cooperation" (E/2014/77).

27   Benjamin J. Richardson, "Sovereign wealth funds and the quest for sustainability: insights from Norway and New Zealand", *Nordic Journal of Commercial Law*, vol. 2, pp. 1–27 (2011).

28   See "Agreement on the new development bank", VI BRICS Summit, 15 July 2014, available from http://brics6.itamaraty.gov.br/media2/press-releases/219-agreement-on-the-new-development-bank-fortaleza-july-15.

29   Stephany Griffith-Jones, "A BRICS development bank: a dream coming true", UNCTAD Discussion Paper, No. 215 (March 2014). Geneva. March. Available from http://unctad.org/en/PublicationsLibrary/osgdp20141_en.pdf.

Figure III.3
Growth in annual disbursements of selected regional and national development banks, 2000–2013

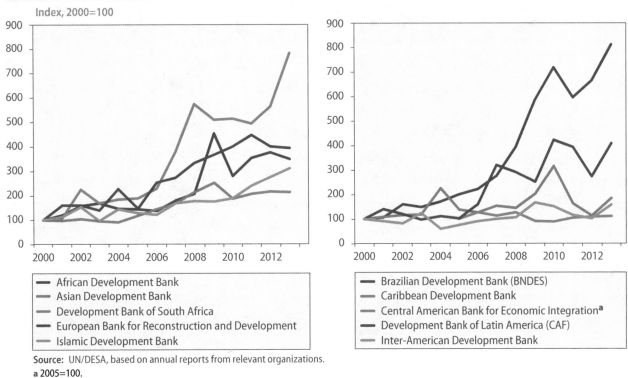

Source: UN/DESA, based on annual reports from relevant organizations.
a 2005=100.

Similarly, the new AIIB has an initial authorized capital base of $100 billion and $10 billion as the initial paid-in capital. China is expected to provide half of the capital. AIIB intends to launch operations in 2015 for infrastructure finance, and is planned to work in concert with the Asian Development Bank and the World Bank. Given that China has the highest credit rating among the BRICS countries, its outsized capital contribution may result in a better credit rating for the AIIB, and may enable it to borrow on better terms than the BRICS NDB. This could potentially enable AIIB to disburse higher volumes of loans compared to the BRICS NDB, particularly for infrastructure investment.

The continued growth in existing regional development banks and sovereign wealth funds, and the emergence of new institutions such as the NDB and AIIB, can provide additional resources for investment in sustainable development. These institutions may also issue long-term bonds to finance investment in infrastructure and green growth. As many institutional investors, such as pension or insurance funds, are typically unable to invest directly in infrastructure projects, the long-term bonds issued by these development finance institutions could be useful in channelling institutional savings into sustainable development.

...and their long-term bonds to finance infrastructure investments are likely to attract institutional investors

Starting up and scaling up sustainably

The volume of resources cannot be the only consideration for development banks to facilitate investment in sustainable development. There needs to be stronger consideration of the quality of financing and investment, as well as how international financing can increase synergies across economic, social and environmental dimensions of sustainable development. One lesson from past experiences with development finance has been the importance

Table III.2

Sovereign wealth funds owned by developing countries and economies in transition with assets above $15 billion

Country	Fund Name	Assets (billion dollars)	Inception
United Arab Emirates - Abu Dhabi	Abu Dhabi Investment Authority	773.0	1976
Saudi Arabia	SAMA Foreign Holdings	757.2	
China	China Investment Corporation	652.7	2007
Kuwait	Kuwait Investment Authority	410.0	2008
Hong Kong SAR[a]	Hong Kong Monetary Authority Investment Portfolio	400.2	1993
Singapore	Government of Singapore Investment Corporation	320.0	1981
Qatar	Qatar Investment Authority	170.0	2005
United Arab Emirates - Abu Dhabi	Abu Dhabi Investment Council	90.0	2007
Russian Federation	National Wealth Fund of the Russian Federation	88.0	2008
Russian Federation	Reserve Fund	86.4	2008
Kazakhstan	JSC Samruk-Kazyna	77.5	2008
Algeria	Revenue Regulation Fund	77.2	2000
Korea, Republic of	Korea Investment Corporation	72.0	2005
United Arab Emirates - Dubai	Investment Corporation of Dubai	70.0	2006
United Arab Emirates - Abu Dhabi	International Petroleum Investment Company	68.4	1984
Libya	Libyan Investment Authority	66.0	2006
Iran (Islamic Republic of)	National Development Fund of Islamic Republic of Iran	62.0	2011
United Arab Emirates - Abu Dhabi	Mubadala Development Company	60.9	2002
Malaysia	Khazanah Nasional	40.5	1993
Brunei Darussalam	Brunei Investment Agency	40.0	1983
Azerbaijan	State Oil Fund of the Republic of Azerbaijan	36.6	1999
Iraq	Development Fund for Iraq	18.0	2003
Timor-Leste	Timor-Leste Petroleum Fund	16.6	2005
Chile	Economic and Social Stabilization Fund	15.2	2007
Total		**4468.4**	

Source: Sovereign Wealth Fund Institute.

a Special Administrative Region of China.

of country ownership, with excessive conditionalities undermining the effectiveness of development finance.[30] So far, non-conditionality and horizontality are important features of SSC and potentially that of new development banks, affording the flexibility to support existing and evolving key priorities in host-country national development programmes.[31]

Absent effective public policies, regulation and monitoring, there is also a risk that new lending may breed inefficiencies and negatively impact social or environmental objectives. Appropriate lending standards (not necessarily conditionalities) will thus be crucial for achieving positive development impact. New development finance institutions could incorporate existing intergovernmental commitments, including internationally agreed labour and environmental standards, in their lending practices to bolster sustainable devel-

---

30   See, for example, World Bank, Independent Evaluation Group, "The World Bank's country policy and institutional assessment: an evaluation", available from http://ieg.worldbankgroup.org/Data/reports/cpia_eval.pdf; IMF, Independent Evaluation Office, "Structural conditionality in IMF-supported programs", available from http://www.ieo-imf.org/ieo/pages/CompletedEvaluation111.aspx.

31   United Nations, "Report of the Secretary-General on trends and progress in international development cooperation" (E/2014/77).

opment impacts and synergies. Ensuring policy coherence at an early stage of institutional development, and learning from past experience, can also strengthen the new institutions' legitimacy and credibility, as well as improve sustainable development outcomes.

Additionally, information on all forms of development cooperation, including from emerging public institutions, should be readily available to policymakers and stakeholders. The 2014 Development Cooperation Forum (DCF)[32] discussed the imperatives of enhancing transparency and accountability in development cooperation, and instilling trust among development partners. Timely data that is understandable and accessible to all was a key discussion point. Since the 2009 United Nations Conference on South-South Cooperation, a number of developing-country partners from the South have decided to further strengthen their work, including through evaluation and additional analysis of evidence. Under the auspices of the DCF, a group of southern partners are sharing information on the quantity and quality of SSC, while the United Nations Office for South-South Cooperation continues to strengthen SSC. Better and more consistent data would facilitate greater understanding of SSC and give more visibility to its positive contributions to sustainable development finance.

Enhancing the stability of the international financial architecture

Along with changes in the development landscape, there have been significant efforts at reforming the international financial architecture, which include strengthened financial market regulations, efforts to improve tax cooperation, and reforms of global economic governance. Yet more concerted efforts are needed to ensure the stability and sustainability of financing for sustainable development.

Financial regulations need to be strengthened, particularly for the too-big-to-fail financial institutions, shadow banking and over-the-counter derivatives market, but also to ensure adequate access to financing. Greater international cooperation can enhance domestic revenue mobilization, which is constrained by international tax avoidance and evasion. Reform and institutional innovation in the areas of sovereign debt resolution can reduce the risks of default and crisis and facilitate greater investment in sustainable development. Achieving such changes would also require revamped governance arrangements to give more voice and representation to countries and interests currently underrepresented in the international monetary and financial decision-making processes.

Reforming financial sector regulation

The financial system intermediates the flow of funds between savers and borrowers and allocates these funds to productive uses within and across economies. Safety and soundness of both individual institutions and the system as a whole are crucial for economic growth and sustainable development. The financial system also needs to broaden the access to credit and other financial services to facilitate sustainable investments. Managing the trade-offs in reducing risks while promoting access to resources presents a complex challenge for policymakers. For example, in an extreme version of a safe financial system, credit would only

---

32   The biennial Development Cooperation Forum is one of the principal new functions of a strengthened Economic and Social Council (ECOSOC) of the United Nations.

flow to AAA borrowers, such as the developed-country sovereigns, but this clearly would be inadequate for promoting sustainable development worldwide.

Global actions have enhanced the resilience of the financial sector, but more concerted efforts are needed

In recent years, the international community has taken important steps to strengthen the resilience of the financial sector and reduce the risk of future crises through regulatory reforms. To date, these reforms have focused on ensuring safety and soundness of the financial system, primarily through regulation of the banking sector through Basel III. These have been supplemented by a series of recommendations and initiatives by the Financial Stability Board (FSB), which include improved oversight of the shadow banking system, recovery and resolution planning for systemically important institutions, and regulation of the over-the-counter derivatives market.

Reforming the banking system

Basel III has introduced important reforms on solvency and liquidity

Through Basel III, which will come fully into force in 2019, the Basel Committee on Banking Supervision (BCBS) has introduced new measures aimed to bolster both solvency and liquidity of banks. The pillars of Basel III include: pillar 1 on capital and risk coverage and containing leverage; pillar 2 on risk management and supervision; and pillar 3 on measures to strengthen what the Bank for International Settlements (BIS) refers to as market discipline, including regulations of both on- and off-balance-sheet exposures and disclosures of financial intermediaries.

A new leverage ratio will take effect in January 2015

As part of the first pillar, banks adopting Basel III must increase their minimum common equity capital ratio to 4.5 per cent of the net risk-weighted assets (RWA).[33] Tier 1 capital must grow from 4.5 per cent to 6.0 per cent.[34] Banks will have to add a conservation buffer of 2.5 per cent to their total minimum capital, raising the rate to 10.5 per cent. Along with traditional microprudential approaches, which focus on reducing risks of individual banks, Basel III attempts to strengthen the macroprudential policy framework through the introduction of a countercyclical capital buffer. This buffer, comprised of common equity, will be determined by the relevant regulator in each jurisdiction within a range of 0.0 to 2.5 per cent, and it would kick in when a regulator would consider credit growth has led to an unacceptable build-up of systemic risk. However, it is unclear whether this will be strong enough to achieve its objective. Basel III also introduces a leverage ratio, a separate and additional requirement from the binding Basel risk-based capital requirements,[35] which is currently set at 3 per cent, subject to further calibration.[36] The first globally consistent definition of the leverage ratio—which is aimed at adequately capturing on- and off-balance-sheet sources of banks' leverage—was agreed in January 2014 and its disclosure requirements will take effect in January 2015.[37] Other areas of regulation include risk coverage, risk management and supervision, as well as market discipline.[38]

---

[33] "Common equity capital" refers to common stock, retained earnings, and other assets that allow a firm to withstand financial stress by offering liquidity.

[34] Bank for International Settlements, "Basel Committee on Banking Supervision: Basel III phase-in arrangements", available from http://www.bis.org/bcbs/basel3/basel3_phase_in_arrangements.pdf.

[35] The Basel III leverage ratio is defined as the capital measure (the numerator) divided by the exposure measure (the denominator), with this ratio expressed as a percentage.

[36] Bank for International Settlements, "Basel Committee on Banking Supervision: Basel III leverage ratio framework and disclosure requirements", January 2014.

[37] Financial Stability Board, "FSB Chair's letter to G20 Ministers and Governors on financial reforms—Completing the job and looking ahead", 21 September 2014.

[38] Bank for International Settlements, "Basel Committee on Banking Supervision: Seventh progress report on adoption of the Basel regulatory framework", October 2014.

Basel III calls for a minimum liquidity coverage ratio that will require banks to have sufficient high-quality liquid assets to withstand a 30-day stressed funding scenario specified by supervisors. It further introduces a net stable funding ratio (NSFR)—a longer-term structural ratio designed to address liquidity mismatches. It will cover the entire balance sheet and provide incentives for banks to use stable sources of funding. The liquidity framework also includes a common set of monitoring metrics to assist supervisors in identifying and analysing liquidity risk trends at both the bank and system-wide levels.[39] In September 2014, the Basel Committee published the results of its latest Basel III monitoring exercise, which showed that banks now meet the Basel III risk-based minimum capital requirements (table III.3).

Table III.3
Basel III stress test from end-2013

	Weighted average LCR		Average NSFR	Percentage of banks with NSFR > 90%
	End-2013	Mid-2013		
Large banks[a]	119	114	111	88
Small banks	132	132	112	

Source: Bank for International Settlements, September 2014, "Basel III Monitoring Report as of 31 December 2013".
a With Tier 1 capital of more than 3 billion euro.

Challenges with banking regulatory reform

As banks implement Basel III, there are concerns about its potential impact on access to credit and sustainable development finance, as well as about its efficacy in creating a more stable financial system. The growth in complexity of regulations is a cause for concern. Regulations on Basel I were summarized in 30 pages, while Basel III regulations are captured in almost 1,000 pages, a number that multiplies rapidly when translated into national rulebooks. Generally, complex regulations can be difficult to implement, supervise and enforce, especially in developing countries where regulatory and supervisory capacities are limited. This argues for broad-based, simpler regulations that incorporate both on- and off-balance-sheet exposures, such as the leverage ratio, along with additional countercyclical buffers.

Basel III may impact access to credit and sustainable development finance...

Through generally raising the cost of credit, the Basel III rules may have the effect of discouraging riskier lending. Indeed, the rules are designed to impose higher costs on riskier activities. Longer-term lending, lending to entities with low credit ratings, as well as investment in locations where it is more costly to get information (for example, where there is insufficient data on default histories) are deemed risky and subjected to higher capital requirements and provisioning costs.[40] Yet, some of the sectors deemed as higher risks in Basel III are precisely the sectors that would need more investments for achieving sustainable development. There has been particular concern regarding the impact of these regulations on infrastructure lending, trade finance, investments in innovation and green technologies, financing of small and medium-sized enterprises (SMEs), as well as lending to

---

39   Bank for International Settlements, "Basel Committee on Banking Supervision reforms—Basel III", available from http://www.bis.org/bcbs/basel3/b3summarytable.pdf.

40   The Financial Stability Board finds that "it remains too early to fully assess their impact on the provision of long-term finance or changes in market behaviour in response to these reforms." See Financial Stability Board, "Update on financial regulatory factors affecting the supply of long-term investment finance", Report to G20 Finance Ministers and Central Bank Governors, 16 September 2014.

developing countries in general. In response to these risks, a number of countries have made some adjustments. For example, the European Union (EU) excluded SME exposures from the calculation of the capital conservation buffer requirements in order to avoid reducing lending to SMEs.[41]

Furthermore, variability in RWA calculations across countries has led to large differences in capital held by banks with similar portfolios, a challenge the Basel Committee intends to address next year. There is thus a tension between countries adjusting regulations to reflect domestic needs and policy objectives and the uniformity of outcomes. There are also concerns that differing regulations can create room for regulatory arbitrage, particularly with regard to implementation of regulations in developing and emerging economies. Although the Basel III rules are primarily designed for financial institutions in major advanced economies, the Basel Committee has reached out to countries that are not members of the FSB to facilitate a wider implementation of Basel III rules. The relevance and potential impact of the full range of Basel III rules on developing and emerging economies remains unclear.

...any may continue to promote procyclicality

Although Basel III includes a countercyclical buffer, there is a risk that the overall package will continue to promote procyclicality. Capital requirements are, by nature, procyclical; they treat financial risk as exogenous and only capture risk after it is realized, and not when financial imbalances actually build up. In that context, the dependence of some of the rules of Basel III on credit ratings is a further source of concern, although this is being addressed in many jurisdictions. Recent research shows that credit-rating standards are generally procyclical, as rating standards tend to be stricter during a recession than in economic expansions.[42] However, regulators need to be careful not to restrict the emergence of new rating agencies in developing countries, which could create more locally relevant risk assessments and contribute to more diverse perspectives on risks associated with long-term, sustainable investments.

Concerns over too-big-to-fail financial institutions remain

Systemic risks associated with very large financial institutions still need to be adequately addressed. In this regard, in November 2014, the G20 leaders agreed to strengthen the oversight and regulation of global systemically important financial institutions (G-SIFIs) and welcomed a framework, proposed by the FSB, that includes a requirement for additional loss-absorbing capacity for banks (a capital buffer above the minimum requirements of Basel III) and enhanced supervisory intensity for G-SIFIs.[43]

Progress in regulating shadow banking

The term "shadow banking" was originally introduced to refer to activities of financial intermediaries that are involved in facilitating credit creation but are not subject to regulatory oversight. In recent years, the term has been used more broadly to refer to any type

---

41   See Bank for International Settlements, "Basel Committee on Banking Supervision: International Convergence of Capital Measurement and Capital Standards: A Revised Framework—Comprehensive Version", para. 231; and European Union, Regulation (EU) No. 575/2013 on prudential requirements for credit institutions and investment firms, Article 501.

42   Jun Kyung Auh, "Procyclical credit rating policy", November 2013, available from http://siteresources.worldbank.org/INTFR/Resources/JunKyungAuhJan212014.pdf.

43   G20 Leaders' Communiqué, Brisbane Summit, 15–16 November 2014.

of credit intermediation outside the conventional banking system.[44] In the build-up to the crisis of 2008, highly leveraged but unregulated financial intermediaries were holding large portfolios of illiquid assets financed by short-term liabilities, exposing the risks inherent in an unregulated shadow banking sector.

While the advanced economies continue to have the largest non-bank financial systems by absolute size, emerging markets showed the most rapid increases in non-bank financial system assets, outstripping the growth in the formal banking sector. However, shadow banking in many developing countries is often of a different nature than its counterpart in developed countries. For example, to the extent that the growth in the non-bank financial system in developing countries represents the development of capital markets and improvement in financial inclusion, it could have positive impacts on sustainable development finance. Even in developed countries, various non-bank financial intermediaries—investment funds in particular—provide long-term credit in the absence of significant bank lending.[45] The question, though, is how these activities should be regulated, taking into account the full scope of activities while balancing risk mitigation objectives with the imperative of increasing access and financial inclusion.

Regulating rapidly growing shadow banks remains a challenge

The discussions on shadow banking often do not pay adequate attention to its linkages to the repo market for sale and repurchase of securities, where loans are granted against collateral, generally government bonds and notes. Although the maturities of the repurchase agreements range from one night to one year, the market is heavily skewed towards overnight to one-month repos. In other words, the repo market provides borrowers with short-term leverage. The market is used by banks, but also by shadow banking entities such as institutional money managers, insurance companies, and hedge funds to manage their cash flows, and is often used to finance longer-term assets. Some experts have expressed concerns that the repo market appears to reinforce the maturity mismatches in the assets and liabilities of financial intermediaries.[46] The systemic risk in the repo market is partially induced by the size of "haircuts", which are additional collateral that the lending institutions request, taking into account the movements in the value of the collateralized securities. These haircuts reflect the risk when the cash realized by the liquidation of securities may turn out to be less than the value of the loan. Consequently, larger haircuts can help restrain the build-up of excessive leverage. Haircuts are, however, procyclical, since they tend to be low during booms and very large in moments of crisis, leading to liquidity shortfalls for institutions relying on the repo market for financing. To deal with the procyclicality of haircuts, the FSB published a new set of minimum standards for their calculations in October 2014.[47] However, debate is ongoing as to whether these standards are insufficient and their coverage too limited.

Major efforts are needed to move the shadow banking sector under a coherent regulatory framework to minimize systemic risks and potential spillover effects. The BCBS has final-

Coherent regulatory frameworks are needed for all financial intermediaries to manage risks and spillover effects

---

[44] IMF, *Global Financial Stability Report: Risk Taking, Liquidity, and Shadow Banking: Curbing Excess While Promoting Growth*, Washington D.C., October 2014.

[45] Ibid.

[46] Matthias Thiemann, and Stephany Griffith-Jones, "Limiting financial crises: demands upon the new financial architecture", *Brot für die Welt*, 20 October 2014, available from https://info.brot-fuer-die-welt.de/sites/default/files/blog-downloads/thiemann_and_griffith-jones_final.pdf.

[47] Financial Stability Board, "Regulatory framework for haircuts on non-centrally cleared securities financing transactions", October 2014.

ized its supervisory framework for large exposures (and risk-sensitive capital requirements) of banks' equity investments in funds to mitigate the spill-over effects between banks and shadow banking entities. The FSB is currently designing a framework for managing systemic risks in the shadow banking system with the goal of preventing these risks from impacting the regulated banking sector. It has also established an annual monitoring exercise to assess global trends and risks of the shadow banking system, and has put forward a calendar for national implementation of these new regulations with a peer review set for 2015.

Although these regulatory challenges are complex, they have a large potential impact on financial stability and may amplify the fragility of the financial systems if they are not designed and implemented effectively. More broadly, careful monitoring of the growth of non-bank financial activities needs to be part of the broader macroprudential regulatory framework to avoid significant increases in risks associated with excessive financial leverage.

Derivatives

Over-the-counter derivatives transactions are yet to be settled through central clearinghouses in most countries

In a major step forward, the G20 agreed that all standardized over-the-counter derivatives should be traded on formal exchanges or electronic platforms and cleared by central counterparties, with a view to reducing risks in the over-the-counter derivatives transactions, including lack of transparency in counterparty exposures, insufficient collateralization, uncoordinated default management, and concerns about market misconduct. Although this was meant for implementation by the end of 2012, progress has been slow. The majority of jurisdictions have announced that they have completed their legislative reforms or expect to have necessary legislative frameworks in place in 2014. Recent disagreements between the EU and the United States of America on the treatment of clearinghouses have further stalled progress. Clearinghouses are meant to prevent a market-wide collapse by ensuring either party in a derivatives transaction would get paid in case the other side defaults. While the goal is to establish a system to ensure that home-country rules for clearinghouses are largely equivalent across borders, different views persist regarding whether or not the United States clearinghouses are regulated equivalently to those in the EU.[48]

International tax cooperation and illicit financial flows

Domestic revenue is the largest and most reliable source for investment in sustainable development. While the primary responsibilities for mobilizing domestic resources lie with national Governments, international rules, policies and cooperation play an important role in ensuring that Governments have the ability to raise sufficient revenue domestically. Current rules and conditions, particularly regarding illicit flows, as well as tax avoidance, often limit what Governments can raise as domestic revenues.

Illicit financial outflows pose a formidable challenge to domestic revenue mobilization in many developing countries

There is no agreed definition of illicit financial flows (IFFs),[49] but it is generally used to mean three different types of flows: (i) the proceeds of commercial tax evasion; (ii) revenues from criminal activities; and (iii) flows from public corruption. IFFs have become a matter of major concern because of the scale and systematic adverse impact of such flows on global governance and the development agenda. While improved domestic policies in tax administration are vital to increasing revenue collection for sustainable investment, there

---

48 Andrew Ackerman, Katy Burne and Viktoria Dendrinou, "U.S., Europe hit impasse over rules on derivatives", *Wall Street Journal*, 26 September 2014.

49 This definition stems from Raymond W. Baker, *Capitalism's Achilles Heel: Dirty Money and How to Renew the Free-Market System*. Hoboken, New Jersey, USA: John Wiley & Sons, Inc.

is a limit to what they can achieve based on the existing international policy environment within which IFFs have blossomed.

While it is difficult to estimate the size of IFFs, one estimate of untaxed off-shore wealth holdings puts the amount between $21 trillion and $32 trillion on the high end, which if taxed at the floor rates, would yield $189 billion a year in new revenues globally.[50] On the low end, other studies estimated off-shore wealth holdings between $5.9 trillion and $8.5 trillion in different years.[51] It is also difficult to assess the relative sizes of the different components of IFFs with any accuracy, although some researchers have argued that commercial tax evasion, which involves cross-border activity to hide money from tax administrations, is one of the main types of IFFs.[52] Others have argued that corruption is a more important source of IFFs in developing countries and that the various types of IFFs are intrinsically linked.[53] While the amount of money lost to IFFs is subject to much debate, all available evidence suggests that it is significant and poses a systemic problem that impedes the mobilization of domestic resources needed for investment in sustainable development.

Multinational enterprises often engage in transfer mispricing (i.e., the mispricing of cross-border intra-group transactions) to evade taxes. They can shift profits to low-tax or no-tax jurisdictions, while shifting losses and deductions to high-tax jurisdictions and thereby reducing their profits and tax liabilities in the latter. National and international tax codes interact in a way that offers loopholes to companies engaged in cross-border trade, and existing standards to prevent double taxation insufficiently address the cases of no or low taxation. The pricing of intangibles, such as intellectual property rights, are particularly subject to transfer mispricing because of the ease of transferring ownership internationally and the difficulty in valuing unique intangibles. The provision of other intra-group services, including management, information technology and financial services, are frequently subject to transfer mispricing. The past decades of growing international trade and capital mobility have increased the levels of cross-border economic activity, resulting in greater potential for mispricing. Multinational enterprises also engage in aggressive tax planning, including making use of complex corporate structures to exploit mismatches and loopholes in tax systems. These tax avoidance activities may be legal under existing tax codes, but undermine the volume of revenues that a government can collect to make public investment in sustainable development.

> Existing tax codes and weak enforcement foster transfer mispricing and tax evasion

Furthermore, tax avoidance and evasion distort markets and prevent fair competition. There are unfair advantages granted to multinational enterprises that operate across borders and can cherry-pick jurisdictions to minimize their tax liabilities and achieve unfair cost competitiveness (often by so-called tax-treaty shopping and other means to lower their own tax bills). Domestic enterprises may be unable to take advantage of the same methods of tax avoidance and evasion, increasing their relative cost base and thus limiting their opportunities for growth.

---

50   James S. Henry, "The price of offshore revisited", Tax Justice Network, July 2012, available from http://www.taxjustice.net/cms/upload/pdf/Price_of_Offshore_Revisited_120722.pdf.

51   Gabriel Zucman, "The missing wealth of nations: are Europe and the US net debtors or net creditors?", *Quarterly Journal of Economics*, vol. 128, No. 3, pp.1321–1364.

52   See, for example, Global Financial Integrity, "Illicit financial flows from Africa: hidden resource for development", Washington, D. C., March 2010.

53   David Chaikin, and J. C. Sharman, *Corruption and Money Laundering: A Symbiotic Relationship*. New York/London: Palgrave Macmillan.

The competition often
fails to attract long-term
investment

Harmful tax competition among governments also presents a challenge to the realization of sufficient revenue for investment in sustainable development. International tax competition involves not only comparison over headline tax rates, but also the application and duration of tax incentives and tax holidays. Recent studies find an increase in tax cooperation, although tax competition remains a challenge, with the potential for a race to the bottom.[54] The policy of giving tax holidays or lower tax rates to particular sectors or under particular circumstances is rarely successful in attracting long-term sustainable development investment in developing countries. While taxation is one factor in investment decisions, investors also take into account factors such as political stability, growth, market size, human capital and infrastructure in the host economy.[55] "Good" tax policies can foster rather than deter foreign direct investment, as taxpayers seeking long-term partnerships with countries tend to welcome effective and predictable tax administrations. Effective tax policy and administration with few or minimal tax holidays and incentives—and which are transparent, carefully considered beforehand and kept under review—can ensure an even playing field for investors, both foreign and domestic.

The international community has started to address the problems of raising sufficient tax revenue with more concerted efforts to enhance international cooperation on tax matters. Existing initiatives, such as the OECD/G20 base erosion and profit-shifting project, have tried to improve international tax cooperation through the development of a 15-point action plan.[56] The G20, in its Brisbane Summit held in November 2014, committed to finalizing this work in 2015, including transparency of taxpayer-specific rulings that constitute harmful tax practices. At the United Nations, the Committee of Experts on International Tax Cooperation[57] continues to address ways of ensuring a revenue return for countries where economic activities occur, such as through limited but practicably enforceable withholding taxes, and by recognizing the practical differences between goods-based and increasingly services-based economies. IMF has also contributed important expertise on tax policies and spillovers.[58] Additionally, there are existing multilateral instruments, such as the OECD-hosted Convention on Mutual Administrative Assistance in Tax Matters. While the convention was opened to non-OECD countries for signature in 2010, it was negotiated within the OECD and the Council of Europe, and all G20 countries agreed to sign the convention. In some regions, such as in Europe, there are discussions on harmonizing corporate tax bases. Ireland recently announced a change in tax residency rules that is intended to make it more difficult for multinational enterprise (MNE) profits to remain untaxed through complex financial structures set up in the country. However, many areas of international tax policy require improvements and effective cooperation to enhance the ability of developing countries to raise revenue for sustainable development investment.

---

54   Philipp Genschel, and Peter Schwarz, "Tax competition: a literature review", *Socio-economic Rev*, vol. 9, No. 2, pp. 339–370.

55   See, for example, World Bank , "Does *Doing Business* matter for foreign direct investment?", available from http://documents.worldbank.org/curated/en/2013/01/18142493/doing-business-2013-doing-business-matter-foreign-direct-investment; Era Dable-Norris, and others, "FDI flows to low-income countries: global drivers and growth implications", IMF Working Paper, No. WP/10/132 (June 2010). Washington, D.C.

56   For more information, see http://www.oecd.org/ctp/beps.htm.

57   For more information, see http://www.un.org/esa/ffd/ffd-follow-up/tax-committee.html.

58   IMF, "Spillovers in international corporate taxation", IMF Policy Paper, 9 May 2014.

Key issues

Skills and capacity gaps are large in the tax authorities of many developing countries, although not uniformly so.[59] International assistance, such as through ODA, could help overcome these problems. Researchers estimate that investment in tax administration and enforcement capacity offers high returns on investment. In the United States, the Department of Treasury estimates that $1 of investment in enforcement yields $6 in direct revenue, plus additional indirect revenue from deterrence. Technical assistance for tax capacity-building in El Salvador, for example, helped raise the tax-to-GDP ratio from 11 per cent in 2004 to 14.1 per cent in 2007.[60] Based on past experience, well targeted international assistance to enhance the capacities of tax administration is likely to have a strong positive impact on domestic resource mobilization efforts. Yet it is estimated that only $120 million of ODA from OECD/DAC donors in 2012 was targeted at tax-related activities, less than 0.07 per cent of the total.[61]

ODA can play a critical role in strengthening capacities of tax administration in developing countries

A key issue is how to determine the location of multinational enterprise value added for the purposes of taxation. In September 2013, the G20 endorsed the statement that "profits should be taxed where economic activities are performed to derive the profits and where value is created".[62] Multinational enterprises often transact across borders through multiple subsidiaries, which are expected to apply the principle of arm's-length transfer pricing.[63] There is a debate about whether the best way to prevent transfer mispricing is through better implementation of the arm's-length pricing mechanism, including through capacity-building of tax administrations, or through a change towards formulary apportionment, wherein the global profits of a multinational enterprise would be divided up by jurisdiction according to a fixed formula agreed in advance and intended as a proxy for the level of economic activity in each jurisdiction.

The proposals for formulary apportionment, which are supported by many civil society organizations, would see MNE profit taxes divided up between jurisdictions based on some metrics such as sales volume, turnover or even employee headcount. Other similar proposals include the idea of unitary taxation of multinational enterprises.[64] Switching from arm's-length pricing to an apportionment formula would affect the corporate tax base of all countries in the world, as the current incidence of taxation does not align with the

---

59   See "Supporting the development of more effective tax systems", Report to the G-20 Development Working Group by the IMF, OECD, UN and World Bank.

60   Organization for Economic Cooperation and Development, "Tax and development: aid modalities for strengthening tax systems", DCD/DAC(2012)34, available from http://www.oecd.org/official-documents/publicdisplaydocumentpdf/?cote=DCD/DAC(2012)34&docLanguage=En.

61   Organization for Economic Cooperation and Development, *Development Co-operation Report 2014: Mobilising Resources for Sustainable Development*. Paris.

62   G20 Leaders' Declaration, Saint Petersburg, September 2013.

63   According to the arm's-length principle, transfer prices charged between associated enterprises reflect prices charged between independent entities at arm's length, taking into account the circumstances specific to the transaction at hand. See United Nations, "Practical manual on transfer pricing for developing countries" ST/ESA/347, p. 11.

64   Sol Picciotto, "Towards unitary taxation of transnational corporations", Tax Justice Network, 9 December 2012; and United Nations, *Global Governance and Global Rules for Development in the Post-2015 Era*. Policy Note of the Committee for Development Policy (United Nations publication, Sales No. E.14.II.A.1).

factors being proposed for inclusion in a fixed formula to apply in unitary taxation.[65] It is as yet unclear what effect this would have on tax revenues in individual countries or on different groups of countries, such as the LDCs. There are also distinct problems of political will in moving in this direction, as well as serious concerns about auditing consolidated MNE profit statements and potential abuse of the system. Some proposals have included implementing unitary taxation on regional bases.[66]

On the other hand, many Governments and the United Nations Committee of Experts on International Tax Cooperation have argued for the more effective implementation of the arm's-length pricing mechanism. The Committee developed and published a practical manual on transfer pricing in 2013, "recognizing the practical reality of the widespread support for, and reliance on, the arm's-length standard among both developing and developed countries".[67] The level of complexity and the information, knowledge and resources required in administering transfer pricing legislation can put a tremendous strain on national tax authorities, especially in countries where tax administrations tend to lack human and other resources. Tax administrations are also confronted with information asymmetry vis-à-vis multinational enterprises. These are areas for further policy development concerning the implementation of the arm's-length pricing standards.

Third, another important debate is the role of tax information. While the need for reliable information for effective and efficient tax administration is well recognized, tax administrators and decisions makers are asking what information should be public, what information should be shared among tax authorities, and how that information should be shared. The G20 has explicitly "committed to automatic exchange of [tax] information as the new global standard, which must ensure confidentiality and the proper use of information exchanged".[68] The G20 countries and other members of the OECD Global Forum expect to automatically exchange tax information among themselves by the end of 2017, and have committed to making sure that developing countries benefit from these new initiatives.[69] In 2013, civil society campaigners worked with the Government of the United Kingdom to ask both the Group of Eight (G8) and the G20 to introduce public beneficial ownership registries[70] so that anyone could access information on corporate and trust ownership.[71] However, the G8 and G20 countries could not agree on this point, although the G8 did agree to make general information on beneficial ownership of all

While the G20 has improved information sharing in tax matters, a global standard would be preferred

---

65   Alex Cobham, and Simon Loretz, "International distribution of the corporate tax base: impact of different apportionment factors under unitary taxation", February 2014.

66   Alex Cobham, "The impacts of illicit financial flows on peace and security in Africa", available from http://www.tanaforum.org/index.php?option=com_docman&task=doc_download&gid=44&Itemid=219.

67   United Nations, "Practical manual on transfer pricing for developing countries" ST/ESA/347, available from http://www.un.org/esa/ffd/wp-content/uploads/2014/08/UN_Manual_TransferPricing.pdf.

68   G20 Leaders' Declaration, Saint Petersburg, September 2013.

69   Organization for Economic Cooperation and Development, "Global forum on transparency and exchange of information for tax purposes: statement of outcomes", October 2014, available from http://www.oecd.org/tax/transparency/statement-of-outcomes-gfberlin.pdf.

70   See "PM letter to the EU on tax evasion", 25 April 2013, available from https://www.gov.uk/government/news/pm-letter-to-the-eu-on-tax-evasion.

71   See, for example, work by Global Witness, available from http://www.globalwitness.org/campaigns/corruption/anonymous-companies.

entities available to law enforcement officials.[72] At the Summit meeting in November 2014, the G20 reaffirmed its commitment to improve the transparency of public and private sector entities and of beneficial ownership by implementing the G20 High-Level Principles on Beneficial Ownership Transparency. Public transparency is supposed to help track and deter tax avoidance and evasion, but if introduced unilaterally may prove a competitive disadvantage to any individual country. A global standard and common introduction would mitigate the negative competitive effects of such a measure. While exchange of information is an important factor in the fight against tax evasion, the rules of information exchange may not adequately reflect the reality of developing countries in terms of their capacity to administer such rules. Developing countries also may not have the capacity to obtain the most relevant information or the analytical capacity to make the best use of information received. Capacity-building in this area can address these problems, but designing rules or norms in a forum that includes developing countries can ensure that information exchange will benefit all countries.

Considerations for reform

There are important distributional implications among Member States, depending on the design and implementation of reforms in international tax cooperation. Potential changes in the global distribution of tax revenues will have implications on the level of domestic resources across countries, with important consequences for financing sustainable development. For example, implementing unitary taxation on multinational enterprises and then distributing the tax revenue according to MNE payroll levels would likely result in high gains in taxation in rich countries, where most multinational enterprises maintain their headquarters and senior staff, and potential losses for developing countries. There is insufficient research on the impact of different types of tax reform on the distribution of tax revenues, particularly the implications of reforms on low-income and least developed countries as groups. Further research in this area would make an important contribution to tax reform discussions, but is constrained by insufficient public information about the distribution of MNE profit reporting and tax payments.

> A better understanding of the distributional consequences of international tax reforms could contribute to global discussions

There are also political economy concerns. MNEs often exert influence on their home Governments and attempt to influence the direction of public policies. This may influence decision makers in countries with many MNEs to prefer certain reforms over others, or no reforms at all. Thus a key impediment to international tax reform would be the incentives of decision makers, who may not agree to reforms that are perceived as harming the competitiveness of some of their strong interest groups. Other interest groups, however, which may make less use of tax avoidance strategies, may see stronger rule enforcement as being in their interest and can be potential partners in improving tax systems. The balance of interests in each political environment will be important for policymakers and stakeholders to understand. If tax reforms proceed on a voluntary basis, then countries that do not accept or participate in new frameworks may distort the distribution of gains and losses. This should also be a priority area for future study.

Reforms to the international framework for tax cooperation, which do not properly assess or address distributional impacts, will carry the risk of being counterproductive.

> The United Nations can provide a universal platform for reaching agreement on reforms in international tax cooperation

---

72   G8 Leaders' Communiqué, Lough Erne, 2013, available from https://www.gov.uk/government/uploads/system/uploads/attachment_data/file/207771/Lough_Erne_2013_G8_Leaders_Communique.pdf.

Forums for discussion of these reforms in which developing countries are not well represented will lack legitimacy. While intergovernmental cooperation on tax matters occurs in many forums, there is no current forum where all developing countries participate on equal terms with developed countries. For example, there was limited representation from developing countries, and no representation from special categories such as the LDCs, small island developing States, or even for small economies, in the negotiation of the OECD Convention on Mutual Administrative Assistance in Tax Matters.[73] Without equal representation, developing-country priorities, such as source-country taxation mechanisms, are less likely to be prioritized. Additionally, new rules, such as those being proposed on beneficial ownership registries, are less likely to consider administrative complexity and the cost of compliance issues. Intergovernmental tax cooperation at the United Nations, which has a universal membership and strong legitimacy, could play a key role in such efforts, building on the intergovernmental cooperation model that has worked at the OECD. It could also facilitate enhanced cooperation among international organizations, including regional institutions.

Improving financial safety nets and surveillance

The global financial safety net comprises global, regional and bilateral arrangements that provide resources to prevent a financial crisis or mitigate the adverse effects of a crisis when it unfolds. Reliable financial safety nets continue to play an important role in ensuring global financial stability. They provide liquidity in times of systemic crisis and reduce incentives for countries to accumulate excess reserves as a protection against external shocks. At the meeting of the G20 Finance Ministers and Central Bank Governors in Cairns in September 2014, the G20 Finance Ministers committed to ensuring the continued effectiveness of global financial safety nets.[74]

Financial safety nets are stronger than before, but remain inadequate and fragmented

Progress at the global level includes the quadrupling of the lending resources of the IMF since 2008 and reforming its lending toolkit. Importantly, a number of regional mechanisms have also considerably improved their ability to respond to a crisis (table III.4). In July 2014, BRICS member countries established the Contingent Reserve Arrangement (CRA) with an initial size of $100 billion.[75] This arrangement—which allows member countries to draw on each other's reserves—is likely to have a positive precautionary effect, help countries forestall short-term liquidity pressures, strengthen the global financial safety nets and complement existing international arrangements. The regional financial safety net for South-East Asia, the Chiang Mai Initiative Multilateralization (CMIM), was boosted in October 2014 when the member countries upgraded the ASEAN+3 Macroeconomic

---

73   Organization for Economic Cooperation and Development, "Convention on mutual administrative assistance in tax matters", October 2014, available from http://www.oecd.org/ctp/exchange-of-tax-information/conventiononmutualadministrativeassistanceintaxmatters.htm (accessed 14 November 2014).

74   Communiqué meeting of G20 Finance Ministers and Central Bank Governors, Cairns, 20–21 September 2014, available from https://www.g20.org/sites/default/files/g20_resources/library/Communique%20G20%20Finance%20Ministers%20and%20Central%20Bank%20Governors%20Cairns.pdf (accessed 23 October 2014).

75   See "Treaty for the establishment of a BRICS contingent reserve arrangement", VI BRICS Summit, 15 July 2014, available from http://brics6.itamaraty.gov.br/media2/press-releases/220-treaty-for-the-establishment-of-a-brics-contingent-reserve-arrangement-fortaleza-july-15 (accessed 23 October 2014).

Research Office (AMRO) into an international organization that will be responsible for surveillance of systemic risks in the member countries. This will complement the lending activities of the CMIM.[76]

Despite these improvements, the safety net mechanisms are still inadequately equipped (table III.4) given the structure of the world economy, where crises are increasingly generated or transmitted on capital and financial accounts. Compared to the magnitude of international capital flows (table III.1)—which still remain below their peak in 2007—the resources of global and regional financial safety nets remain inadequate. When the establishment of the European Stability Mechanism did not sufficiently calm market reactions to the euro area debt crisis in 2012, it required the European Central Bank President's announcement that the institution would do whatever it takes to reduce interest rate spreads and avert a full-blown crisis in the euro area.

Expanding its financial safety nets, the IMF has enhanced the flexibility of its existing instruments for low-income countries. This includes easing timing restrictions on access under the Standby Credit Facility, providing options for Extended Credit Facility arrangements with longer initial durations, offering more flexibility in the phasing of disbursements, and relaxing the requirements for poverty reduction strategy documentation. The IMF can now disburse with reduced conditionalities and at a zero interest rate under the Rapid Credit Facility, although the interest rate is scheduled for review by the end of 2014.

Improved coordination of swap arrangements can also improve the predictability of the current ad hoc arrangements in bilateral financial safety nets, while still respecting the

> Swap arrangements among central banks can strengthen financial safety nets

Table III.4
Fund size and paid-in capital for global and regional financial agreements

In billions of United States dollars and percentage

	Fund size	Paid-in capital	Paid-in ratio
Arab Monetary Fund	2.7	2.6	96%
Latin American Reserve Fund (Fundo Latino Americano de Reservas, FLAR)	3.3	2.3	70%
EURASEC Anti-Crisis Fund (Central Asia)	8.5	8.5	100%
European Union Balance of Payments Facility	63.5	63.5	100%
European Financial Stabilization Mechanism (European Union)[a]	76.2		
BRICS Contingency Reserve Agreement	100.0		
Chiang Mai Initiative Multilateralization (ASEAN+3)	240.0		
European Financial Stability Facility (euro area)[a]	558.8		
European Stability Mechanism (euro area)[a]	635.0	101.6	16%
International Monetary Fund (IMF)	1,362.0	362.0	27%

Source: IMF; Rhee, Changyong, Lea Sumulong and Shahin Vallée (2013). Global and regional financial safety nets: lessons from Europe and Asia. Bruegel Working Paper, 2013/06. Brussels: Bruegel. November, available from http://www.bruegel.org/publications/publication-detail/publication/801-global-and-regional-financial-safety-nets-lessons-from-europe-and-asia/.

a Since September 2012, all loans for euro area members are under the European Stability Mechanism. The European Financial Stability Facility and the European Financial Stabilization Mechanism will continue to manage the previously approved loans to Greece, Ireland and Portugal.

76   ASEAN+3 Macroeconomic Research Office, "AMRO Director's statement regarding the completion of the signing of the agreement establishing ASEAN+3 Macroeconomic Research Office", 10 October 2014, available from http://www.amro-asia.org/wp-content/uploads//2014/10/141010-Press-release-AMRO-Directors-statement-on-signing-of-the-AMRO-Agreement.pdf (accessed 23 October 2014).

unique roles of central banks. The Fed has set up a number of permanent swap arrangements; however, they are limited to a few high-income countries such as with Canada and Japan, and the European Central Bank. China has established more than 25 bilateral currency swap arrangements, including with a number of ASEAN countries and Australia, Switzerland and the United Kingdom.

Regional mechanisms will need to enhance their precautionary and lending capacities as well as their surveillance efforts. Proposals for strengthening the linkages between the IMF and regional arrangements include a review of IMF options to lend directly to regional structures that are in the position to contribute significantly to surveillance. Another suggestion is for regional arrangements to look beyond their regional interest and facilitate cooperation with the IMF, especially in terms of programme design, surveillance and monitoring. While improving cooperation between global and regional financial safety nets will be important, each structure will also have to be strengthened individually.

Stronger coordination in multilateral surveillance is needed

The multilateral surveillance framework comprises the IMF and the G20 along with several standard-setting bodies such as the World Bank, the BCBS or the Financial Action Task Force. In 2009, the G20 introduced the Mutual Assessment Process (MAP)—a new approach to policy collaboration—to identify objectives for the global economy, the policies needed to reach them, and their spillover effects on other countries and the global economy. MAP envisaged an in-depth analysis of the nature and causes of countries' imbalances to identify impediments to adjustment and recommend appropriate policy actions. Compared to IMF surveillance under Article 4, MAP presented stronger country ownership as it is directly under the leadership of the G20 member states. However, the MAP process lost traction because major deficit and surplus countries could not agree on how to manage the imbalances.

The IMF has significantly improved its surveillance mechanisms

The IMF strengthened its surveillance mechanisms in the past years to address shortcomings in its pre-crisis surveillance framework. This has included a stronger focus on interconnections within and between economies; improved integration of bilateral and multilateral surveillance; strengthening analysis beyond exchange-rate movements when assessing spillovers; improved risk assessments; building expertise in financial stability analysis; stronger awareness of the comprehensiveness of external stability measures; and stronger cooperation with Member States. In the 2014 Spillover Report, the IMF extended country coverage by analysing spillovers resulting from the withdrawal of unconventional monetary policies in advanced economies and the declining growth rates in emerging markets.[77] A review of the Financial Sector Assessment Program (FSAP), which assesses the stability of countries with systemically important financial sectors, was released in September 2014.[78] As many as 144 member countries have undergone assessments under the programme since 1999, most of them more than once. The review found that since 2009 FSAP reports improved in all dimensions, including stress tests that covered a broader set of risks, and an increasing analysis of spillovers and macroprudential policy frameworks.

---

[77]   IMF, "IMF multilateral policy issues report: IMF Spillover report", IMF Policy Paper, 29 July 2014, available from http://www.imf.org/external/np/pp/eng/2014/062514.pdf (accessed 23 October 2014).

[78]   IMF, "Review of the financial sector assessment program: further adaptation to the post crisis era", September 2014, available from http://www.imf.org/external/np/pp/eng/2014/081814.pdf (accessed 23 October 2014).

In October 2014, the IMF completed its latest Triennial Surveillance Review (TSR).[79] The review analysed the consistency and focus of the IMF policy advice and found that the IMF had not taken full advantage of the synergies between and among bilateral and multilateral surveillance. In particular, it found that stronger efforts are required to identify how risks map across countries and how domestic vulnerabilities are exacerbated by rapid spillovers across sectors. The TSR also raised the question whether the IMF mandate is sufficient to support a stronger role of the Fund in global cooperation. Concerns remain that IMF surveillance is too strongly focused on overall comprehensiveness instead of identifying risks that bear the biggest threats to the global economy. A better understanding of individual country situations and risks will help the IMF offer customized advice to its 188 member states.

The efficacy of multilateral institutional arrangements for both safety nets and surveillance is still constrained by the underrepresentation of developing countries. The fragmentation of the international financial system further undermines policy coordination and causes time delays. Therefore, reforms that allow for more inclusiveness and efficiency gains will have to be explored.

Greater representation of developing countries can further strengthen multilateral surveillance

Governance reform

The governing bodies of both the IMF and the World Bank Group agreed to governance reforms in 2010 with a view to improving representation, responsiveness, and accountability in these two organizations. The FSB, created in 2009, has a more inclusive governance structure compared to its predecessor, the Financial Stability Forum, and recently reviewed its structure of representation.[80] Still, the need for governance reform leading to strengthened global coordination remains urgent. FSB remains an exclusive body without universal representation and without clear rules for membership in its various subsidiary bodies. The World Bank Group reforms would result in an increase in voting power for developing and transitional countries in the International Bank for Reconstruction and Development and the International Finance Corporation for Part II members, but have so far not been fully implemented. The proposed reforms of the IMF executive board, which require an amendment of the IMF Articles of Agreement, have also not entered into force because they have not yet been ratified by the United States. This has stalled the implementation of the IMF quota increases and voting rights reforms that were agreed in 2010.

Governance reforms are urgently needed to foster an enabling financing framework for sustainable development

The underrepresentation of developing countries in global economic decision-making bodies needs to be addressed to enhance the effectiveness of global partnership for sustainable development. While member states have asked the IMF to explore other options for reforms given the impasse over implementation of the 2010 reforms, more can be done to reform the global economic decision-making processes. Building on the current momentum created by the preparations for the upcoming third International Conference on Financing for Development in July 2015, the United Nations, by providing an inclusive forum for policy dialogues and coordination, can play an increasingly critical role in strengthening global economic cooperation, enhancing global financial stability and creating a financial architecture that enables sustainable development.

---

79 IMF, "2014 Triennial Surveillance Review", 15 October 2014, available from https://www.imf.org/external/np/spr/triennial/2014/index.htm (accessed 23 October 2014).

80 Financial Stability Board, "Report to the G20 Brisbane Summit on the FSB's review of the structure of its representation", 6 November 2014.

Chapter IV
Regional developments and outlook

Developed market economies

The developed market economies are expected to gradually strengthen over the forecast period, with growth of gross domestic product (GDP) projected to be 2.1 and 2.3 per cent in 2015 and 2016, respectively, up from the estimated 1.6 per cent in 2014 (see annex table A.1). There is an increasing divergence of performance within the group. The United States of America, Canada and the United Kingdom of Great Britain and Northern Ireland are experiencing a period of relatively strong growth, while growth is much weaker and more at risk in the economies of the euro area and Japan. Inflation rates reflect this varying performance: Japan continues to struggle to end its deflationary past and push inflation towards its 2 per cent target while the euro area increasingly flirts with entering deflation. Policy stances also reflect this divergence. The euro area and Japan continue to strengthen highly accommodative monetary policies, while the United States and the United Kingdom contemplate the beginning of policy normalization, bringing policy to a more neutral stance. This policy divergence was reflected in strong currency movements in the latter half of 2014, which are expected to continue in the forecast period.

North America

The United States: growth prospects continue to improve

The economy of the United States is expected to expand in 2015 and 2016 at the pace of 2.8 and 3.1 per cent, respectively. While robust growth in business investment will be the major driver, household consumption is also expected to strengthen, along with a continued improvement in employment. The fiscal drag on GDP growth from cuts in government spending will remain, but the pace of the spending reductions will be much milder than in the previous few years. The United States Federal Reserve (Fed) is expected to start raising interest rates from mid-2015 on, but the monetary policy stance will continue to be accommodative until the end of 2016. Inflation is expected to stay benign. The contribution from the external sector to GDP growth will be limited, as export growth is expected to be curbed by the strong appreciation of the dollar. The downside risks for the economy are mainly associated with the possible increase in financial volatility in response to the normalization of monetary policy. Sizeable corrections in equity prices and bond yields could produce significant adverse effects on the growth and stability of the real economy.

Business investment, particularly investment in equipment, has been strengthening and is expected to expand at a pace of about 6 per cent in 2015–2016, with investment in industrial equipment leading at a pace of 8–9 per cent. Most firms in the United States are

Investment strengthens as firms are in solid financial positions

in solid financial positions. For instance, companies in the Standard & Poor's 500 index have the lowest ratio of net debt to earnings in two decades, more than $3 trillion in cash and record earnings per share. With long-term interest rates at record lows, companies have the potential to boost investment more than projected if the prospects for aggregate demand strengthen further and uncertainties about economic policy diminish. Meanwhile, housing investment, which continued to recover in 2014, although at a subdued pace compared with 2013, is expected to improve further in 2015–2016.

Growth in consumer spending has been moderate, at an estimated pace of 2.2 per cent in real household consumption for 2014, lower than the previous year. Real household consumption is projected to grow by 2.7 and 3.0 per cent in 2015 and 2016. While personal income increased by about 4.0 per cent in 2014, the household saving rate also increased slightly, to 5.1 per cent from 4.9 per cent in 2013, reflecting a certain degree of precaution taken by middle-income households with regard to their spending.

The labour market holds
the key to household
consumption

Five years after the Great Recession, payroll employment in the United States has finally exceeded the pre-crisis peak registered in January 2008. Increases in payroll employment in 2014 have averaged 230,000 per month, up from the monthly pace of 190,000 during 2012–2013. The unemployment rate has declined more than 4 percentage points from its peak in 2009, to below 6 per cent in late 2014, although the rate of underemployment remains above 11 per cent. The proportion of long-term unemployment (27 weeks or longer) has also been declining from the peak of 46 per cent in 2009 to 31 per cent in 2014, but is still notably higher than the pre-crisis level.

The decline in the unemployment rate has also been accompanied by a steady drop in the rate of labour force participation, although this stabilized during 2014. Labour force participation had actually begun to decline in early 2000, well before the Great Recession, partly reflecting the ageing of the baby boom generation; however, the pace of decline accelerated with the recession of 2008–2009. The drop in the participation rate since 2008 can be attributed to increases in four factors: retirement, disability, school enrollment and worker discouragement. These changes are a combination of both structural and cyclical movements, the latter due to the recession and slow recovery. The stabilization of the labour force participation rate since 2013 could partly reflect the return of discouraged workers to the labour force in response to the improvements in the labour market. Employment is expected to continue increasing at an average monthly rate of more than 200,000, with the unemployment rate dropping to 5.5 per cent by 2016 (see annex table A.7).

The current-account
deficit has declined but
is expected to stabilize
going forward

Growth in both exports and imports has been sluggish in the past two years, at an annual pace of 2–3 per cent. Some moderate improvement is expected, increasing to a rate of about 5–6 per cent in 2015–2016. Growth in the exports of the United States will continue to be driven by increasing foreign demand for capital goods and industrial supplies, while imports of the United States will continue to undergo a structural change, with the trend of declining petroleum imports continuing as domestic energy production rises. The United States dollar has appreciated significantly in 2014, but a continued appreciation of the dollar may curb export growth of the United States in the future. The current-account deficit of the United States has been narrowing to $420 billion in 2014, or less than 2.5 per cent of GDP. The deficit is expected to stabilize around this level in 2015–2016, as the effects of a strong dollar on the deficit are offset by the continued decline in imports of petroleum.

Fiscal policy has been tightening in the United States since 2011, with government spending in real terms declining by about 13 percentage points cumulatively in the past four years. In the outlook for 2015–2016, fiscal policy is expected to remain restrictive, but less severe than in 2014. Real federal government spending is expected to decline by less than 1 per cent in 2015–2016. The debt ceiling is expected to be increased in the forecast period.

The Fed is expected to gradually normalize its monetary stance during 2015–2016, from the extremely accommodative "anti-recession" mode to a more neutral position, but the stance will remain supportive of growth. The Fed stopped its programme of purchasing long-term government bonds and mortgage-backed securities in late 2014, but will maintain the size of its balance sheet. The Fed will keep the federal funds interest rate within the range of 0.0 to 0.25 per cent until mid-2015 and is expected to start raising its policy interest rate gradually thereafter.

The Fed ends quantitative easing and prepares to withdraw accommodation

Certain risks in the next two years are associated with the uncertainties in monetary policy. The Fed has a dual mandate to promote both maximum employment and price stability, but because inflation has remained tame for the past several years, employment has been the dominant policy concern. The extremely accommodative monetary policy in the past five years has mainly been enacted to confront the challenges in the labour market, but as the economy approaches full employment, the Fed is preparing to normalize its monetary stance. There are two types of risk. First, if the signs of inflation come later than usual in the recovery, maintaining zero interest rates until inflation emerges could be too late, and would be followed by an abrupt and potentially disruptive tightening of policy later on. On the other hand, tightening monetary policy immediately when inflation approaches 2 per cent may prevent labour markets from recovering fully. Another risk is the possibility that the United States will be entrapped in secular stagnation (box IV.1).

Canada: growth depends on exports

Driven by strong growth in exports, together with robust household consumption and some recovery in investment from the contraction in late 2013 and early 2014, Canada's GDP is estimated to have grown by 2.3 per cent in 2014. In the outlook for 2015–2016, exports are expected to continue expanding at a robust pace of about 6 per cent, providing an important support to GDP growth. However, improvement in the labour market has been slow, with employment rising only marginally and mainly in terms of increases in part-time workers. Meanwhile, household indebtedness remains a concern. As a result, consumption spending is expected to be curbed in 2015–2016. Business investment is expected to recover, but only at a slow pace, as surveys show that firms are largely focusing on the replacement of existing equipment rather than new expansion. GDP is projected to grow by 2.6 and 2.8 per cent in 2015 and 2016, respectively.

With consumer price index (CPI) inflation close to 2 per cent—the midpoint of the inflation-targeting range of the central bank—and the output gap continuing to be negative, the Bank of Canada is expected to maintain its policy interest rate at the current level of 1 per cent until the end of 2015, to be followed by a gradual tightening. On the fiscal front, Canada is in one of the better positions among developed countries, with the government deficit currently standing at 1.8 per cent of GDP. In the outlook period, fiscal policy is expected to be in a neutral stance, and the deficit will narrow slightly, to below 1.5 per cent of GDP by 2016.

Box IV.1
Secular stagnation

By historical standards, a full six years after the eruption of the global financial crisis, growth remains subdued in the world economy, particularly in the United States of America and the euro area. This observation has prompted some economists to postulate the hypothesis of "secular stagnation", suggesting the anaemic growth may continue for a considerably long period.

Weak investment demand

Some analysts emphasize weak aggregate demand, as evinced in the conspicuously large output gaps in major developed economies (figure IV.1.1).[a] By this view, in the aftermath of the financial crisis, because central banks cannot lower nominal interest rates below the zero lower bound, real interest rates remain too high to boost sufficient investment demand relative to savings, thus leading to both inadequate employment and aggregate demand. Main policy proposals from these analysts include: (a) the central banks of major developed economies should raise their inflation targets to 4 per cent from the current target of 2 per cent, so as to push down real interest rates; (b) governments should increase public investment in infrastructure.

Figure IV.1.1
Actual and potential GDP in the United States, 2007–2017

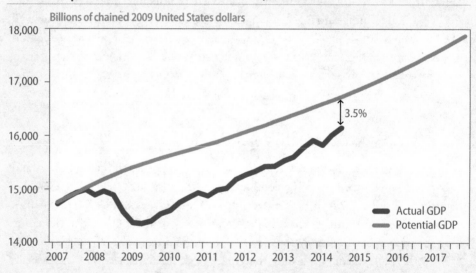

Billions of chained 2009 United States dollars

Source: UN/DESA, based on data from the United States Bureau of Economic Analysis and Congressional Budget Office.

Note: Last data point for the actual GDP is 2014 Q3.

a For example, Lawrence H. Summers, "Reflections on the 'new secular stagnation hypothesis'", in *Secular Stagnation: Facts, Causes and Cures*, Coen Teulings and Richard Baldwin, eds. London: CEPR Press, 2014.

b See Robert J. Gordon, "The demise of U.S. economic growth: restatement, rebuttal, and reflections", NBER Working Paper, No. 19895, Cambridge, Massachusetts: National Bureau of Economic Research.

Supply bottlenecks

Another group of economists focuses on supply constraints as the main factor behind growth stagnation. For instance, Robert Gordon[b] has identified four indicators that may curb the growth of the United States in the next few decades: demography, namely, ageing and stagnant population growth; education, i.e., no further increase in average education levels; widening inequality; and high public debt that makes public services unsustainable. These four bottlenecks may reduce the per capita gross domestic product (GDP) growth rate in the United States from the average of 2.0 per cent in the past century to 0.8 per cent in the next few decades. The policies proposed by this group of economists include reforms of the education system, labour market and social welfare system.

Debate on secular stagnation

The term "secular stagnation" was first coined by the Harvard economist Alvin Hansen in 1938, to describe the gloomy outlook during the Great Depression, but his pessimistic outlook proved to be wrong as growth in the United States accelerated forcefully in the 1940s. Nevertheless, some economists still

(continued)

Figure IV.1.2
Private sector GDP growth rate in the United States, 2001–2014

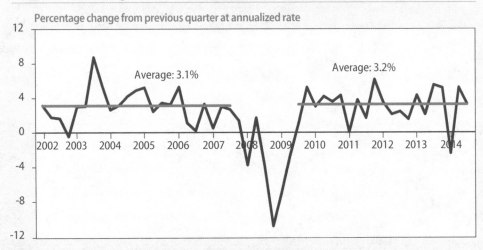

believe that the growth acceleration in the 1940s was stimulated by the surge in government spending during WWII, but currently no such scale of fiscal stimulus is available.

Some critics pointed out that secular stagnation in the United States was not validated, as the growth rates for GDP minus government expenditure in the United States in the aftermath of the financial crisis are actually higher than that in the period prior to the crisis (figure IV.1.2).

Box IV.1 (*continued*)

Source: UN/DESA, based on data from Bureau of Economic Analysis, United States Department of Commerce. Note: Last data point is 2014 Q3.

Source: UN/DESA.

Developed Asia

Japan: policy actions drive the short-term dynamics

In Japan, GDP has been strongly affected by the Government's fiscal consolidation programme. In April 2014, the consumption tax rate was raised by 3 percentage points. In anticipation of this, households brought forward their purchases of durable goods; private consumption therefore expanded significantly in the first quarter at an annual rate of 9.1 per cent, but this reversed in the second quarter with consumption dropping by 18.6 per cent. As a result, GDP fluctuated egregiously, and the economy fell into a technical recession in the second and third quarter. For the year as a whole, GDP is estimated to grow by only 0.4 per cent in 2014 and is projected to expand by 1.2 per cent in 2015 and 1.1 per cent in 2016 (see annex table A.1).

The fiscal stimulus package introduced in 2013 raised public consumption and investment by about 2 per cent in 2013. After the end of the package, the Government introduced a new supplementary budget in early 2014, but the magnitude has not been sufficient to fully offset the negative impact of the higher taxes.

The unconventional monetary policy measures implemented in April 2013 drove down the yields on securities and also guided inflation expectations upward, as the year-on-year change in the CPI climbed from -0.9 per cent in March 2013 to 1.6 per cent at the end of 2013 (figure IV.1). After the sales tax hike, inflation increased further to 3.7 per cent within two months, but then started to decelerate. The Bank of Japan estimated that core inflation, net of the tax effect, was only 1.25 per cent for the third quarter, and, consequently, it expanded monetary easing substantially in October 2014. The annual headline inflation rate for 2014 is estimated to reach 2.7 per cent and is projected to be 1.3 per cent in 2015 and 1.5 per cent in 2016 (see annex table A.4).

The consumption tax hike created turbulence

Monetary easing was expanded

Figure IV.1
CPI inflation in Japan, January 2009–September 2014

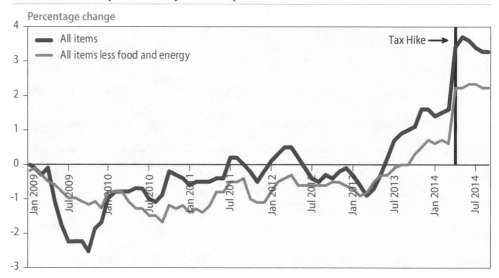

Source: UN/DESA, based
on data from the Bureau of
Statistics, Government of Japan.

**Yen depreciation has a
limited impact on exports**

Monetary easing has led to a strong depreciation of the Japanese yen vis-à-vis all major currencies. In early November 2014, the yen's value against the dollar was about 23 per cent lower than in late 2012. This depreciation has helped to increase inflation through the higher price of imported goods.

The deprecation of the yen starting in late 2012 was expected to provide a boost to exports, but the recovery in exports has been slower than expected. In 2013, total export volumes increased by only 1.6 per cent. With a rebound of more than 7.0 per cent in the first quarter, exports are estimated to grow by 4.4 per cent in 2014, and are forecast to grow by 2.4 per cent in 2015. In the first half of 2014, import volumes increased by more than 10 per cent, owing to the front-loading of consumption. Import growth is expected to mirror that of exports in 2015. Although the trade balance is predicted to remain in deficit, the current-account balance is expected to remain in slight surplus, with the help of a continuous surplus in investment income.

Wages remain tepid

The labour force had been declining since 2000 due to the ageing of the population, but in late 2013, it started to increase as the participation rate rose. After five years of continuous decline, employment has increased since 2013 and is expected to continue to pick up in 2015. The unemployment rate is estimated to have decreased from a level of 4.0 per cent in 2013 to 3.5 per cent in 2014, with a further decline to 3.3 per cent projected for 2015 (see annex table A.7). But the improvement in the labour market has so far led to only tepid increases in the nominal wage rate. For 2014 as a whole, it is estimated that real wages will decline, underpinning weaker private consumption growth.

Australia and New Zealand: growth driven by investment

The Australian economy is estimated to have grown by 3.0 per cent in 2014 and is forecast to grow by about 2.4 per cent in both 2015 and 2016. Export volumes will grow by about 5 per cent per year on average during the outlook period, as new mining facilities enter the production stage. Investment in large mining resources projects is expected to continue expanding until 2015 and sustain the growth in overall fixed investment. Both private and government consumption are predicted to grow by 2.0 to 2.5 per cent in 2015–2016. The consumer inflation rate will remain within the target zone of the central bank over the outlook period.

New Zealand's economy is estimated to have grown by 3.0 in 2014, and will grow by 3.3 per cent in 2015, mainly driven by the solid expansion of capital investment. Private consumption will maintain relatively stable growth in the coming years. Government consumption is expected to be curbed by concerns regarding fiscal deficits. Export growth is expected to increase at about 2.5 to 3.0 per cent in 2015–2016. Import growth will remain high, partly as a consequence of strong investment growth. The Reserve Bank of New Zealand raised its policy rate in 2014 and is expected to tighten further in 2015–2016.

Europe

Western Europe: moderate improvement in the outlook period

Western Europe continues to be held back by the travails of the euro area, where the level of GDP has yet to regain its pre-recession peak, unemployment remains extremely high in many countries, and inflation is at alarmingly low levels. The emergence from recession in the second quarter of 2013 and subsequent strengthening of activity into the beginning of 2014 raised hopes that the euro area had finally entered a period of sustained growth; but activity decelerated sharply in the second quarter and, despite a slight up-tick in the third quarter, the outlook has deteriorated. Some of the initial decline can be attributed to seasonal effects, but the impact of the geopolitical tensions in Ukraine has played a clear role, affecting trade and confidence. This highlights the weakness of the recovery and the ease with which it can be disturbed. In the EU-15,[1] GDP is estimated to have grown by only 1.2 per cent in 2014 and is expected to strengthen only modestly to 1.5 and 1.9 per cent in 2015 and 2016, respectively.

The stresses surrounding the euro area sovereign debt crisis have by now almost completely dissipated, owing in large part to the European Central Bank (ECB) announcement of the Outright Monetary Transactions facility in September 2012, which signalled that the ECB would do whatever it takes to end the crisis. But many legacies of the Great Recession and the subsequent sovereign debt crisis continue to depress activity: Fiscal austerity programmes, while lessened in intensity, remain in place against a backdrop of extremely high debt levels in many countries. Private sector balance-sheet repair, also lessened in intensity, continues to be a drag on activity. The banking system remains under stress and lending conditions remain fragmented, with bank credit in periphery countries, particularly for small to medium-sized enterprises (SMEs), extremely challenging to obtain. Labour markets in many countries are characterized by very high rates of unemployment, which is increasingly becoming long term.

Systemic risks in the euro area have subsided, but activity remains weak and fragile

A reflection of these legacies and structural characteristics—which vary in degree and type across countries in the region—is that in the large economies, the evolution of the level of GDP has been quite diverse in the six years since the onset of the Great Recession: Italy

Country prospects are diverse

---

1   The EU-15 refers to the 15 countries that were members of the European Union (EU) prior to its enlargement on 1 May 2004. The countries are: Austria, Belgium, Denmark, Finland, France, Germany, Greece, Ireland, Italy, Luxembourg, the Netherlands, Portugal, Spain, Sweden and the United Kingdom of Great Britain and Northern Ireland.

and Spain remain well below pre-recession levels, while France, Germany and the United Kingdom have all regained their previous levels (figure IV.2).

Figure IV.2
Western Europe GDP indices, 2008–2014 Q2

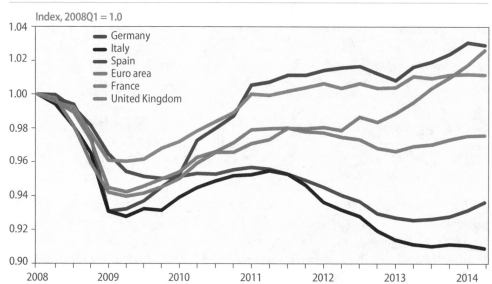

Source: OECD, *Main
Economic Indicators.*

Going forward, economic prospects still differ. Italy is estimated to contract by 0.4 per cent in 2014, the third consecutive year of decline, and is projected to recover by only 0.5 and 1.1 per cent in 2015 and 2016, respectively. France is nearly stagnant, estimated to have grown by only 0.3 per cent in 2014, after growing 0.2 per cent in 2013 and before some acceleration to 0.8 and 1.3 per cent in 2015 and 2016, respectively. Germany started the year strongly but slowed as the geopolitical tensions around Ukraine mounted, with GDP growth estimated to be 1.4 per cent in 2014. Given the poor momentum, growth is expected to be only 1.4 and 1.7 per cent in 2015 and 2016, respectively. A ray of hope exists, however, in that some of the crisis countries have resumed growth. Spain resumed positive growth in mid-2013 and has been strengthening since, growing by 1.2 per cent in 2014 and expected to grow by 2.1 and 2.5 per cent in 2015 and 2016, respectively. In Ireland and Portugal, two of the smaller countries swept into the euro area debt crisis, positive growth has also resumed. In all three cases, recoveries remain extremely fragile and they have yet to recover their pre-recession GDP levels. The only example of more robust growth is outside the euro area, in the United Kingdom, where GDP is estimated to have grown by 3.1 per cent in 2014 and is projected to grow by 2.6 per cent in 2015 and 2.5 per cent in 2016.

*Consumption provides
some support*

Private consumption expenditure is expected to be of modest support to growth in the forecast period, stemming from a number of factors: consumer confidence, despite falling back somewhat in the last few months, has increased significantly since its low point in the final quarter of 2012; energy prices have come down; government austerity programmes have diminished in intensity; and labour markets have finally stabilized with rates of unemployment, albeit extremely high in many countries, coming down somewhat and wages picking up gradually.

Investment expenditure continues to be a major weak spot in the euro area. It is expected to stabilize and gradually pick up, but not to provide much support to growth. Following the easing of euro area problems, industrial confidence had improved significantly, but has seen a reversal since the tensions around Ukraine emerged, particularly in those countries with a strong manufacturing orientation. Capacity utilization has increased significantly since the end of the Great Recession, but remains low by historical standards. Funding conditions vary tremendously across the region; interest rates on loans, particularly to SMEs, are much higher in the periphery countries than elsewhere in the region. Housing investment has started to turn around, but remains a drag on activity in some countries.

Investment remains a weak spot

Exports improved in 2014 and are expected to gradually pick up in 2015 and 2016. The appreciation of the euro during 2013 accentuated the poor performance of exports, but its subsequent reversal in the second half of 2014—and assumed further depreciation in 2015 and 2016—provide a boost. However, the geopolitical tensions around Ukraine will provide another negative impulse to trade. Import volumes continued to rebound from their collapse in 2012, in line with the evolution of income, as the region recovered from the negative headwinds of the sovereign debt crisis; they are expected to gradually strengthen in 2015 and 2016, but will be held back by the depreciation of the euro.

Unemployment remains at high levels in many countries in the region, particularly in the euro area where, after peaking at 12.0 per cent in mid-2013, the rate of unemployment has come down by only 0.5 percentage points as of late 2014. Going forward, a weak growth profile, the continuing need for structural adjustments, and the re-entry of discouraged workers into the labour market as conditions improve, is causing a glacially slow improvement in rates of unemployment. In the EU-15, the rate of unemployment is estimated to have averaged 10.5 per cent in 2014 and is projected to improve to 10.2 in 2015 and 9.9 in 2016. Again, there is tremendous diversity in unemployment in the region, standing at 5.1 per cent in Germany and 6.4 per cent in the United Kingdom, but reaching 10.2 per cent in France, 12.6 per cent in Italy and 24.6 per cent in Spain in 2014.

High rates of unemployment will persist for many countries

These figures also mask the much harsher conditions faced by youth in the region, with unemployment above 23 per cent in the euro area as a whole but above 53 per cent in Spain, 44 per cent in Italy and 35 per cent in Portugal in late 2014. Another major concern is that the persistence of high rates of unemployment in some countries will lead to more workers transitioning to the ranks of the long-term unemployed (defined as being unemployed 12 months or more) or dropping out of the labour force. Long-term unemployment has increased significantly in the aftermath of the Great Recession, up from 3.0 per cent of the labour force in the euro area in 2008 to 6.0 per cent in 2013.

Headline inflation decelerated almost continuously in the euro area during 2014, registering 0.4 per cent year over year in October and raising fears that the region would fall into deflation. To some extent, this results from temporary effects such as the decline in energy and food prices and the earlier appreciation of the euro; however, weak economic activity is the major cause, as core inflation has also drifted down, remaining below 1 per cent since May 2014. This low rate of inflation for the euro area as a whole meant that individual countries that were adjusting their competitive positions, such as Greece, Italy, Portugal and Spain, were already in deflation.

Inflation continues to decelerate, raising deflation fears

Inflation is expected to gradually pick up but remain low. Output gaps are still substantial and expected to close only slowly in the outlook period. Wages are expected to increase modestly, but not much in excess of productivity gains. Oil prices are expected to remain low in 2015 and 2016. Some upward pressure on inflation will come from the depreciation of the euro. The harmonized index of consumer prices for the euro area is estimated to have reached 0.7 per cent in 2014 and is expected to rise modestly to 1.2 and 1.7 per cent in 2015 and 2016, respectively.

The ECB adds new stimulus measures

Over the past year, the ECB made a number of policy adjustments, both conventional and unconventional. It cut its policy interest rates twice, bringing its main refinancing rate to 0.05 per cent, its marginal lending rate to 0.30 per cent, and introducing a negative interest rate of -0.20 per cent on its Deposit Facility Rate. The ECB also announced four new or enhanced unconventional policies: i) an extension of the existing unlimited short-term liquidity provided by main refinancing operations until at least 2016; ii) a new policy of targeted longer-term refinancing operations, where banks will be able to borrow money at highly favourable terms, but on condition that they meet lending benchmarks; iii) another new policy of purchasing asset-backed securities; and iv) a revival of the covered bond purchase programme. The aim is to bring the ECB balance sheet back to the levels prevailing at the beginning of 2012, about 3 trillion euro, which means a total increase of about 1 trillion euro.

In the outlook period, it is assumed that the ECB will keep policy interest rates at their current levels through mid-2016, followed by a gradual increase. Unconventional policies will be carried out as announced and the central bank balance sheet will return to 2012 levels through the end of 2016. There will be no new programme of sovereign bond buying. The Bank of England, facing a very different economic environment, is expected to embark on a path of policy normalization beginning in early 2015.

Fiscal policy maintains its emphasis on deficit reduction

Fiscal policy in the region is still heavily biased towards deficit reduction. In the euro area, the Stability and Growth Pact (SGP) requires most countries to consolidate their budgets, but the pressure has eased considerably, with a number of countries granted additional time to reach their budget targets. At the aggregate level, progress has been made: the deficit-to-GDP ratio for the euro area as a whole has gone from 4.2 per cent in 2011 to 2.5 per cent in the second quarter of 2014.

But 8 out of the 20 regional economies remain under the Excessive Deficit Procedure, so the pressure continues. In addition, the Fiscal Compact, which entered into force in 2013, adds additional budgetary requirements to those in the SGP. Structural government budget deficits should be less than 0.5 per cent of GDP (or less than 1 per cent of GDP if their debt-to-GDP ratio is below 60 per cent) and debt ratios above 60 per cent will require remedial action. The conclusion is that government budgets will remain under pressure for an extended period.

In the outlook period, it is assumed that, for a majority of regional economies, fiscal policy will continue to be focused on reducing fiscal imbalances. The degree of consolidation will be less onerous than in the past few years. The debt crisis countries will continue their adjustment programmes, and any shortfalls due to growth underruns will not be made up; rather, the timetable for achieving targets will be extended. Finally, it is assumed that no countries will ask for formal assistance under the European Stability Mechanism.

The euro depreciates as policy divergence among the major economies widens

During the first half of 2014, the dollar/euro exchange rate ranged from 1.35 to 1.40, but has since depreciated significantly to near 1.25. The major cause is the recent announcements of additional stimulus by the ECB, together with evidence that the euro area recovery is faltering and the anticipation of the beginning of policy normalization by the Fed due to a strong recovery in the United States. The euro is expected to continue to depreciate against the dollar from an average of 1.34 in 2014 to 1.25 in 2015 and 1.21 in 2016.

The underlying growth momentum in the region has decelerated to the point where an exogenous event could lead to a return to recession. The current tensions around Ukraine have already had a serious negative impact on activity and confidence. The weak state of the recovery is characterized by extremely high unemployment in many countries, which becomes more entrenched as the number of long-term unemployed increase, and by dangerously low inflation that could turn into Japan-style deflation. Aside from being exceptionally difficult to exit, deflation would also increase real government debt burdens and perhaps reignite the debt crisis as fiscal targets become increasingly difficult to achieve.

Risks are once again tilted to the downside

The new EU members:[2] slow but stable recovery amid geopolitical tensions

The new EU member States continue to recover from the long-lasting consequences of the global economic and financial crisis and a sharp slowdown of growth in 2012. This recovery solidified in 2014, thanks to emboldened domestic demand, easing of fiscal austerity, a turnaround in the inventory cycle, and, in the first quarter, rising economic dynamism in the EU-15. This moderate but stable growth path is expected to continue despite downgraded prospects for the EU-15, as domestic demand becomes an increasingly important driver of growth. Although households' foreign-currency-denominated debt still remains a major macroeconomic problem in some of those countries, record-low inflation and increasing real wages, along with improving labour markets, have boosted households' confidence. Investment is benefiting from the expansion in public sector projects, in particular utilizing EU funds, and declining financing costs. Nevertheless, the region still remains heavily dependent on the external environment: the upcoming policy normalization of the Fed may lead to more volatile capital flows; deleveraging by foreign banks is not completely over yet; and the geopolitical tensions in the region create additional risks.

All countries are estimated to register positive growth rates in 2014, with the exception of Croatia, where a confluence of factors—including tight fiscal policy to meet the requirements of the SGP and the loss of duty-free access to the Central European Free Trade Agreement (CEFTA) markets of the neighbouring countries—led to a contraction in output. The aggregate GDP of the new EU member States is estimated to have grown by 2.6 per cent in 2014, and projected to grow by 2.9 per cent in 2015 and 3.3 per cent in 2016.

The unfolding geopolitical conflict around Ukraine and the sanctions imposed between the Russian Federation and many leading Organization for Economic Cooperation and Development (OECD) economies have certain repercussions for the region, apart from weak growth in the EU-15. The restriction on supplying deep-water drilling equipment to the sanctioned Russian oil companies will impact some of the countries in Central Europe, which are integrated into the production chain of the embargoed products. The Russian ban on food imports, imposed initially for one year, will affect the Baltic States and, to a smaller extent, Poland, through direct losses by the agricultural sector, effects on the logistics system, state budgets, and banks exposed to agricultural borrowers. However, at the macroeconomic level, those effects are not expected to be very large in 2015, unless the geopolitical tensions escalate further.

Geopolitical tensions present risk but did not have a large impact

The lower energy and food prices and cuts in administered utility prices drove inflation in the new EU members to record-low levels in 2014, with repeated incidents of defla-

Inflation reaches record lows

---

2   This subsection mainly refers to the new EU member States in Central and Eastern Europe.

Figure IV.3
**Inflation dynamics in selected new EU member States,
November 2013–September 2014**

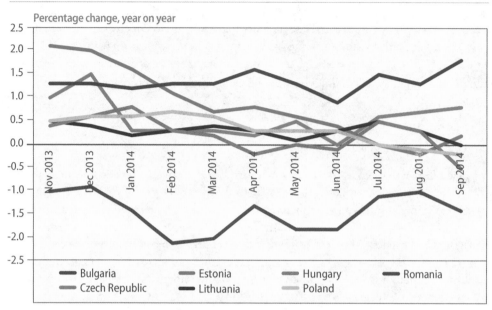

Percentage change, year on year

Legend: Bulgaria, Czech Republic, Estonia, Lithuania, Hungary, Poland, Romania

Source: Eurostat.

tion in a number of countries (figure IV.3). Annual inflation in the region is expected to be well below the respective targets set by the central banks and negative in some cases. A moderate strengthening in domestic demand is likely to add a percentage point to annual inflation in 2015. This outlook is subject to the potential risks of higher energy prices in case of disruptions in natural gas supply through Ukraine.

Labour markets strengthened

Positive trends in the region's labour markets continued in 2014, although the progress was uneven across countries. In the Czech Republic, Hungary (where the public works programme had an impact), Poland and Slovakia, unemployment rates dropped by a percentage point or more over the course of the year. In the Baltic States, both net outward migration and the increased employment figures contributed to the improvement in labour markets. In Croatia, however, there was little tangible progress, as fiscal policy is contractionary, output is contracting, and some companies, losing duty-free access to the CEFTA markets, have outsourced production to countries with a cheaper labour force. Positive trends are expected to continue in 2015. For example, the entitlement of the citizens of Bulgaria and Romania to employment in any EU country since 2014 should somewhat mitigate pressure in the labour markets of those countries. There are, however, risks that employment gains in the sectors exposed to trade with the Russian Federation (such as agriculture or food processing) may be reversed. Given the largely structural nature of unemployment in the region, achieving any tangible progress will require committed policy actions.

Fiscal austerity is gradually abandoned

Fiscal austerity in the new EU members is being gradually phased out, as most of those countries have succeeded in rebuilding their public finances. The impact of fiscal policy on growth in 2014 may be expansionary in some cases. However, certain countries, including Poland, still have budget deficits exceeding 3 per cent of GDP and are subject to the excessive deficit procedure of the EU. The recapitalization of several domestic banks in Slovenia in 2014 imposed heavy costs on public finances. As a consequence, the high-deficit countries will have to remain on the track of fiscal consolidation in the near term. In addition, the Governments in the region, often facing pressure from the EU, are aiming at long-term fiscal sustainability and have serious public finance reforms on their agenda for 2015 and beyond. Nevertheless, most of the region will face less fiscal drag in 2015. A modest pickup in growth will favourably affect public revenues, and in certain areas, public spending will support growth.

Monetary policy remains the main instrument for macroeconomic stimulus in the new EU members. In the countries with flexible currencies (the Czech Republic, Hungary, Poland and Romania), policy interest rates are at record-low levels after a series of reductions in 2013 and 2014. The much-improved current-account positions mitigate the vulnerability of those countries to external shocks. Apart from maintaining the record-low policy rates, a number of central banks in the region use additional measures. These include direct interventions in the currency market (in case of the Czech National Bank) and channelling funds to SMEs through commercial banks (in the case of the Hungarian National Bank). Those countries which are members of the euro area (Estonia, Latvia, Slovakia and Slovenia) maintain the low policy rate of the ECB. Lithuania is set to join the euro area in 2015. Loose monetary policy is likely to continue in 2015, as a spike in inflation is unlikely, although the weaker currencies adversely affect the holders of foreign-currency-denominated loans. However, if the Fed raises interest rates in the second half of 2015, the region's central banks may be forced to adjust their policies.

Interest rates are at record lows

The region's credit markets, however, are still stagnating, with minor exceptions, as the asset quality of domestic banks remains low and credit demand is recovering slowly. The attempts to resolve household indebtedness in Hungary and some proposed banking regulations may affect profitability of the banking sector, restricting its lending ability.

The current-account positions of the new EU members are much healthier than in the pre-crisis period, thanks to trade surpluses run by several economies in the region and increasing transfers from the EU. Even if deficits slightly increase in 2015—in particular because of a deficit in investment income—they should not endanger macroeconomic stability in the near term.

Current accounts are in healthy positions

A renewed protracted slowdown in the EU-15 remains the major macroeconomic risk for the region. A potential disruption in the flow of Russian natural gas through Ukraine would also have detrimental consequences for the industries of the new EU members. Strengthening of the balance sheets of EU-15 banks as a result of the recent stress tests, or losses incurred in the Russian Federation or Ukraine, may prompt them to limit their exposure to the region.

Economies in transition

Amid a challenging external environment, aggregate GDP growth in the Commonwealth of Independent States (CIS) and South-Eastern Europe further decelerated to a mere 0.8 per cent in 2014, down from 2.0 per cent in 2013 (see annex table A.2). This slowdown reflects weakness in both regions. In the outlook period, aggregate growth is forecast to recover to 1.1 per cent in 2015 and 2.1 per cent in 2016.

South-Eastern Europe: slow recovery derailed by natural disasters

After returning to growth in 2013, overall economic activity in South-Eastern Europe slowed down in 2014. Floods in May had a severe impact in Bosnia and Herzegovina and

Serbia, causing significant damage to housing and infrastructure (including bridges, roads, and energy and telecommunications grids) and hampering economic activity; as a result, the Serbian economy contracted in 2014. In the rest of the region, economic performance improved, helped by a mild strengthening of activity in the EU. Growth is expected to pick up in 2015, boosted by reconstruction work in flood-affected areas, planned infrastructure projects and continued recovery in the EU. The aggregate GDP of South-Eastern Europe increased by only 0.7 per cent in 2014 and growth rates of 2.7 per cent and 3.0 per cent are expected for 2015 and 2016, respectively.

After contracting for two years, a modest recovery of domestic demand also took place, with the notable exception of Serbia. Infrastructure, tourism and energy projects have supported economic expansion in the region. However, high unemployment, ongoing fiscal adjustments and elevated indebtedness constrain growth.

Unemployment declines, but remains high in most countries

Labour markets in South-Eastern Europe are characterized by very high unemployment and low employment rates, especially in Bosnia and Herzegovina and the former Yugoslav Republic of Macedonia. Despite some decline, unemployment still remained close to 20 per cent in Serbia. In the former Yugoslav Republic of Macedonia, some growth in employment led to a marginal improvement in the unemployment rate amid growing economic activity. In Albania, the gap between male and female participation rates, which runs at about 20 percentage points, increased further.

Low inflation persists, owing to weak demand

Inflation remained low in the region, owing to weak domestic demand. In Serbia, lower food prices and the stability of the exchange rate contributed to the deceleration of inflation in 2014. In Bosnia and Herzegovina, prices declined for a second consecutive year. Deflationary pressures were also strong in Montenegro, despite increases in electricity prices. Low inflation prompted monetary easing in Albania and a series of interest rate cuts were undertaken in Serbia.

Substantial fiscal problems linger

Large fiscal gaps persist throughout the region, resulting from slow growth and large spending commitments. In Albania, progress in clearing government arrears has improved the business climate and boosted demand. In Bosnia and Herzegovina, fiscal consolidation continued under an International Monetary Fund (IMF) programme, but the floods and the electoral calendar have complicated adjustment plans. There was no progress in reducing the large public deficit in Serbia, despite some wage and pension cuts that were accompanied by the elimination of the solidarity tax. In the outlook period, the countries are likely to face fiscal drag, as they implement cuts in public sector wages and subsidies to state-owned enterprises in a bid to reduce fiscal deficits.

Large external imbalances continue

Export growth slowed in 2014 in Serbia, where the floods in May destroyed industrial capacity. By contrast, sluggish wage increases and a weak currency raised competitiveness and boosted exports in Albania. Export growth also accelerated significantly in the former Yugoslav Republic of Macedonia. The current-account deficits widened in most countries in the region. In Albania, the double-digit current-account deficit as a percentage of GDP increased further, driven by faster import growth. In Montenegro, the current-account deficit—the largest in the region—also widened further, reflecting the impact of the bankruptcy of the KAP aluminium smelting factory on export capacity. In the former Yugoslav Republic of Macedonia, the external gap rose sharply, but remained the lowest in the region.

Significant structural fragilities remain

The region's future economic performance will largely depend on the outlook for the European economy and the possibilities for higher exports and remittances in a context where significant structural fragilities exist. The uncertain situation in the euro area thus presents the main downside risk for the region. High unemployment rates will continue to put a brake on domestic demand. Policy space is restricted by the presence of large public debts and fiscal deficits. The banking sector remains in poor shape, in particular in Bosnia and Herzegovina and Serbia. Poor infrastructure and a still challenging business environment limit the ability to attract investment to boost growth and raise productive capacity.

The Commonwealth of Independent States:[3] uncertainty damages economic prospects

Economic growth in the CIS slowed down sharply in 2014. Despite some improvement in global activity, geopolitical tensions resulted in a difficult external environment with high levels of uncertainty. Economic activity in the Russian Federation, the largest economy in the CIS, came to a standstill, thus reducing growth prospects in the region. In Ukraine, a severe output contraction followed years of sluggish expansion. A mild recovery in aggregate output growth is expected in 2015, provided that geopolitical tensions ease and output stabilizes in Ukraine. The aggregate GDP growth of the CIS and Georgia decelerated from 2.0 per cent in 2013 to 0.8 per cent in 2014, and is projected to strengthen modestly to 1.1 per cent in 2015 and 2.1 per cent in 2016.

A sharp slowdown pervades CIS economic activity

Sluggish domestic demand drove the slowdown in the region in 2014. In the Russian Federation, investment plummeted as a result of higher financing costs and uncertainty linked to the sanctions imposed by, among others, the United States and the EU. The pace of expansion of household consumption decelerated markedly, reflecting declining wage and retail lending growth. Net external demand, boosted by the devaluation of the rouble, prevented the economy from falling into a recession; near-zero growth is expected in 2015 with serious downside risks and a persisting problem of capital outflows (box IV.2) In Ukraine, GDP contracted sharply, as the conflict in the south-east affected economic activity in the industrial regions of Donetsk and Luhansk and weighed negatively on investment. Despite the recovery of potash exports and a good harvest, growth was sluggish in Belarus. In Kazakhstan, spillovers from the Ukrainian crisis depressed economic activity, as the Russian Federation and Ukraine are major export destinations for the country. A decline in oil extraction contributed to the slowdown in Azerbaijan. By contrast, rapid growth followed the development of the Galkynysh gas field in Turkmenistan. Lower remittances from the Russian Federation have constrained consumption in the region's lower-income countries.

Uncertainty weighs on investment

Despite the slowdown in economic activity, the labour market in the Russian Federation remained tight, with the unemployment rate continuing to edge downwards and reaching historical lows during the year as the employment level increased. In Kazakhstan, the unemployment rate remained unchanged, as job creation absorbed the increase in the active population. By contrast, unemployment rose rapidly in Ukraine, amid a severe contraction of economic activity. Unemployment also increased sharply in some Central Asian countries, which had seen lower remittances.

Unemployment in the Russian Federation continues to decline

Currency depreciations (figure IV.4) created upward price pressures in many countries, including the Russian Federation, where food import bans also contributed to inflation. In Belarus, the weakening of the exchange rate boosted the already high inflation. In Ukraine, inflation surged as the national currency plummeted, bringing the rate of annual change to double digits, in sharp contrast with the mild deflation observed in 2013. In

Inflation accelerates in many countries

---

3   Georgia is not a member of CIS, but its performance is discussed in the context of this group of countries for reasons of geographic proximity and similarities in economic structure.

Box IV.2

The Russian Federation: a net external creditor in need of financing

The Russian Federation has posted persistent, albeit declining, current-account surpluses over the last decade, averaging almost 6 per cent of gross domestic product (GDP) per year in 2005–2013. Mirroring the current-account surpluses, the country has seen net accumulation of foreign assets by the private and public sectors and increases in reserves. Substantial resources have been channelled into the existing sovereign wealth funds (accounting for 9.6 per cent of GDP by the end of September 2014) and invested in liquid foreign assets, which are part of international reserves.

In most years, private capital outflows have been much higher than current-account surpluses (figure IV.2.1). The difference between the net purchase of foreign assets by the private sector and the current-account surplus was equivalent to an annual average of 3.6 per cent of GDP in 2007–2013. This creates a financing gap that needs to be covered by drawing down reserves, raising foreign financing (i.e., ensuring private capital inflows) or a combination of both mechanisms.

Figure IV.2.1

Current-account balance and private capital flows in the Russian Federation

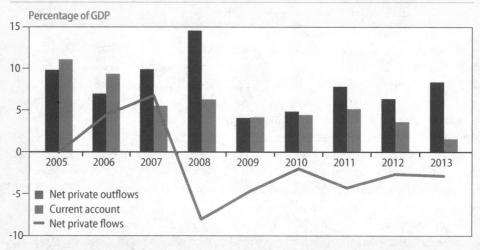

Source: Central Bank of the Russian Federation.
Note: A positive sign for net private outflows implies an exit of capital. Net private flows (line) are the difference between net private inflows and net private outflows. A positive sign indicates an entry of capital and a net acquisition of foreign liabilities.

Percentage of GDP

- ■ Net private outflows
- ■ Current account
- ▬ Net private flows

Private capital outflows partly reflect a desire for portfolio diversification. The internationalization of Russian corporations has led to the acquisition of foreign companies. Some outflows are associated with "round-tripping"—that is, Russian capital that returns to the country under the cover of a different nationality. Offshore financing structures have been used to provide protection against a still challenging business environment and obtain other advantages. The authorities are now promoting "de-offshorization" initiatives to limit capital outflows, while seeking to apply Russian taxation to structures that use offshore companies administered from the Russian Federation. Outflows are also the result of the negative assessment of investment opportunities in the country.

In addition to legitimate, registered outflows, there are a number of unrecorded capital outflows, which would correspond to a narrow definition of capital flight. The Central Bank of the Russian Federation includes an estimate of fictitious transactions in the balance of payments, which were equivalent to 45.0 per cent of the current-account surplus and 2.2 per cent of GDP on average during the period 2005–2013. As these flows are considered unlikely to return to the country, they are excluded from the statistics on the international investment position.

Given this continued leakage, access to foreign financing remains important. There were sizeable private capital inflows in 2005–2008, averaging 11 per cent of GDP annually. However, the global financial crisis of 2008–2009 marked a significant retrenchment, alerting Russian banks and corporations about the risks of rising foreign financing and reduced investor appetite for Russian assets. In 2010–2013, average annual private capital inflows were only 3.9 per cent of GDP, well below outflows of 6.8 per cent of

(continued)

GDP. Russian banks have now moved into a positive net foreign asset position, as the growth of assets, mainly in the form of deposits abroad and loans, has outstripped the increase in liabilities.

Credits from foreign banks represented 2.3 per cent of fixed capital investment in 2010, but this ratio fell to 1.2 per cent by 2012. In addition, foreign banks' claims on the Russian Federation's non-bank private sector fell by $12.2 billion in 2009–2012, in sharp contrast with the $87.5 billion increase observed in 2004–2007. While funding has declined, corporations' access to external financing remains important in overcoming the limitations of the domestic financial system regarding the availability and cost of long-term financing. The current geopolitical tensions have created a more adverse external environment for raising capital. The conflict in Ukraine has had a negative impact on investor sentiment and led to the introduction of sanctions by a number of countries, thus restricting the ability of Russian companies and banks to access international capital markets and increasing the cost of financing. About one quarter of bank and corporate external debt (a total of $650 billion) needed to be repaid or refinanced in the next twelve months, according to data from the end of the first quarter of 2014. As was the case during 2008–2009, the authorities have deployed substantial foreign reserves to alleviate the situation. In addition, they are also seeking financing from other non-Western sovereigns.

The capital of state-owned banks targeted by the sanctions is being boosted by public equity injections, including $5.4 billion for the major bank, VTB, in order to shore up banks' positions in a worsened economic climate which is accompanied by loss of access to capital markets. Funding from the repayment of state subordinated loans granted to shore up the banking sector during the 2008–2009 financial crisis is being used to finance those equity purchases. The authorities also plan to use the National Wealth Fund ($83 billion by the end of September 2014) to provide long-term support to corporations affected by the sanctions. In addition, the Central Bank of the Russian Federation is providing foreign-exchange liquidity to the sector. Overall, the direct implication of the sanctions has been an increase of the influence of the state on financial intermediation in the Russian Federation.

These initiatives provide a temporary cushion against ongoing turbulence. Addressing structural problems, including the persistent leakage of the financial account, would require more sustained reforms that promote financial development, including local currency financing, and boost confidence in investment opportunities in the country. Increased monetary credibility, leading to lower inflation, would facilitate the emergence of long-term financing sources. The consolidation of a larger domestic institutional investor base would increase domestic financing options, adding to the possibilities offered in a financial system that is primarily bank-based.

Box IV.2 (*continued*)

Source: United Nations Economic Commission for Europe.

Kazakhstan, despite the devaluation of the currency, inflation remained within the target range, supported by a good harvest.

Depreciation pressures have constrained monetary policy in many countries in the region. In the Russian Federation, the central bank raised policy rates several times and maintained its commitment to greater exchange-rate flexibility, despite earlier interventions to offset the impact of geopolitical tensions. The National Bank of Ukraine was forced to hike policy rates sharply and introduced restrictions on foreign-currency transactions in order to stem capital outflows and currency depreciation. By contrast, the authorities of Kazakhstan prompted the devaluation of the tengue, despite growing foreign-exchange reserves, to preserve competitiveness. Despite slowing economic activity, Tajikistan raised rates in response to mounting inflation. By contrast, rates were lowered repeatedly to stimulate the economy in Belarus, contributing to the weakening of the currency. Armenia also cut rates, as the inflationary pressures linked to gas price increases in 2013 abated.

Currency turbulence prompts tightening

Energy-producing countries had some policy space to address the economic slowdown. In the Russian Federation, fiscal revenues were boosted by the depreciation of the rouble, thus offsetting the impact of a lacklustre economic performance. Real public expenditure increased, after declining in 2013, which provided some lift to economic activity. There are plans to introduce a wage freeze in the 2015 federal budget, which will negatively affect growth. Despite conservative fiscal plans, sharply lower prices would force the authorities to

Fiscal expenditures increase

Figure IV.4
Depreciation of currencies in the CIS, 2014

Index for daily exchange rate versus the United States dollar: 01 January 2014 = 100

- Armenia
- Kyrgyzstan
- Republic of Moldova
- Russian Federation
- Tajikistan
- Uzbekistan

Source: UN/DESA, based on data from relevant central banks.
Note: An upward movement represents a depreciation of the national currency against the United States dollar.

tap into the reserve fund to finance planned expenditures. Kazakhstan deployed resources from its sovereign wealth fund to finance a stimulus programme. In Ukraine, economic contraction and conflict-related costs resulted in a larger deficit, including a sizeable gap at the state oil and gas company Naftogaz, which accounts for about one fourth of the total deficit.

The current-account surplus widens

External balances have improved, as a result of the contraction of imports, which has been accompanied by a deceleration in the growth of exports. In the Russian Federation, the devaluation of the rouble, import restrictions and continuing energy export revenues led to a widening of the current-account surplus, thus reducing pressures on reserves from growing capital outflows. In Ukraine, falling domestic demand and the depreciation of the national currency led to a large reduction of the current-account deficit, despite the worsening in the terms of trade. The large devaluation of the Belarusian rouble helped to keep the trade deficit down. Past gains in closing the external gap in Georgia were reversed, amid strengthening domestic demand. In the Kyrgyz Republic, the poor performance of exports to non-CIS countries and lower remittances widened the current-account deficit. The establishment of the Eurasian Economic Union, on the basis of the existing Customs Union of the Russian Federation, Belarus and Kazakhstan, will require further harmonization of economic regulations in the CIS area and should bolster intraregional economic ties in the forecast period.

Downside risks dominate

Economic prospects depend largely on the evolution of the geopolitical situation. Easing of tensions would facilitate access to finance, reduce risk premia and improve investment sentiment. By contrast, further escalation would have detrimental consequences for the region, through trade, investment and remittances channels. The Russian Federation has substantial foreign-exchange reserves to withstand current turbulence, but continued instability would affect investment for an extended period of time. This would make it more difficult to address emerging supply constraints and raise potential growth. Fragilities in the banking sector persist in some countries (with the share of non-performing loans exceeding 30 per cent) and may get worse in the current environment, as many loans are denominated in foreign currencies. The region also remains vulnerable to declines in commodity prices, which would compound the effect of other negative influences on growth and reduce policy choices.

Developing economies

Developing economies experienced a slowdown in GDP growth in 2014 as the protracted weakness in external demand was accompanied by increasing challenges on the domestic front. These factors were further exacerbated by global crises, such as the Ebola outbreak and geopolitical conflicts. Average GDP growth in developing economies decelerated from 4.8 per cent in 2013 to 4.3 per cent in 2014 (see annex table A.3). This was the slowest pace since the global financial crisis and the second-slowest since 2003. Among the different regions, only South Asia saw a marked strengthening of economic activity, led by a recovery in India. By contrast, growth weakened notably in Latin America and the Caribbean, where lower international commodity prices, structural constraints and, in some cases, macroeconomic imbalances resulted in a downturn in investment. Economic growth also decelerated in East Asia, where China continued to move towards lower, but more balanced and sustainable growth, and in Western Asia, where activity was held back by lower oil prices, the intensification of conflicts and external imbalances. In Africa, growth was stable, but well below potential and with large differences among the various subregions. In the outlook period, developing economies are forecast to see a gradual strengthening of growth, with aggregate GDP projected to increase by 4.8 per cent in 2015 and 5.1 per cent in 2016. Growth in all developing regions, except East Asia, is projected to improve in 2015–2016. However, the outlook is subject to significant uncertainties and downside risks, including a further escalation of geopolitical crises, a sharper-than-expected slowdown in China and a severe tightening of global liquidity conditions in the face of a normalization of United States monetary policy.

Africa: solid aggregate growth accompanied by significant downside risks

Africa's overall growth momentum is set to continue, with GDP growth expected to accelerate from 3.5 per cent in 2014 to 4.6 per cent in 2015 and 4.9 per cent in 2016.[4] Growth in private consumption and investment are expected to remain the key drivers of GDP growth across all the five subregions and all economic groupings, underpinned by increasing consumer confidence, the expanding middle class, improvement in the business environment and the reduction in the cost of doing business. Government consumption will remain high, due mainly to increased spending on infrastructure. However, its contribution to growth will decrease because of fiscal consolidation measures, mostly in Central, Southern and West Africa. Net exports will continue to have a negative contribution to growth across all the subregions as significant investments in infrastructure, commodity exploration and increasing domestic demand drive rising imports. Oil-exporting countries are expected to see a rebound from low growth of 3.2 per cent in 2014 to 4.8 per cent in 2015. Underpinning the slowdown in 2014 were moderating oil prices coupled with disruptions in oil production and political unrest in parts of North (Libya) and West Africa (Central African Repub-

Africa continues to see robust growth, driven by private consumption and investment

---

4   These growth rates exclude Libya, owing to unreliable data amid the unstable situation in the country.

lic and Mali). Oil-importing countries' growth will improve from 3.7 per cent in 2014 to 4.4 per cent in 2015. Mineral-rich countries are expected to build on their growth momentum and accelerate from 3.4 per cent in 2014 to 4.1 per cent in 2015. This is mainly owing to increased investment and new mineral discoveries in countries such as Sierra Leone (in iron ore and diamond production), Zambia (in copper mining), Botswana (in copper, coal and diamonds), Namibia (in uranium and diamonds), Angola (in coal mining) and Ghana and Liberia (in gold mining). Africa's non-oil and non-mineral-rich economies, the fastest-growing countries on the continent, will see their growth momentum strengthen further. Growth will increase from 3.9 per cent in 2014 to 4.8 per cent in 2015, driven by a strong expansion in services, agriculture and spending on infrastructure in countries such as Ethiopia.

North and Southern Africa will see a marked increase in growth

Growth is expected to vary significantly across subregions. North[5] and Southern Africa are expected to experience some acceleration in growth, from 2.7 per cent and 2.9 per cent in 2014 to 3.6 per cent and 3.6 per cent in 2015, respectively. The enhanced growth prospects for North Africa are underpinned by improving political stability in Egypt and Tunisia. In the Southern African subregion, although Angola, Mozambique and Zambia will continue to be the fastest-growing economies, the 2015 growth acceleration is expected to be mainly driven by more investment in the non-diamond sector in Botswana, a recovery in private consumption in South Africa and increased investment in mining and natural gas exploration in Mozambique.

Central and West Africa are expected to experience a more moderate increase in growth, from 4.3 per cent and 5.9 per cent in 2014 to 4.7 per cent and 6.2 per cent in 2015, respectively, with increased political instability and terrorism in some of the countries in this region (e.g., Central African Republic, Mali, Nigeria) preventing an even stronger expansion. The Ebola outbreak in West Africa (box IV.3) and possible increased political instability in the run-up to elections in Nigeria constitute major downside risks for the outlook in the subregion.

East Africa will be the fastest-growing subregion

Regional integration in the East African Community is expected to continue to boost GDP growth of this subregion, from 6.5 per cent in 2014 to 6.8 per cent in 2015, making it the fastest-growing African subregion. Kenya and Uganda will be the key drivers of growth between 2014 and 2015. Kenya's growth will benefit from the rapid expansion in banking and telecommunications services, the rise of the middle class, urbanization and investment in infrastructure, particularly railways, while Uganda's growth will be supported by increasing activity in sectors such as construction, financial services, transport and telecommunications.

Inflation will moderately decelerate

Inflation in the African region is expected to remain constant at an average of 6.9 per cent in 2015 and moderate slightly to 6.8 per cent in 2016 (figure IV.5). Inflation has come down since its peak in 2012, thanks to the moderating global prices in commodities, food, oil and industrial imports. Increasingly prudent monetary policies across the region are also credited for the subdued inflation. Oil-importing countries are expected to be the major beneficiary of falling prices of oil and other commodities. Inflation is estimated to fall slightly from 5.6 per cent in 2014 to 5.4 per cent in 2015 in these countries (see annex table A.6). Oil-exporting countries continued to see high inflation in 2014 at 8.1 per cent and will likely see a slight increase to 8.2 per cent in 2015. Mineral-rich countries are expected to experience a slight decrease in inflation. The risk remains that declining commodity and oil prices and tighter monetary policies in the United States could negatively weigh on the currencies of both oil- and commodity-exporting countries, leading to imported inflation.

---

5   These growth rates also exclude Libya.

Box IV.3

The economic and social impacts of the Ebola virus disease outbreak

West Africa is currently experiencing the largest and most complex outbreak of the Ebola virus disease (EVD), with the number of deaths—4,950 as of 4 November 2014—exceeding the fatalities of all previous outbreaks combined. The EVD first appeared in 1976 in Nzara, Sudan, and Yambuku, Democratic Republic of the Congo. Since then, more than 20 outbreaks have been registered, mainly in rural areas of East and Central Africa. The first episode in West Africa was recorded in March 2014 in Gueckedou, Guinea. The disease then spread to the capital city Conakry and to the neighbouring countries of Liberia and Sierra Leone, which today form the epicentre of the disease. As of 4 November, a total of 13,241 cases have been recorded in the three countries, with Liberia accounting for almost 50 per cent of the cases and Sierra Leone for almost 40 per cent. The spread of the EVD to major urban centres together with the weak capacity of public health systems are important factors in explaining the severity of the outbreak. A limited number of cases have also spread to Mali, Nigeria, Senegal, Spain and the United States of America, but have been contained. While the immediate concern is to save lives and contain the spread of the disease, a comprehensive response to the epidemic must take into account that the epidemic causes impacts which go beyond public health concerns.

Economic impacts

Since the beginning of the outbreak, the dramatic worsening of the economic prospects for Guinea, Liberia and Sierra Leone have led to a spiral of downward revisions in gross domestic product (GDP) growth. The estimated GDP growth for Guinea in 2014 is 2.3 per cent, Liberia 5.1 per cent and Sierra Leone 8.5 per cent, with the latter two both having registered double-digit growth in the previous year. While it is too early to come to a final assessment of the impact of the EVD outbreak on economic growth, the observed trends and disruptions of economic activity are worrisome. The outbreak has resulted in increased labour absenteeism and unemployment, changes in consumption patterns and reduced investments. Opportunities to do business have shrunk with the closure of markets for weeks and cross-border trade is heavily reduced by the restraints on people's movements. The economic performance at the sectoral level has been affected as well, as economic activity in the key sectors of agriculture, mining and services has been seriously hit. In particular, farmers have abandoned their farms and most international expatriates have left the affected countries. Meanwhile, disruptions in international and national transport constrain the service sector and some businesses and banks have reduced their hours of operation. Stocks are declining, prices are rising and government revenues have been reduced, generating important shortfalls in public budgets at the very time when the fight against Ebola actually requires increases in public expenditures.

Despite the severe consequences for the directly affected countries, the economic impact on the West African subregion and Africa as a whole is expected to be limited in view of the small size of the affected economies, as long as a further spread of the disease across borders can be prevented. In 2013, the combined GDP of Guinea, Liberia and Sierra Leone accounted for only 2.42 per cent of West Africa's GDP and 0.68 per cent of Africa's GDP. In recent years, average growth in West Africa has been leaping ahead of Africa as a whole, with growth rates of 6.7 per cent for 2012 and 5.8 per cent for 2013, compared with 4.0 per cent and 3.7 per cent for Africa.[a] Notwithstanding the consequences of the EVD outbreak, the economic prospects for West Africa as a subregion remain positive, with a moderate increase in growth to 6.2 per cent expected in 2015.

Social impacts

Beyond the suffering of the EVD patients and their families, the affected countries also risk a rise in morbidity and mortality from diseases other than Ebola. The containment of Ebola patients requires a refocusing of funds and medical personnel. Before the EVD crisis, there was one physician in Guinea, to cover the health concerns of 10,000 persons. In Liberia and Sierra Leone, there were only 0.1 and 0.2 physicians per 10,000 persons, respectively. The loss of medical personnel and the diversion of funds due to EVD have further reduced the capacity of these already weak public health systems. In addition, those in need of medical attention may avoid health centres, fearing quarantine, stigma and the possibility of contracting the disease.

The provision of other social and educational services has also been restricted. Schools have been closed in the three heavily affected countries, with no clear timeline for the resumption of normal activity. This and other disruptions in the provision of public services may have consequences that reach far beyond the immediate impacts. In particular, progress towards the Millennium Development Goals in the domains of education and health is at risk of being undone owing to the crisis.

a Growth numbers for Africa exclude Libya.
Source: United Nations Economic Commission for Africa/Sub-Regional Office for West Africa.

Figure IV.5
Consumer price inflation in Africa by region, 2013–2016

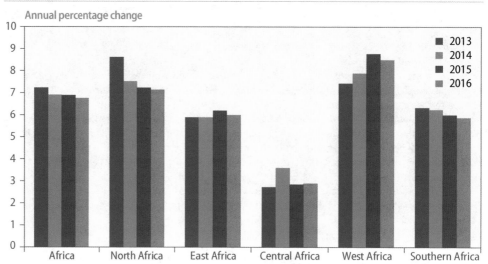

Source: UN/DESA.
Note: Data for 2014 are estimates, data for 2015–2016 are forecast.

Central Africa will register the lowest inflation rates in the region

At the subregional level, Central Africa is set to continue seeing the lowest inflation rates in the region as well as the biggest decline between 2014 and 2015, mainly because most countries in this region pursue a similar monetary policy, which is based on pegging their common currency, the Communauté Financière Africaine (CFA) franc, to the euro. In Southern Africa, inflation is expected to decrease from 6.2 per cent in 2014 to 6.0 per cent in 2015, owing to lower oil and global food prices. Other factors that will contribute to inflation reduction include the improvement in domestic food supply in Malawi and Zambia, tight monetary policy in Lesotho and South Africa, and appreciation of the currency in Botswana and Zambia.

In East Africa, inflation is expected to rise slightly, from 5.9 per cent in 2014 to 6.2 per cent in 2015. In Kenya, inflation will be lower, but will continue to be driven by the outcome of the rainy season. In the United Republic of Tanzania, inflation will come down slightly, but will continue to remain at about 6 per cent, driven by a weakening shilling and rising electricity tariffs. In West Africa, inflation is expected to increase from 7.9 per cent in 2014 to 8.8 per cent in 2015. Nigeria is likely to be the key driver of West Africa's inflation, due to fiscal expansion in the run-up to the 2015 elections and the growing consumer demand. In Ghana, increases in water and power tariffs, which caused inflation to peak at 17.5 per cent in 2014, will continue to be a source of inflationary pressures even into the first quarter of 2015. Nevertheless, given public backlashes, additional tariff increases may be postponed until after the 2016 elections, resulting in lower although still relatively high inflation in 2015.

North Africa will see a fall in inflation

North Africa is expected to register a further fall in inflation from 7.5 per cent in 2014 to 7.2 per cent in 2015, while West Africa overtakes it as the subregion with the highest inflation in Africa. Falling global food prices will particularly benefit Algeria and Mauritania, where food and commodity prices constitute a large proportion of the inflation basket. Morocco is likely to continue to have low inflation, due to moderating domestic demand, falling international food prices and mild currency appreciation against the United States dollar. In Egypt and Libya, disruptions in supply chains caused by political instability are expected to continue being a major challenge for monetary authorities. Cuts in food and energy subsidies and high minimum wages for government employees will also drive infla-tion in Egypt.

Fiscal balances for African countries are set to remain negative as countries maintain their investment in infrastructure, expenditure on public sector wage bills, transfers and subsidies, and other social sector projects. However, the region's fiscal deficit is expected to slightly decline in 2015. This decline is expected to be driven by decreases in East, North and Southern Africa. In South Africa, the fiscal deficit is estimated to decrease from 4.4 per cent of GDP in 2014 to 3.7 per cent of GDP in 2015, as fiscal authorities have undertaken measures to reduce the fiscal deficit by minimizing corruption and inefficiencies and by cutting allocations to non-essential expenditures. In Botswana, the buoyant revenue from mineral taxes, income and value-added taxes, and the Southern African Customs Union revenue-sharing scheme will improve the fiscal surplus from 1.2 per cent of GDP in 2014 to 1.5 per cent in 2015. Nigeria's fiscal deficit is expected to increase by 0.1 percentage points to 2.1 per cent of GDP, owing to increased expenditure in the lead-up to elections. Egypt, Ghana and the United Republic of Tanzania face fiscal sustainability issues, with their fiscal deficits expected to average about 11 per cent, 8 per cent and 6 per cent of GDP, respectively, between 2014 and 2016.

All the economic groupings in Africa are expected to experience an improvement in fiscal balances in 2015. However, oil-importing and mineral-rich countries are expected to register the largest improvement of 1.2 and 1.3 percentage points, respectively, because of lower oil prices. Other factors that will contribute to these improvements in fiscal bal-ances include fiscal consolidation, the emergence of new sources of revenue and innovative resource mobilization in some economies such as Botswana, Cameroon, the Republic of the Congo and South Africa. However, at the individual country level, fiscal balances may deteriorate in Nigeria, Sudan and the United Republic of Tanzania because of increased spending in the lead-up to national elections scheduled for 2015.

Oil-exporting countries will continue to have current-account surpluses, although moderating oil prices will trim these surpluses in 2015. On the other hand, current-account deficits of oil-importing countries will decrease as a result of this moderation. Mineral-rich countries will continue to have the largest current-account deficits because of deficits on services and other intangible trade, due to the reliance on imported services. Moreover, as the mining sectors are dominated by multinational companies, mineral-rich countries face structural deficits on the income account when these companies pay external debt and repatriate profits.

Current-account balances of open economies such as Botswana, Kenya, Nigeria and South Africa could benefit from increasing net exports as their currencies weaken owing to tighter monetary policy in the United States. However, this will depend on whether the weakened currencies will not affect competitiveness through their effect on imported inflation. South Africa is expected to reduce its current-account deficit from 5.4 per cent of GDP in 2014 to 4.7 per cent of GDP in 2015. Despite falling oil prices, Nigeria's current-ac-count balance is expected to remain positive, benefiting partly from higher remittances from its large diaspora population. A major impact on the trade patterns of Africa could emanate from the Economic Partnership Agreements that are being negotiated with the EU (box IV.4).

Despite the continuation of relatively robust growth across the region, a number of internal and external risks may derail Africa's medium-term economic performance. First, a more drastic fall in oil and commodity prices, a renewed weakening in the developed

The aggregate fiscal balance will remain in deficit

The moderating oil price will affect current-account balances

Downside risks include weakening trade and tighter financial conditions

Box IV.4

Economic Partnership Agreements and their implications for structural transformation in Africa

Africa's exports and imports have expanded more than fourfold over the last twelve years. However, this expansion has mostly stemmed from an increase in prices rather than volumes, while the growth of exports in volume terms was increasingly outpaced by that of imports. Even more importantly, over the last 10–15 years, the composition of Africa's exports has become increasingly skewed towards primary commodities. Even in sectors where the continent displays revealed comparative advantages, African producers are often relegated to low-value-added products.[a]

Against this background, it is clear that the impact of the Economic Partnership Agreements (EPAs) between the European Union (EU) and African, Caribbean and Pacific (ACP) countries needs to be considered in the context of the latter's structural transformation and industrialization agenda.[b] In this context, the long-term economic impact of EPAs will be determined especially by the pronounced and multifaceted asymmetries between the two parties. These refer not only to the economic size and level of development of the two regions, but also to two key facets of their bilateral trade relations:

1. Although it has been declining, the weight of the EU as an export market for Africa continues to significantly exceed the corresponding importance of Africa as an export market for Europe.

2. Africa's exports to the EU continue to be concentrated in a narrow range of mostly primary commodities, whereas EU exports to the region are significantly more diversified.

This lopsided pattern of bilateral trade relations has persisted for several decades, despite the preferential market access granted by the EU to exports from ACP countries.

The negotiations on the EPAs were launched in 2002 as part of the Cotonou Agreement, with the aim of making the trade relations between the two parties compatible with World Trade Organization principles.[c] The focus has been on a reciprocal but asymmetric free trade agreement, whereby the EU would immediately grant 100 per cent duty-free access to ACP-originated exports, whereas ACP countries would progressively liberalize "substantially all trade" with the EU.[d] ACP countries have approached negotiations grouping themselves into seven blocks, five of which are in Africa, namely West Africa, Central Africa, Eastern and Southern Africa, the East African Community (EAC) and the Southern African Development Community (SADC). In parallel, it is noteworthy that the least developed countries (LDCs), which include as many as 34 African economies, have in any case duty-free and quota-free access to the EU market under the Everything but Arms (EBAs) initiative, a unilateral preferential scheme of the EU for LDCs.

Leaving aside the limited differences in the negotiating text of the various African blocks, EPAs have traditionally raised a number of concerns. First, they have created tension between LDCs and non-LDCs, in so far as LDCs would ultimately have to open up their economies to EU products without any significant gain, whereas only non-LDCs would actually have improved access to the EU market. This situation, coupled with the structural asymmetries in trade relations, suggests that export gains for Africa are likely to be confined to a relatively narrow range of countries and products, while the EU could expand its exports to a wide range of countries and for a broader array of products. Second, EPAs could derail Africa's progress towards regional trade integration for two main reasons:

a. Africa's negotiating configuration of country groupings in the EPAs is not consistent with the existing Regional Economic Communities (REC), thereby hampering the establishment of REC-level Custom Unions, especially in presence of overlapping memberships;

b. The EPAs could adversely affect intra-African trade, since in some African countries, EU-originated products may ultimately face lower tariffs than similar African products originated outside a country's REC.[e]

(continued)

a United Nations Economic Commission for Africa, "Building trade capacities for Africa's transformation: A critical review of Aid for Trade", Addis Ababa, 2013.

b Northern African economies are not included in the ACP group, and their trade relations with the EU are regulated under the Euro-Mediterranean Partnership Agreement, rather than under the EPAs.

c Unilateral preferences previously accorded by the EU to ACP-originating goods represented a breech to the general WTO principle of most favoured nation and, hence, needed a specific waiver to be granted by other WTO members.

d Although there is no precise definition of "substantially all trade", the expression has commonly been interpreted as meaning approximately 80 per cent of trade.

e Precisely for this reason, it is imperative that African countries accelerate their progress towards the reduction of trade barriers not only within each REC, but also across RECs, working towards the establishment of the Continental Free Trade Area.

Box IV.4 (*continued*)

Third, even though the EU has pledged to support African countries in facing the adjustment costs of EPAs, these costs are likely to entail revenue losses from lower import duties and export taxes, sources of public revenues which play a significant role for a number of African countries. Fourth, some controversial provisions in the text of the EPAs may curtail African countries' policy space, in particular with regard to export taxes and the pursuit of trade liberalization agreements with other significant trade partners.

Against this background, progress in the EPA negotiations has been mixed across African regions and countries. While negotiations have already been concluded in West Africa and the SADC, a few outstanding issues remain in the case of the EAC. Progress has been slower in Central Africa and Eastern and Southern Africa, although most non-LDC countries in these regions have already concluded an interim EPA with the EU and, therefore, are not at risk of losing trade preferences.[f]

f Interim EPAs have been signed by Cameroon, Madagascar, Mauritius, Seychelles and Zimbabwe. All information concerning the status of Economic Partnership Agreement negotiations is taken from official EU documents, updated as of October 2014.

Source: United Nations Economic Commission for Africa.

economies, or a further slowdown in demand for commodities in China would negatively weigh on Africa's trade earnings. Second, tighter global financial conditions in developed economies (such as the United States) might result in the outflow of private capital and increase the volatility of currencies. Third, the Ebola outbreak is a major risk for West Africa's medium-term growth prospects. In addition to the severe human toll, the outbreak has already had a significant negative impact on trade in both goods and services (particularly travel and tourism) in the West African subregion. Fourth, political instability and terrorism in a number of African countries and civil and labour unrest in other countries will continue to be a source of pessimism, disruption and damage, and negatively weigh on investment, trade and tourism on the continent. However, the aggregate number of armed conflicts in Africa has decreased since 2000, and more initiatives are being undertaken at the continental level to address issues of peace and security.[6] Finally, weather-related shocks will continue to be a source of downside risks, given that most African economies are still dependent on agricultural production.

East Asia: growth projected to remain robust

East Asia remains the world's fastest growing region, even as GDP growth slowed from 6.4 per cent in 2013 to 6.1 per cent in 2014. The outlook for the region as a whole is robust, with growth projected at 6.1 per cent in 2015 and 6.0 per cent in 2016. China's transition to more moderate growth is expected to be offset by higher growth in other economies, such as Indonesia, Singapore, Thailand and Viet Nam. In many economies, investment and exports are projected to pick up in the forecast period, supported by government programmes and a gradual recovery in developed countries. Household consumption is expected to remain strong on the back of subdued inflation, robust labour markets and generally low real interest rates. Fiscal policy remains moderately supportive of growth and most countries have sufficient space to provide additional stimulus, if necessary. The key downside risks for East Asia are related to the upcoming tightening of global liquidity conditions—which could result in weaker growth of domestic consumption and investment—and to a sharper-than-expected slowdown in China.

---

6   United Nations Economic Commission for Africa, "Frontier markets in Africa: misperceptions in a sea of opportunities", Addis Ababa, 18 July 2014.

China's growth is
projected to further
moderate in 2015–2016 as
authorities focus on the
quality of development

China's economy, which accounts for two-thirds of East Asia's total output, is transitioning to a more consumption- and service-oriented and more environmentally sustainable system, which has resulted in lower headline GDP growth. In 2014, the economy expanded by an estimated 7.3 per cent, down from 7.7 per cent in 2013, as growth in exports and investment slowed. A further gradual deceleration to 7.0 per cent in 2015 and 6.8 per cent in 2016 is forecast. This lower growth trajectory is in line with the Government's focus on raising the quality of development and partly reflects policy measures aimed at curbing financial risks. The slowdown in China has negatively impacted growth in other East Asian economies, especially Hong Kong Special Administrative Region of China, where business investment weakened and tourist spending dropped over the past year. Indonesia and Thailand also saw growth decelerate in 2014 owing to country-specific factors. In Indonesia, domestic demand weakened, following policy measures to curb inflation and reduce the current-account deficit, and net exports contributed less than in 2013 (figure IV.6). Market sentiment improved, however, following presidential elections in July, and the economy is likely to gain some strength in 2015 and 2016. Thailand's economy contracted in the first quarter of 2014 and was flat in the first half of the year as political instability weighed heavily on domestic demand, in particular investment (figure IV.6). Full-year growth in 2014 remained subdued at an estimated 1.1 per cent; further strengthening of activity depends critically on the implementation of public investment projects. In the baseline outlook, a moderate improvement to 3.9 per cent growth is forecast for 2015. In the Republic of Korea, growth picked up to 3.4 per cent in 2014, although high household debt, a stagnant property market, subdued consumer sentiment and sluggish exports weighed on activity. Easier monetary policy and a gradual improvement in external demand are expected to support activity in 2015–2016, with growth forecast to strengthen slightly. Malaysia and the Philippines were among the best-performing countries in East Asia in 2014, following strong consumption and investment demand. While overall conditions in both countries are expected to remain benign, a moderation in growth is projected for 2015. Viet Nam is expected to see a gradual strengthening of growth in the forecast period, mainly owing to stronger investment, whereas Papua New Guinea is set to record a jump in GDP growth in 2015 as it starts to export liquefied natural gas.

Labour markets are expected to remain robust amid stable growth

Given the region's solid growth outlook, the labour market situation is likely to remain robust. With few exceptions, official unemployment rates in the region are low. In the region's higher-income economies, average unemployment rates in 2014 ranged from 2.0 per cent in Singapore to 4.0 per cent in Taiwan Province of China. In the Republic of Korea, unemployment edged up in 2014, partly as a result of an increase in the labour force participation rate (see annex table A.8). In China, despite slower economic growth, the unemployment rate in 31 large and mid-size cities remained at about 5 per cent in 2014 as employment growth, particularly in the service sector, has been faster than expected. The unemployment rate rose marginally in Thailand in 2014, while declining slightly in Indonesia and the Philippines. In most countries, the jobless rate for those aged 25 to 29 continued to be two to three times higher than for the other age groups. Widespread vulnerable employment remains a particular concern in the region's lower-income economies, notably in Indonesia, the Philippines and Viet Nam.

Falling commodity prices keep consumer price inflation low

Average consumer price inflation in East Asia fell to 2.4 per cent in 2014, down from 2.8 per cent in 2013 owing to further declines in international commodity prices and limited demand pressures (see annex table A.6). In most countries, inflation is within or below the target ranges set by the central banks. Recent trends in inflation varied across the region, largely corresponding to the strength of domestic demand. In China, average inflation declined from 2.7 per cent in 2013 to 2.1 per cent in 2014, in line with slower eco-

Figure IV.6
East Asia: contributions of expenditure components to real GDP growth, January 2013–June 2014

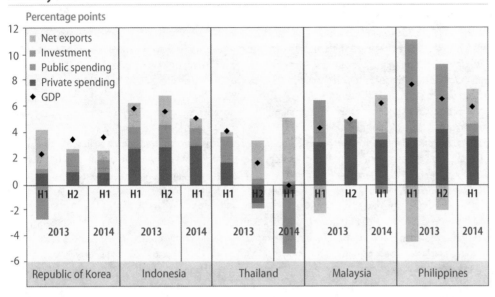

Source: UN/ESCAP, based on data from CEIC database (accessed 23 September. 2014). Note: Investment refers to gross capital formation, i.e., outlays on additions to the fixed assets of the economy plus net changes in the level of inventories. Differences between GDP growth and the sum of components are due to statistical discrepancies.

nomic growth and stable food prices. Inflation also slowed in Hong Kong Special Administrative Region of China, Indonesia, Singapore and Viet Nam, but accelerated in Malaysia and the Philippines, consistent with above-trend economic growth. Inflation is expected to temporarily rise in Malaysia as a result of the introduction of a new consumption tax and in Indonesia, where a further reduction of fuel price subsidies is planned. For the region as a whole, consumer price inflation is expected to accelerate gradually in the outlook period, rising to 2.7 per cent in 2015 and 2.9 per cent in 2016.

Monetary policy remained generally accommodative across East Asia. The moves by central banks in the past year reflect the different macroeconomic trends in the region. For much of 2014, China's central bank opted for only targeted measures to support the economy, rather than generalized policy easing. However, in late November, the authorities cut interest rates for the first time in more than two years in a bid to boost growth. The Republic of Korea, Thailand and Viet Nam also cut their main policy rates during the year in an attempt to revive domestic demand. In contrast, the central banks of Malaysia and the Philippines raised interest rates amid strong growth and rising inflationary pressures. At the same time, monetary and financial authorities in a number of countries used macroprudential measures to address financial sector risks, such as curbs on real estate lending. An increasing number of East Asian central banks are expected to gradually tighten monetary policy in the latter part of the forecast period in the face of improving global conditions, higher interest rates in the United States, and a pickup in domestic inflation.

Monetary policies move in different directions as macroeconomic trends diverge

Fiscal policy was generally supportive of growth across East Asia. In several countries, the Governments tried to further stimulate economic activity. In China, the authorities implemented measures to support domestic demand, including tax relief for small firms and accelerated fiscal and infrastructure spending. In July, the Government of the Republic of Korea announced a stimulus package of $11.7 billion, targeting low-income households, small firms and the property market, and introduced for 2015 the most expansionary budget since 2009. In Thailand, the military Government unveiled plans to spend $75 bil-

Several Governments provide additional fiscal stimulus to support growth

Box IV.5

Reprioritizing public expenditure for sustainable development in East Asia[a]

Many East Asian countries are in the process of making existing public expenditure more efficient and of reprioritizing public expenditure towards inclusive growth and sustainable development. These policy measures are aimed at freeing significant amounts of financial resources by improving expenditure management of their budgets. Critically, the huge savings from curbing non-developmental expenditures and removing, or reducing, subsidies should allow policymakers to be more ambitious in their inclusive growth programmes.

A significant amount of non-developmental expenditure is devoted to military spending, which totalled over $258 billion in 12 countries of the East Asia region in 2013. Military expenses often exceed those on health and education combined.[b] Significant resources are also spent on subsidies, especially for energy. In East Asia alone, fossil fuel consumption subsidies totalled about $76 billion in 2012. Fuel subsidies amounted to 3.0 per cent of GDP in Brunei Darussalam and Indonesia, 2.6 per cent in Thailand, 2.5 per cent in Viet Nam and 2.4 per cent in Malaysia.[c] In most cases, these subsidies present a drain on government financial resources and impede the Government's capacity in other fields.

Moreover, energy subsidies tend to mostly benefit the wealthier groups in society; they inherently encourage wastage, and result in fuel-intensive production. Importantly, poorly targeted energy subsidies have had little impact on either enhancing inclusive growth or reducing extreme poverty. However, curbing increasing levels of non-development expenditure and removing or reducing harmful subsidies is politically challenging. In several countries, the removal of subsidies has sparked protests, especially from influential interest groups.

Rationalizing subsidies is a key reform that would raise public financial resources for productive investment and sustainable development in the region. According to the United Nations Economic and Social Commission for Asia and the Pacific, estimates for savings of individual countries—including Indonesia, Malaysia, the Philippines and Thailand—from these subsidies would be sufficient to finance, for instance, a comprehensive policy package comprising income security for older persons and all those with disabilities, as well as providing universal access to health and education.

At the national level, several countries have started to introduce policy measures and multifaceted reform agendas, which include a reduction in energy subsidies and an expansion of public expenditure on education, health and social protection. These policy measures will provide further support for fiscal consolidation, while also releasing financial resources for inclusive growth policies.

For example, Indonesia and Malaysia rationalized energy price subsidies and/or raised electricity tariffs to restore medium-term fiscal sustainability. Indonesia decided in mid-2013 to cut fuel subsidies to curb its fiscal deficit, while Malaysia reduced fuel subsidies in September 2013 and again in October 2014. Indonesia faced steep price increases as subsidy rationalization pushed up prices of gasoline and diesel by 44 per cent and 22 per cent, respectively. In the case of Malaysia, the initial impact on inflation has been more moderate as the price increase in 2013 took effect when overall inflationary pressure was low. In both countries, the Government limited the direct negative impact of the subsidy reduction on low-income households by providing assistance through compensatory cash transfers and increased welfare payments. In Indonesia, the fiscal savings from the initial subsidy cuts have been lower than expected (partly due to a weaker currency). However, further subsidy rationalization should boost fiscal resources for social spending on items such as the country's universal health-care plan, which was launched in 2014 and aims at complete coverage by 2019.

One important caveat is that policymakers must avoid one-size-fits-all approaches in the case of removal or reduction in subsidies. Rather, policy reforms need to take into account the net welfare effects, especially on poor and vulnerable households. The removal of energy subsidies—which are often regressive and tend to hinder public spending on education, health, social protection and physical infrastructure—should be complemented by policy reforms that include targeted cash transfers to ensure that poor and vulnerable households are not put in even worse positions. In contrast, policymakers may need to approach food subsidies differently as these generally benefit low-income groups.

a This box is based on analyses in United Nations Economic and Social Commission for Asia and the Pacific, *Economic and Social Survey of Asia and the Pacific 2013: Forward-Looking Macroeconomic Policies for Inclusive and Sustainable Development* (United Nations publication, Sales No. E.13. II.F2) and in "Sustainable development financing: perspectives from Asia and the Pacific", background paper prepared for the Asia-Pacific Outreach Meeting on Sustainable Development Financing, held in Jakarta on 10-11 June 2014, available from http://www.unescap.org/sites/default/files/UNESCAP-SDF-Paper-1July2014-share.pdf.

b Stockholm International Peace Research Institute (SIPRI) Military expenditure database, available from http://www.sipri.org/research/armaments/milex/milex_database, accessed 5 November 2014.

c International Energy Agency data, available from http://www.iea.org/subsidy/index.html

Source: United Nations Economic and Social Commission for Asia and the Pacific.

lion over eight years to improve transport infrastructure. Most East Asian economies have the fiscal space to further boost investments in human and physical capital. Public debt as a share of GDP ranges from less than 40 per cent in Indonesia and the Philippines—which have reduced debt over the past decade—to 45 to 60 per cent in Malaysia and Thailand. Moreover, countries are reprioritizing expenditures and pursuing tax policy and administration improvements. In particular, several countries, such as Indonesia and Malaysia, are in the process of reforming their energy subsidy systems (see box IV.5).

East Asia's trade and current-account surpluses have narrowed since the global financial crisis. In 2013, the region's combined current-account surplus stood at about 3.0 per cent of GDP, compared with a high of 8.3 per cent in 2007. The trend towards lower surpluses marginally reversed in 2014 as import growth slowed more rapidly than export growth. Several countries, such as Malaysia, the Philippines and Viet Nam saw dynamic export growth in 2014, led by strong international demand for electrical and electronic products. Export growth was less buoyant, but still solid, in other parts of the region, including China, the Republic of Korea, Singapore and Taiwan Province of China. These economies saw export revenues (in dollar values) grow by an estimated 3–5 per cent in 2014. By contrast, export revenues contracted slightly in Indonesia and Thailand during this period. The decline in Indonesia can be attributed to weak international commodity prices and new regulations banning the export of unprocessed minerals. The decline in Thailand mainly reflects the impact of the political turmoil and a shift in global demand for some electronic products. Imports generally grew at a slower pace than exports in 2014, largely owing to a weakening of investment activity in the region and lower international commodity prices. China saw import spending rise only marginally in 2014, while Indonesia and Thailand experienced marked declines. Net capital inflows to the region were slightly higher than in 2013, despite considerable outflows at the beginning of 2014. Most currencies registered gains against the euro and the yen, but significant losses against the dollar, which began appreciating sharply in mid-2014.

Exports present a mixed picture

The key downside risks for East Asia are related to the upcoming tightening of global liquidity conditions and to the slowdown of China's economy. The Fed's upcoming increase in interest rates could lead to a marked adjustment in credit conditions for East Asia's emerging economies, resulting in weaker investment and consumption growth than currently anticipated. This risk factor is particularly relevant for countries with high household or corporate debt, such as the Republic of Korea, Malaysia and Thailand, and for economies with potential housing-market bubbles, including Hong Kong Special Administrative Region of China, Singapore and Thailand. A sharper-than-expected slowdown in China would have a severe impact through trade and finance channels on other economies in the region, in particular commodity exporters such as Cambodia and Indonesia.

Tightening of global liquidity conditions and slowdown in China pose downside risks

South Asia: growth set to strengthen, led by gradual recovery in India

South Asia's economic growth is set to reach a four-year high of 5.4 per cent in 2015, up from an estimated 4.9 per cent in 2014 and well above the 4.1 per cent recorded in 2013. For 2016, a further acceleration to 5.7 per cent is forecast. The recovery is expected to be led by a pickup in growth in India, which accounts for about 70 per cent of regional output. Other economies, such as Bangladesh and the Islamic Republic of Iran, are also projected to see stronger growth in the forecast period. Along with robust external demand, growth is expected to be underpinned by a moderate strengthening of domestic consumption and investment as several countries benefit from improved macroeconomic conditions. Governments have started to make some progress in implementing economic policy reforms, thus providing support to business and consumer confidence. The growth projections for 2015 and 2016 rest on several key assumptions, including normal monsoon conditions, stable or slightly moderating global food and energy prices, a limited impact of higher international interest rates on regional credit conditions and continued policy reforms.

Growth in India picks up as government reforms encourage investment

India's economy expanded by an estimated 5.4 per cent in 2014, an improvement from growth of 5.0 per cent recorded in 2013, but still significantly below the 8.0 per cent pace of the pre-crisis period. The recovery is partly the result of improved market sentiment after the new Administration took office in the second quarter of 2014 and announced plans to reform the bureaucracy, labour laws and public subsidies. The authorities implemented reforms to ease restrictions on foreign direct investment (FDI), speed up investment in large-scale projects and lift state control on diesel prices. After years of sluggishness, fixed investment has started to gain strength. This has also been reflected in a mild recovery in the manufacturing and construction sectors. A subpar monsoon, along with fiscal constraints, has, however, weighed on economic activity. Going forward, India is projected to see a gradual acceleration in growth, with GDP forecast to expand by 5.9 per cent in 2015 and 6.3 per cent in 2016. Meanwhile, Bangladesh and Sri Lanka maintained strong growth of 6.2 per cent and 7.8 per cent, respectively, in 2014, amid buoyant household consumption and investment. Both economies are expected to expand at a strong pace in 2015 and 2016 as favourable conditions remain largely intact. Although Pakistan's GDP growth rebounded to an estimated 4.2 per cent in 2014 after robust private and public consumption, macroeconomic fundamentals remain fragile in the face of ongoing security concerns and low fixed investment that is constrained by the shortage of domestic savings. Growth is forecast to decline slightly in 2015, before picking up again in 2016. The Islamic Republic of Iran is estimated to have seen a return to mildly positive growth in 2014 as macroeconomic conditions stabilized and the partial lifting of sanctions helped non-oil exports. A more robust recovery depends, however, on a comprehensive nuclear agreement and further sanctions relief, especially for oil exports and the financial sector.

Cross-country differences in unemployment rates are large

India's manufacturing sector registered employment gains through June 2014. A weak start in 2014 was more than offset by a strong second quarter, when several sectors, such as textiles, metals and information technology, saw marked increases in employment levels. In general, the job market situation in South Asian countries appeared to be relatively stable in 2014, although data are limited and do not fully reflect the reality of the employment situation. The differences in official unemployment rates between countries have remained large as growth trends continued to diverge. In the Islamic Republic of Iran, the unemployment rate was estimated at 10.7 per cent in the second quarter of 2014 as economic activity remained weak. Unemployment in Sri Lanka, by contrast, declined further to 4.1 per cent in the first quarter of 2014 amid robust domestic demand. In countries with available data (including India, the Islamic Republic of Iran, Pakistan and Sri Lanka), unemployment rates remained significantly higher for women than for men. In the Islamic Republic of Iran, the female unemployment rate was estimated at 19.4 per cent in the second quarter of 2014, compared to 9.0 per cent for men. This is particularly alarming since the labour force participation rate is much lower among women than men. The share of vulnerable employment, defined as unpaid family workers and own-account workers, is as high as 60 per cent in Pakistan and 80 per cent in India. This illustrates the magnitude of the employment challenges the region is facing and highlights the importance of generating quality employment.

Average consumer price inflation in South Asia (figure IV.7) declined considerably from 14.7 per cent in 2013 to 9.2 per cent in 2014. Falling international prices of oil and other commodities, vigilant monetary policies and limited demand pressures contributed to lower inflation, offsetting the impacts of a late monsoon arrival and floods in certain parts of the region. India's consumer price inflation rate fell below 7.0 per cent year on year in the third quarter, compared to 10.4 per cent in the final quarter of 2013. This also helped bring down price pressures in Nepal, which is closely tied to India through the exchange-rate peg and strong trade flows. In Sri Lanka, inflation declined to a multi-year low of 3.5 per cent in the third quarter of 2014. In the Islamic Republic of Iran, consumer prices were up by an estimated 17.8 per cent in 2014, after a 40 per cent surge in 2013, when the international sanctions had led to significant supply shortages and a sharp devaluation of the rial. In most countries of the region, food inflation remained slightly higher than overall inflation. Going forward, average inflation in the region is expected to moderate further to 7.8 per cent in 2015 and 7.2 per cent in 2016, as commodity prices will likely remain subdued and domestic demand picks up only gradually. There are, however, notable upside risks to the baseline inflation forecast. Given the dominance of traditional agriculture and the reliance on imported commodities, South Asia is very vulnerable to weather conditions and global price developments. Further reductions of subsidies, (in Pakistan, for example) and a new round of currency weakness could also push inflation rates above current projections.

> Inflation is trending down amid lower oil prices and limited demand pressures

Amid slowing inflation and a slight recovery in growth, monetary policy in South Asia remained fairly stable in 2014. The Reserve Bank of India (RBI) has kept its key policy interest rate at 8 per cent, following upward adjustments in response to inflation pressures and capital outflows between mid-2013 and early 2014. India's monetary authorities emphasized that while inflation has slowed, the balance of risks was still to the upside. The RBI is expected to maintain its firm anti-inflationary stance, but could start easing mone-

> India's central bank maintains a firm anti-inflationary stance

Figure IV.7
Consumer price inflation in South Asia, January 2012–September 2014

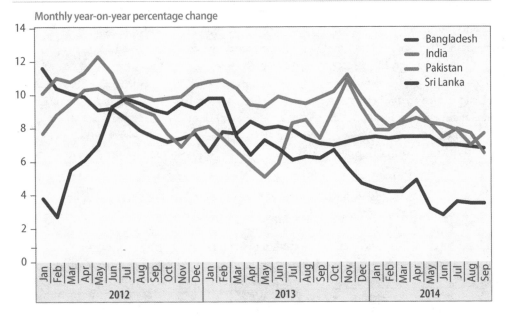

Monthly year-on-year percentage change

Source: UN/DESA, based on national data.

tary policy in the course of 2015. As in India, policy rates were also left unchanged in Bangladesh, Pakistan and Sri Lanka in 2014 and no significant changes to the monetary policy stance are expected for 2015–2016. Bangladesh's central bank raised the cash reserve ratio by 50 basis points to 6.5 per cent in June to curb excess liquidity in the banking system, and Sri Lanka's central bank increased the pressure on commercial banks to cut lending rates.

Mildly expansionary fiscal policy has supported economic growth over the past year, but persistently large fiscal deficits add risk to medium-term debt sustainability. Fiscal deficits generally trended down in 2014, but remained high at about 4 per cent of GDP in India, 5 per cent in Bangladesh and Sri Lanka, and 7 per cent in Pakistan. Military spending and heavy price-subsidy bills accounted for a significant portion of total government expenditures in these countries. In the outlook period, most countries are expected to see a further slight improvement in their fiscal balances (relative to GDP), as efforts to rationalize subsidy bills and to expand the tax base yield some results and economic growth picks up (box IV.6). Deficit reduction, however, will likely be slow and most Governments will struggle to meet their announced targets.

Most South Asian economies, including Bangladesh, India, the Islamic Republic of Iran and Sri Lanka, recorded solid export growth in 2014. India's exports benefited from the marked depreciation of the rupee in 2013, and Bangladesh and Sri Lanka registered expansions of garment exports amid robust demand in developed economies. As some of the sanctions against the Islamic Republic of Iran were suspended, exports started to recover in 2014, albeit at only a moderate pace. Pakistan's exports, by contrast, remained weak in 2014, held back by persistent power shortages and poor infrastructure. On the import side, South Asia's economies generally benefited from the decline in fuel prices in 2014. Moreover, some country-specific measures, such as an import duty on gold and silver in India, helped curb total import spending. Current-account positions thus improved in 2014 in most economies. Bangladesh, Nepal, Pakistan and Sri Lanka recorded a further increase in workers' remittances, which account for more than 5 per cent of GDP in these economies. Similarly, tourist arrivals continued to rise, although tourism revenues remain small relative to merchandise exports, except in Nepal. India's current-account deficit moderated from a peak of 6.1 per cent in the last quarter of 2012 to 0.2 per cent in the first quarter of 2014. International reserves increased in most of the region's economies and currently range from close to four months of imports in Pakistan to nine months in Nepal. Except in Sri Lanka, the share of external debt in total debt is also relatively low.

There are significant downside risks to the baseline outlook for South Asia, related to the continuing fragility of the global economy and country-specific weaknesses, such as volatile security conditions, agricultural dependency on the monsoon and difficulties in implementing structural reforms. A decline in global liquidity, along with a re-emergence of domestic inflationary pressures, could lead to a tightening of domestic credit, particularly in India and Pakistan, which would likely weaken consumption and investment activity.

Western Asia: weak economic recovery is projected, but significant downside risks remain

In Western Asia, GDP growth is projected to pick up in many countries, albeit to relatively modest levels compared with previous years (figure IV.8). After slowing from 4.0 per cent

Box IV.6

Mobilizing domestic tax revenues for development in South Asian countries[a]

Governments have a range of options for augmenting fiscal space for productive and countercyclical spending to support sustainable development. Among these options, strengthening tax revenues is critical, particularly in South Asia, where average tax revenues of the central Government reached only 10.7 per cent of gross domestic product (GDP) in 2011/12. Such low levels of tax revenue limit the ability of Governments to address the region's large development needs. In Afghanistan, Bangladesh, Bhutan, the Islamic Republic of Iran and Pakistan, tax-to-GDP ratios were close to, or at, single-digit levels, much lower than in other developing countries in Asia and the Pacific (figure IV.6.1).

Figure IV.6.1

Central government tax revenue in selected East and South Asian economies

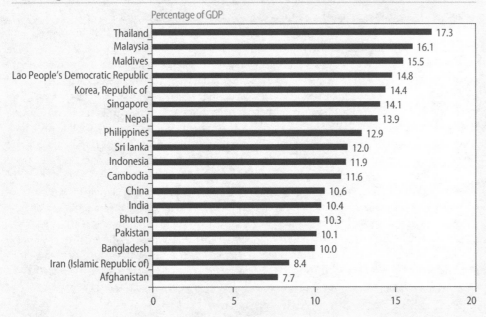

Percentage of GDP

Thailand	17.3
Malaysia	16.1
Maldives	15.5
Lao People's Democratic Republic	14.8
Korea, Republic of	14.4
Singapore	14.1
Nepal	13.9
Philippines	12.9
Sri lanka	12.0
Indonesia	11.9
Cambodia	11.6
China	10.6
India	10.4
Bhutan	10.3
Pakistan	10.1
Bangladesh	10.0
Iran (Islamic Republic of)	8.4
Afghanistan	7.7

Source: World Bank and IMF Government Finance Statistics.
Note: Data refer to the most recent available year (2012 or 2011). For Bhutan and the Islamic Republic of Iran, data refer to 2009.

One reason for the low levels of tax revenue is that many people are exempt from taxes due to low incomes; also, a high proportion of people work informally or in agriculture—activities on which it is more difficult to collect taxes, especially income tax. But even wealthier individuals pay little income tax, owing to high tax avoidance and non-compliance, as well as inadequate institutional mechanisms to ensure payment of taxes. The tax gap between the de jure tax objective and the actual revenue is caused by underreporting of taxable income, voluntary taxpayer registration and various individualized tax exemptions, all combined with poor tax administration, namely insufficient inspection and auditing. In Bangladesh and Pakistan, for example, only about 1 per cent of the population pays income tax; in India that proportion is only 3 per cent.

Many countries therefore collect more tax from corporations than from individuals, as is the case in Bhutan, the Islamic Republic of Iran, Maldives and Sri Lanka, where corporate income tax accounts for more than three quarters of direct tax revenues. Yet, corporate tax bases are often eroded by numerous tax exemptions and allowances that are granted to attract foreign direct investment (FDI) and private inflows. For instance, preferential tax treatment is offered in Sri Lanka to the tourism and construction sectors, in India to insurance service providers, and in Pakistan to power-generating companies.

a This box is based on analysis in United Nations Economic and Social Commission for Asia and the Pacific, *Economic and Social Survey of Asia and the Pacific 2014: Regional Connectivity for Shared Prosperity* (United Nations publication, Sales No. E.14.II.F.4).

(continued)

Box IV.6 (*continued*)

Tax revenues have also been negatively affected by government measures that liberalize trade and reduce trade-related taxes and/or duties in order to encourage trade and investment flows. In the Maldives and Pakistan, for instance, tax revenues from international trade declined by over 5 per cent of GDP between 1990 and 2011. Most countries have increased consumption taxes, such as on goods and services through a value added tax (VAT) or a general sales tax, to offset declines in taxes and/or duties on trade flows. Yet, the collection efficiency of VAT is quite low, particularly in Bangladesh, India and Pakistan, indicating tax exemptions and difficulties in implementing the complex tax system. In Afghanistan, Pakistan and Sri Lanka, the revenue from consumption taxes has been unable to offset declines in revenues generated from trade.

A number of countries are resorting to innovative tax measures to raise additional revenue. For instance, in India a "super tax" is levied on individuals whose annual income exceeds about $170,000. India has also introduced a 3 per cent education levy (or "cess") on income tax, corporate tax, excise and customs duties and service tax to finance universal access to basic education. It has also introduced a securities transaction tax to stop avoidance of the capital gains tax. In Sri Lanka, a deemed dividend tax is designed to encourage boards of companies to increase dividends, while in Bangladesh, VAT has been extended to private education and health providers.

The good news is that the tax potential is sizeable in South Asia, reaching several percentage points of GDP. Using an econometric analysis that captures structural and developmental factors (such as the value added in the agricultural sector, GDP per capita and the degree of trade openness in a country) and that allows for differences between developing regions, the United Nations Economic and Social Comission for Asia and the Pacific (ESCAP) estimated that current tax revenues were significantly lower than their potential (table IV.6.1).[b] Fully utilizing the tax potential would thus boost tax revenues in most South Asian economies, making valuable resources available for development.

To strengthen tax revenues, countries clearly need to broaden tax bases and rationalize rates. They also need to tackle tax evasion and tax fraud more forcefully and improve tax administrations.

Greater regional cooperation is also of critical importance as it would enable countries to harmonize taxes and combat competition for FDI, which is creating a "race to the bottom" in terms of taxation of profits. Such cooperation would help avoid double taxation and also tackle the problem of transfer pricing, used by multinational corporations to divert profits to low-tax countries through subsidiaries. Regional cooperation could also be a useful tool to deal with tax havens. ESCAP has proposed creating an Asia-Pacific tax forum to share best practices in tax policies, tax administration and tax reforms.

b The tax-to-GDP ratios in table IV.7.1 are taken from the Economic and Social Survey of Asia and the Pacific 2014, ibid., and differ slightly from those provided in figure IV.6.1. For more details on the computation of the tax potential, see chap. 3 of the ESCAP report.

Table IV.6.1

Estimated tax potential in selected South Asian economies

	Year	Tax-to-GDP ratio (percentage)		Tax gap (percentage points)	Tax gap as a proportion of current revenue (percentage)
		Actual	Potential		
Afghanistan	2011	8.8	15.0	6.2	70.5
Bangladesh	2013	10.5	18.0	7.5	72.1
Bhutan	2009	9.2	16.0	6.7	72.9
Iran (Islamic Republic of)	2013	5.8	13.1	7.2	124.5
Pakistan	2012	10.3	12.1	1.8	17.3

Source: UN/ESCAP.   **Source:** Economic and Social Survey of Asia and the Pacific 2014: Regional Connectivity for Shared Prosperity, ESCAP.

in 2013 to 2.9 per cent in 2014, GDP growth is expected to reach 3.7 per cent in 2015 and 4.3 per cent in 2016. Nevertheless, there are important downside risks to this forecast, in particular if oil prices decline further and if armed conflicts in Iraq and the Syrian Arab Republic escalate.

In Turkey, the biggest economy in the region, real GDP growth decelerated from 4.1 per cent in 2013 to 2.7 per cent per cent in 2014. The slowdown is mainly due to deceleration of private consumption and investment. Private consumption increased only by 0.4

The Turkish economy is expected to improve moderately in 2015, driven by government spending and exports

Figure IV.8
GDP growth in Western Asia, 2013–2016

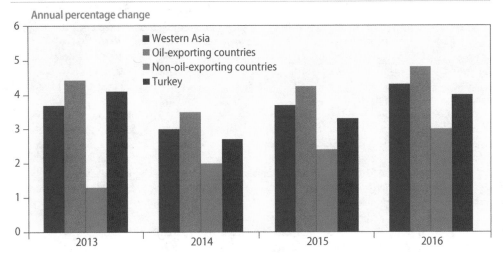

Source: UN/DESA.
Note: Data for 2014 are estimates, data for 2015–2016 are forecast.

per cent in the second quarter of 2014, after a 3.2 per cent increase in the previous quarter, compared with 5.1 per cent in 2013. This overall slowdown in private demand largely reflects tighter monetary policy, which started in January 2014 to fight currency depreciation and inflation. In the outlook period, a moderate economic recovery is expected, with GDP growth averaging 3.7 per cent a year in 2015–2016, supported by government spending and stronger external demand, provided that the depreciation of the national currency will continue to help the export sector.

Oil-exporting countries, in particular, member countries of the Cooperation Council for the Arab States of the Gulf (GCC), namely Bahrain, Kuwait, Oman, Qatar, Saudi Arabia and the United Arab Emirates, are expected to continue growing faster than non-oil exporters. Despite lower oil prices, demand from East and South Asia strengthened through increased interregional trade linkages. At the same time, several economies in the region were able to limit the negative impact of the subdued oil sector by increasing fiscal spending and stimulating domestic demand. For instance, Saudi Arabia is expected to register the same GDP growth in 2014 as in 2013. The forecast for this subgroup remains fairly positive, despite expected lower oil prices in 2015. Domestic demand will remain strong, stimulated by ongoing public investment in infrastructure, as many of the countries enjoy sizeable financial reserves to cope comfortably with lower oil prices. Qatar and Saudi Arabia are both expected to register slightly faster GDP growth in 2015, at 6.7 per cent and 4.2 per cent, respectively.

Oil-exporting countries will continue to grow faster than non-oil-exporting countries, supported by expansionary fiscal policies

For Iraq, another oil-exporting country, limited data prevent confident assessment of the current economic situation. Despite stable crude oil exports, the collapse of non-oil-sec-

Box IV.7

The impact of the Iraqi crisis on neighbouring countries' current accounts

On 10 June 2014, a powerfully armed militant group, the "Islamic State" in Iraq and the Levant—or ISIL—seized control of Mosul, the main city of Northern Iraq. This incursion marked a major escalation of the armed violence and the beginning of a crisis situation in Iraq, in addition to the conflict in the neighbouring Syrian Arab Republic. By mid-September, 1.8 million Iraqis in need of assistance were internally displaced,[a] amplifying the humanitarian crisis in the region. The Iraqi economy was seriously impacted, particularly in the region of the Kurdish Regional Government, which had been on a stable economic development path—more than any other provincial regions within Iraq. Despite international intervention, the situation has yet to see any concrete political stabilization.

The economic impact of the present crisis has been mostly felt through the disruption of intra-regional trade, even though concerns over Iraq's oil-exporting capacity received broader attention. Major transport routes from Turkey and Jordan to Iraq were forced to close for formal commercial activities with few exceptions. For instance, the Syrian Arab Republic and Iraq host truck routes which link the member countries of the Cooperation Council for the Arab States of the Gulf and the rest of Western Asia. As transport routes through the Syrian Arab Republic had already been severed, the closure of Iraqi routes seriously hampered the intraregional trade networks on the ground.

This situation more severely affected neighbouring countries, for which Iraq is one of the most important export markets. While Iraq's exports consist mostly of crude oil[b], the country imports a variety of goods, such as electronic machinery, vehicles, raw materials, and food products, from its neighbouring countries, and has become a growing destination market for exporters in the region. In 2013, Iraq was the largest export destination for Jordan, the second largest for Turkey and the fourth for Lebanon.

Those neighbouring countries have registered sizeable bilateral trade surpluses with Iraq in recent years. Considering the chronic overall current-account deficits in these countries (figure IV.7.1-A), their trade surplus with Iraq has been crucial. In a hypothetical scenario where there had been no bilateral trade with Iraq, the current-account deficit would have widened by 28.9 per cent in Jordan, 18.1 per cent in Turkey and 4.7 per cent in Lebanon in 2013 (figure IV.7.1-B).[c] This shows the extent to which bilateral trade with Iraq is important for the countries' current accounts and balance of payments.

The loss of export earnings from the Iraqi market in 2014 is estimated to reach $360 million for Jordan, $110 million for Lebanon, and $4.5 billion for Turkey. As a result, current-account deficits are estimated to widen by 8.4 per cent in Jordan, 1.7 per cent in Lebanon, and 8.0 per cent in Turkey, compared to the initial forecast values. Although Jordan, Lebanon and Turkey hold sufficient levels of foreign reserves that can be used in case of severe foreign-exchange constraints, weaker external positions make these countries more vulnerable to the increasingly uncertain international financing conditions due to the anticipated normalization of the monetary policy in the United States of America.

a United Nations High Commissioner for Refugees (UNHCR) Iraq, "Operational update: internally displaced persons", 1-15 September 2014, available from http://reliefweb.int/sites/reliefweb.int/files/resources/UNHCR_Iraq-IDP_Update_1-15_Sept_14%5B1%5D.pdf

b The share of oil exports stood at 99.6 per cent in 2013. (Data from ITC Trade Map, based on the UNCTAD COMTRADE database).

c The indicator was calculated with the following formula: (Increase of the current-account deficit in year *i*) = (Current-account deficit in year *i*) - (Net exports to Iraq in year *i*)) / (Current-account deficit in year *i*) x 100. It measures the difference between a counterfactual current-account deficit without trade with Iraq and the actual current-account deficit. Thus, it indicates, ceteris paribus, how much the current-account deficit would deteriorate if there was no bilateral trade with Iraq.

Source 7.I-A: UN/ESCWA, based on national official data.
Source 7.I-B: UN/ESCWA.

Figure IV.7.1-A
Western Asia:
current-account balances
in selected countries

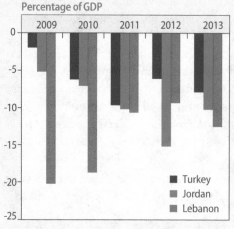

Source: United Nations Economic Commission for Western Asia.

Figure IV.7.1-B
Western Asia: increase of the current-account deficit in selected countries with no bilateral trade with Iraq

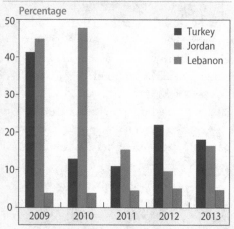

tor activities due to the expanding conflict areas in the country significantly worsened the economic situation and the standard of living. As a result, the economy is estimated to have contracted by 2.6 per cent in 2014. The ongoing armed conflict will continue to hamper the economy, although GDP growth is projected to be positive in 2015, before picking up more firmly in 2016.

Among non-oil-exporting countries, Jordan and Lebanon are experiencing a pace of economic expansion insufficient to accommodate the large influx of refugees from conflict countries in the region. GDP growth is estimated to have accelerated in these two economies in 2014, to 3.5 per cent in Jordan and to 1.8 per cent in Lebanon, driven mainly by strong growth in construction and government spending. In Israel, by contrast, GDP growth decelerated in 2014, partly owing to the conflict in Gaza, but also to lower private consumption and investment. All three countries are expected to see their economies expand at a faster pace during the forecast period.

The Iraqi and Syrian conflicts have significant spillover effects, encumbering economic growth in non-oil-exporting countries

The intensifying armed violence in the Syrian Arab Republic caused substantial losses of capital stock, hampered private investment activities and depressed growth prospects. Besides the heavy human toll, GDP has been contracting for the past three years, by 3 per cent in 2011, by 30.8 per cent in 2012 and by 37.7 per cent in 2013. As a result, the GDP level in the Syrian Arab Republic at the end of 2013 was about 41 per cent of the level in 2010. A further factor in this context has been economic sanctions. In addition, the continuing influx of Syrian refugees overburdened the economic infrastructures of Jordan, Lebanon and Turkey.

The stable domestic demand expansion in GCC countries contributed to the increase in labour demand in those countries. In spite of labour nationalization measures taken by some GCC countries, demand for additional labour in the private sector, both in skilled and unskilled categories, resulted in a growing number of immigrants. Despite job growth in the private sector throughout 2014, unemployment figures will remain high for nationals (i.e., the unemployment rates excluding foreign workers), particularly for youth, whose qualifications do not always match with current job opportunities. Moreover, the intensifying armed conflicts in Iraq, Palestine, the Syrian Arab Republic and Yemen forced workers to be either unemployed or economically inactive. The presence of a larger number of refugees is expected to continue during the forecast period, fuelling high unemployment. In addition, labour nationalization in GCC countries is expected to continue at various levels, which may have negative effects for job seekers from Jordan and Lebanon.

Although labour demand increased in GCC countries, unemployment figures remain high for youth

Reflecting the declining trend in international commodity prices, inflationary pressures were well contained in the region in 2014, with the exception of the Syrian Arab Republic, Turkey and Yemen. In Turkey, despite tighter monetary policy, inflation has trended up, with an anticipated annual increase of 8.9 per cent in 2014, compared with 7.5 per cent in 2013. Yemen's inflation remains in double digits, mainly as a result of fuel and electricity shortages. The average inflation rate for Western Asia increased to 4.7 per cent in 2014 from 4.4 per cent in 2013. During the forecast period, inflation is expected to remain relatively benign as oil and other commodity prices will continue to trend down, and GDP growth will remain modest.

Inflationary pressures are well contained in the region, with the exception of a few countries

Turkey introduced a tighter monetary policy stance in January 2014, in order to prevent further currency depreciation and high inflation. Assuming that inflation is going to remain high, the central bank will keep interest rates relatively close to current levels during the forecast period. In GCC countries, growth-supporting monetary policy regimes with historically low policy interest rates continued throughout 2014, mirroring the monetary policy stance of the United States. In non-oil-exporting countries, monetary policy will

Many countries will continue with loose monetary policies

remain loose, given the anticipated low inflation and modest economic growth. The central banks in Iraq, the Syrian Arab Republic and Yemen placed their policy priority on economic stabilization, aiming to smoothly provide foreign-exchange supplies. Monetary policies in the region will be revised in line with the anticipated interest-rate hike in the United States in 2015, especially in countries where the national currency is pegged to the dollar.

Fiscal balances are expected to weaken in GCC countries

More expansionary fiscal policy is expected in Turkey in 2015–2016. In oil-exporting countries, the fiscal stance is expected to remain expansionary, although less than in previous years, given the sharp decline in oil prices. The forecast oil price of $92 per barrel in 2015 already represents a fiscal breakeven price for several oil exporters in the region. Nevertheless, growth in public expenditure in real terms is expected to continue to be the basis of support for domestic demand expansion in GCC countries. A prudent fiscal policy environment will continue in Jordan, Lebanon and Yemen, where rising government debt is pressuring fiscal balances due to higher interest payments. These countries rely more on foreign aid to carry out public investments.

The current-account deficit in Turkey is expected to improve, whereas in GCC countries surpluses will narrow

The current-account deficit of Turkey is estimated to have narrowed in 2014. This trend is likely to continue during the forecast period, but financing the deficit may become more challenging than in previous years. The trade balance has improved, as exports increased in the first half of 2014 by 8.1 per cent, while imports contracted by 2.1 per cent in the same period. Despite declining oil export revenues, GCC countries, as well as Iraq, are expected to register current-account surpluses in 2014, although narrower than in previous years. The current-account deficits are estimated to edge up in Jordan, Lebanon and Yemen in 2014, mainly owing to a deterioration of exports. In part, the external accounts of Jordan and Lebanon, as well as Turkey, have been affected by the conflict in Iraq (box IV.7). Current transfers, including remittances and foreign aid, partly offset trade balance deficits in non-oil-exporting countries. Despite lower energy and food prices during the forecast period, current-account balances will remain large.

Important downside risks include the expansion of conflict areas and oil prices dropping below an average of $70 per barrel

The outlook is subject to four major downside risk factors. The first factor is the possible expansion of conflict areas in the Syrian Arab Republic and Iraq to other countries in the region. Second, should crude oil prices fall below an average of $70 per barrel in Brent, business confidence in GCC countries would be significantly affected. Third, unanticipated repercussions from monetary tightening in the United States would increase the region's funding costs. Last, any worsening in the growth prospects of Asian economies, such as China, India and the Republic of Korea, will have substantial impact on the region's exports.

Latin America and the Caribbean: moderate recovery expected for 2015, but substantial downside risks remain

Latin America and the Caribbean continues to face challenging economic conditions, amid domestic weaknesses and a less supportive external context, particularly lower commodity prices. After meagre economic growth of 1.3 per cent in 2014, the region is expected to improve moderately to an average growth of 2.4 per cent in 2015 (figure IV.9), although with considerable cross-country differences and significant downside risks. Among the subregions, the economies of Mexico and Central America are forecast to expand by 3.5 per cent in 2015, up from 2.6 per cent in 2014. By contrast, South America is expected to grow by only 1.9 per cent, compared to 0.7 per cent in 2014. The Caribbean economies are expected to expand by 3.8 per cent, similar to 2014.

Figure IV.9
GDP growth in Latin America and the Caribbean, 2010–2015

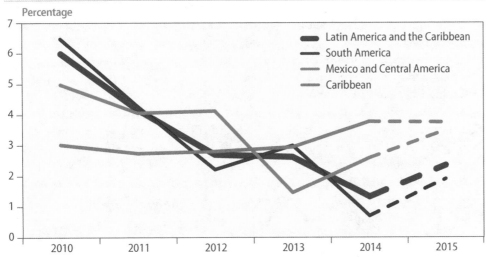

Source: UN/DESA.
Note: Data for 2014 are partially estimated. Data for 2015 are forecast.

Despite considerable heterogeneity among countries, investment demand in the region is estimated to gradually pick up after a continuing slowdown in recent years (box IV.8), led by the implementation of large public investment projects in countries such as Brazil, Chile and Mexico. Accommodative monetary conditions and supportive fiscal stances are also expected to buttress economic activity in some countries. On the external front, a sustained recovery of the United States is projected to further benefit Mexico and Central America through trade, tourism and remittance channels. The depreciation of national currencies may also contribute to increasing the competitiveness of exports.

Among the largest countries, GDP growth in Mexico is expected to accelerate from 2.4 per cent in 2014 to 3.4 per cent in 2015, owing to monetary and fiscal stimulus, previous structural reforms and the strengthening of the United States. After barely expanding by 0.3 per cent in 2014, the Brazilian economy is expected to grow modestly by 1.5 per cent in 2015, still affected by major supply bottlenecks. The Bolivarian Republic of Venezuela is expected to remain in recession, amid political turbulence and enduring economic imbalances, including extremely high inflation. Argentina slowed markedly last year and is expected to grow by a lacklustre 0.8 per cent in 2015, while facing a challenging path to contain inflation. After a noticeable slowdown, with GDP expanding by only 1.9 per cent in 2014, Chile's economy is expected to grow by 3.0 per cent in 2015, following a significant stimulus from monetary and fiscal policies. Other economies such as Colombia, Panama, Paraguay and the Plurinational State of Bolivia are projected to continue registering relatively strong economic growth rates in 2015, above 4.5 per cent. In addition, Peru's economy is expected to resume relatively strong growth of 4.9 per cent in 2015, up from 3.2 per cent in 2014, driven by a recovery in investment demand and resilient private consumption.

Large South American economies continue to face major domestic vulnerabilities

The deteriorating economic conditions significantly reduced job creation, particularly in South American economies. However, unemployment remained relatively low in most countries. Furthermore, regional urban unemployment is estimated to slightly decrease in 2014 compared to the previous year. This trend is driven by a lower participation rate, especially in Argentina, Brazil, Ecuador and Mexico. Meanwhile, progress on improving the quality of employment, as measured by the number of workers covered by contributory

Despite lower job creation, regional unemployment remains close to record lows

social security systems, also decelerated in 2014. Importantly, increases in formal employment have played a significant role in reducing income inequality in the region in recent years. In addition, real wages still increased at a moderate pace in several countries, which, combined with still positive credit growth, sustained a modest rise in household consumption in the region.

Inflation has increased, but unevenly across the region

In 2014, regional inflation moderately increased to an estimated rate of 10.2 per cent, continuing a slow but permanent upward trend that began in mid-2012. However, this trend is highly heterogeneous across subregions and countries. In Mexico and some Central American countries, inflation decreased somewhat and remains relatively stable and low, at about 4 per cent. By contrast, inflation in South American economies accelerated notably, driven by Argentina and Venezuela (Bolivarian Republic of), where inflation in 2014 was about 25 per cent and 68 per cent, respectively, fuelled by the devaluation of their currencies in early 2014. Other countries, such as Brazil and Chile, have also experienced moderate rises in inflation, although at much lower levels. The regional inflation rate is projected to decline slowly, to 8.8 per cent in 2015 and 7.0 per cent in 2016.

Several countries have loosened monetary policy in order to promote economic activity

Across the region, monetary policy is facing the dual challenge of reinvigorating growth while containing inflation pressures, amid the normalization of monetary policy in the United States. Some countries have opted to ease their monetary conditions, such as Chile, Mexico and Peru. By contrast, Brazil has significantly increased interest rates to tackle persistent inflation pressures, further affecting subdued economic activity. Colombia also tightened its monetary stance in the second half of 2014, while some Central American economies tended to reduce the expansion of their monetary base. Given that inflation rates remain above official targets and that real interest rates are already low—or even negative— in some economies, the monetary policy space will be relatively restricted in the case of worsening economic conditions. Meanwhile, domestic lending in the region continued to grow, albeit at lower rates than in recent years. In particular, domestic lending to the private sector slowed in economies that are more integrated in international financial markets, as well as in some Central American economies. However, public bank lending expanded markedly in countries such as Brazil, Ecuador, Mexico, Panama and Peru as authorities sought to stimulate domestic demand.

Fiscal policies are moving to a more supportive stance, but policy space is narrowing

Given the economic slowdown, several countries, such as Chile, Mexico and Peru, are implementing more proactive fiscal policies and have announced sizeable infrastructure programmes and public-private partnership initiatives. Overall, the region's fiscal balance in 2014 is estimated to have reached a deficit of 2.5 per cent of GDP. Thus, regional fiscal balances have noticeably deteriorated, by about 3 percentage points, compared to the situation before the financial crisis, narrowing the policy space for countercyclical policies. Moreover, the general trend towards stable fiscal revenues and increasing expenditures poses a challenge for the fiscal accounts over the medium term, increasing pressures for fiscal discipline in some cases.

Access to external financial markets remains positive

Overall, financial conditions remain positive in the region, including favourable access to external financial markets and relatively strong though volatile capital flows, particularly portfolio bond inflows. Meanwhile, international reserves grew slightly in 2014, with considerable heterogeneity between countries. The economies of the Dominican Republic and El Salvador posted significant increases in reserves, while in Brazil, Mexico, Paraguay and Uruguay, international reserves augmented, although at lower rates. The slower build-up of international reserves at the regional level also reflected their use as a tool to reduce exchange-rate volatility. By early 2014, the central banks of Costa Rica, the Dominican Republic, Peru and Trinidad and Tobago had actively intervened in foreign-exchange

Box IV.8
The recent investment slowdown in Latin America

During the boom years of 2004 to 2008, investment in Latin American countries witnessed a strong recovery, after relatively low growth rates from 1999 to 2003. In the later period, regional investment grew steadily at two-digit levels, with an annual average growth rate of 10.7 per cent. This brought the regional investment rate to almost 22 per cent of gross domestic product (GDP) in 2008. The sharp increase in investment during this period mainly reflected the rise in investment in machinery and equipment. This rise was prompted by strong demand for commodities, robust domestic economic activity and decreasing prices for capital goods in terms of national currency, given the exchange-rate appreciations that prevailed during these years. Real investment in construction increased at an annual average rate of 7.4 per cent over the same period. This can be traced, in part, to rising investment in the retail sector, due to the sustained increase in household consumption. Investment in the residential sector also increased, owing to enhanced access to housing credit and higher incomes resulting from improved labour market indicators. In addition, strongly improved terms of trade contributed to increased national savings in many countries, which translated into higher availability of domestic resources to finance investment and to lower dependency on external financing. Add to this the enhanced access of most Latin American countries to external financing, at lower costs and longer maturities.

However, after the sharp post-crisis decrease in investment rates in 2009 and the subsequent rebound in 2010, investment growth in the region has slowed. While in 2011 regional gross fixed-capital formation increased by 8.9 per cent, average regional investment growth declined significantly to 2.6 per cent during 2012–2013. Despite this aggregate trend, the performance of investment at the country level has been heterogeneous. As of 2013, in South American countries, such as Argentina, Brazil and Venezuela (Bolivarian Republic of), investment rates (relative to GDP) were still lower than in 2008, while in the Plurinational State of Bolivia, Colombia, Ecuador and Peru, they were 3 to 4 percentage points higher. This heterogeneity can also be found in Mexico and Central American countries. After the sharp decrease in investment rates in 2009, investment has been growing at a slow pace; with the exception of Costa Rica and Panama, investment rates in 2013 were still below pre-crisis levels.

The downward trend in investment growth spread throughout the region during 2014, but the heterogeneity across countries remains present. In 2014, Argentina, Brazil, Chile, Mexico and Venezuela (Bolivarian Republic of) registered very low or negative growth rates; in the Plurinational State of Bolivia, Colombia and Panama, investment kept growing at relatively high rates, albeit lower than in 2013. Therefore, the regional investment rate is expected to decrease further in 2014 compared to 2013 (figure IV.8.1).

Figure IV.8.1
Growth of GDP and aggregate demand components in Latin America, 2013 Q1–2014 Q2
Year-on-year-growth rate, constant 2005 dollars

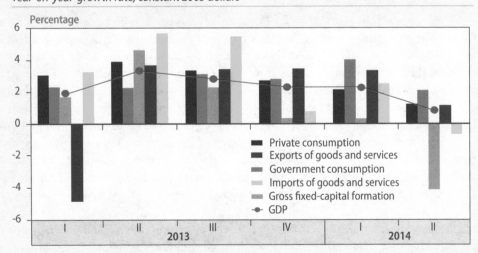

Source: UN/ECLAC, based on official data.

(continued)

Box IV.8 (*continued*)

Investment in machinery and equipment is the main contributor to this decline throughout the region, as imports of capital goods have noticeably contracted. The dynamism of the construction sector has also declined at a fast pace in many economies.

The recent investment slowdown is the result of various factors. For instance, expected lower external demand for commodities coupled with higher operating costs has impacted investment in big mining projects, particularly affecting countries that are specialized in the production and exports of minerals and metals, such as Chile and Peru. The culmination of big investment projects in the mining sector in Peru and in infrastructure in Panama adds to this slowdown. In addition, expectations of weak economic activity and, in some cases, financial constraints have been relevant in countries such as Argentina, Brazil, Ecuador and Venezuela (Bolivarian Republic of). The external context has had an unequal impact on Latin American countries, depending on their exposure to commodity prices, financing needs and policy space to implement countercyclical measures. In some cases, uncertainty about economic policies has further dampened investment.

Investment is expected to pick up for 2015 in several countries, but will grow below the pace seen during 2004–2008. In Mexico, the approved reforms should have a positive impact on investment in the oil and energy sector, while in Chile, local authorities have announced a large infrastructure investment programme. In Brazil, oil and infrastructure concessions and the preparation for the Olympic Games in 2016 are expected to contribute to an investment recovery. In Peru, sustained growth of domestic consumption should support investment in the retail and services sectors.

Source: United Nations Economic Commission for Latin America and the Caribbean.

markets while the Central Bank of Brazil extended the daily currency swap programme introduced in mid-2013. A number of economies have also implemented macroprudential measures to improve regulation and oversight of the financial sector and adjust their management of reserves and capital flows, such as Argentina, Brazil, Colombia, Peru and Trinidad and Tobago.

The pattern of stagnating and gradually falling prices for a number of the region's export commodities continued in 2014. As a result, the terms of trade deteriorated, albeit to varying degrees depending on a country's export structure. Overall, the current-account deficit in 2014 remained at about 2.7 per cent of GDP. Among the subregions, exports and imports increased more strongly in Mexico and Central America. By contrast, exports and imports in South America remained subdued owing to lower external demand, the fall in investment and the slowdown in household consumption. As in previous years, relatively robust FDI inflows, and to some extent bond inflows, continued to play a key role in financing current-account deficits.

A further slowdown in China remains a major risk for the region

There are several downside risks to the regional outlook. On the external front, the major risks are related to a larger-than-expected growth decline in China and thus further reductions in commodity prices, and the potential financial spillovers from the normalization of the monetary stance in the United States, which might reduce even further the policy space to reinvigorate investment and growth. A continuous decline in China's growth would be particularly adverse for commodity exporters in South America, affecting not only external demand and investment prospects but also fiscal positions in several economies.

On the domestic front, large South American countries are facing the challenge to restore economic momentum through coordinated fiscal, monetary, exchange rate, macroprudential and structural policies. For instance, recent structural reforms and infrastructure concession programmes in several countries are expected to generate benefits in the medium term. However, implementation problems or lack of coherence with other policies might derail the investment recovery. Overall, the prevailing internal and external conditions highlight the relevance of additional efforts on the reform agenda to tackle structural constraints and of proactive policies to boost productivity growth and promote the diversification of the productive structure.

Statistical annex

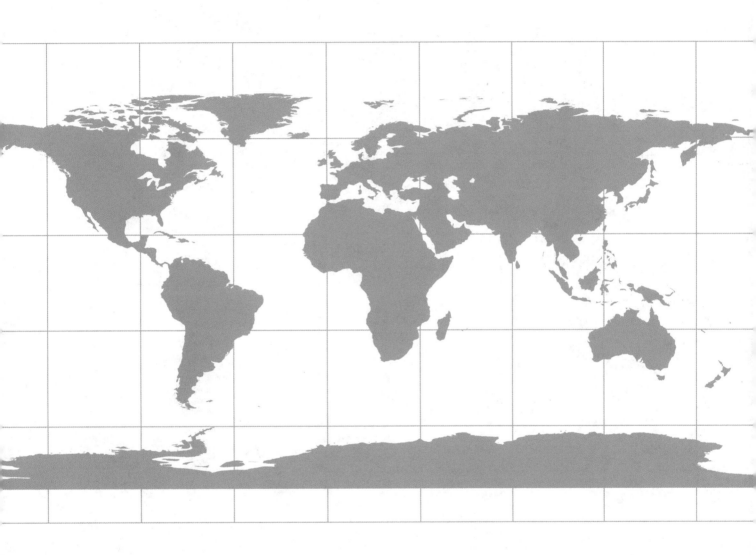

Country classification

Data sources, country classifications and aggregation methodology

The statistical annex contains a set of data that the *World Economic Situation and Prospects (WESP)* employs to delineate trends in various dimensions of the world economy.

Data sources

The annex was prepared by the Development Policy and Analysis Division (DPAD) of the Department of Economic and Social Affairs of the United Nations Secretariat (UN/DESA). It is based on information obtained from the Statistics Division and the Population Division of UN/DESA, as well as from the five United Nations regional commissions, the United Nations Conference on Trade and Development (UNCTAD), the United Nations World Tourism Organization (UNWTO), the International Monetary Fund (IMF), the World Bank, the Organization for Economic Cooperation and Development (OECD), and national and private sources. Estimates for the most recent years were made by DPAD in consultation with the regional commissions, UNCTAD, UNWTO and participants in Project LINK, an international collaborative research group for econometric modelling coordinated jointly by DPAD and the University of Toronto. Forecasts for 2015 and 2016 are primarily based on the World Economic Forecasting Model of DPAD, with support from Project LINK.

Data presented in *WESP* may differ from those published by other organizations for a series of reasons, including differences in timing, sample composition and aggregation methods. Historical data may differ from those in previous editions of *WESP* because of updating and changes in the availability of data for individual countries.

Country classifications

For analytical purposes, *WESP* classifies all countries of the world into one of three broad categories: developed economies, economies in transition and developing economies. The composition of these groupings, specified in tables A, B and C, is intended to reflect basic economic country conditions. Several countries (in particular the economies in transition) have characteristics that could place them in more than one category; however, for purposes of analysis, the groupings have been made mutually exclusive. Within each broad category, some subgroups are defined based either on geographical location or on ad hoc criteria, such as the subgroup of "major developed economies", which is based on the membership of the Group of Seven. Geographical regions for developing economies are as follows: Africa, East Asia, South Asia, Western Asia, and Latin America and the Caribbean.[1]

---

[1] Names and composition of geographical areas follow those specified in the statistical paper entitled "Standard country or area codes for statistical use" (ST/ESA/STAT/SER.M/49/Rev. 4).

In parts of the analysis, a distinction is made between fuel exporters and fuel importers from among the economies in transition and the developing countries. An economy is classified as a fuel exporter if the share of fuel exports in its total merchandise exports is greater than 20 per cent and the level of fuel exports is at least 20 per cent higher than that of the country's fuel imports. This criterion is drawn from the share of fuel exports in the total value of world merchandise trade. Fuels include coal, oil and natural gas (table D).

For other parts of the analysis, countries have been classified by their level of development as measured by per capita gross national income (GNI). Accordingly, countries have been grouped as high-income, upper middle income, lower middle income and low-income (table E). To maintain compatibility with similar classifications used elsewhere, the threshold levels of GNI per capita are those established by the World Bank. Countries with less than $1,045 GNI per capita are classified as low-income countries, those with between $1,046 and $4,125 as lower middle income countries, those with between $4,126 and $12,745 as upper middle income countries, and those with incomes of more than $12,746 as high-income countries. GNI per capita in dollar terms is estimated using the World Bank Atlas method,[2] and the classification in table E is based on data for 2013.

The list of the least developed countries (LDCs) is decided upon by the United Nations Economic and Social Council and, ultimately, by the General Assembly, on the basis of recommendations made by the Committee for Development Policy. The basic criteria for inclusion require that certain thresholds be met with regard to per capita GNI, a human assets index and an economic vulnerability index.[3] As at 30 November 2014, there were 47 LDCs (table F).

WESP also makes reference to the group of heavily indebted poor countries (HIPCs), which are considered by the World Bank and IMF as part of their debt-relief initiative (the Enhanced HIPC Initiative).[4] In September 2014, there were 39 HIPCs (see table G).

Aggregation methodology

Aggregate data are either sums or weighted averages of individual country data. Unless otherwise indicated, multi-year averages of growth rates are expressed as compound annual percentage rates of change. The convention followed is to omit the base year in a multi-year growth rate. For example, the 10-year average growth rate for the decade of the 2000s would be identified as the average annual growth rate for the period from 2001 to 2010.

WESP utilizes exchange-rate conversions of national data in order to aggregate output of individual countries into regional and global totals. The growth of output in each group of countries is calculated from the sum of gross domestic product (GDP) of individual countries measured at 2010 prices and exchange rates. Data for GDP in 2010 in national currencies were converted into dollars (with selected adjustments) and extended forwards and backwards in time using changes in real GDP for each country. This method supplies a reasonable set of aggregate growth rates for a period of about 15 years, centred on 2010.

---

2   See http://data.worldbank.org/about/country-classifications.

3   *Handbook on the Least Developed Country Category: Inclusion, Graduation and Special Support Measures* (United Nations publication, Sales No. E.07.II.A.9). Available from http://www.un.org/esa/analysis/ devplan/cdppublications/2008cdphandbook.pdf.

4   IMF, Debt Relief Under the Heavily Indebted Poor Countries (HIPC) Initiative, available from http://www.imf. org/external/np/exr/facts/pdf/hipc.pdf.

The exchange-rate based method differs from the one mainly applied by the IMF and the World Bank for their estimates of world and regional economic growth, which is based on purchasing power parity (PPP) weights. Over the past two decades, the growth of world gross product (WGP) on the basis of the exchange-rate based approach has been below that based on PPP weights. This is because developing countries, in the aggregate, have seen significantly higher economic growth than the rest of the world in the 1990s and 2000s and the share in WGP of these countries is larger under PPP measurements than under market exchange rates.

Table A
Developed economies

Europe		Other countries	Major developed economies (G7)
European Union	**Other Europe**		
EU-15	Iceland	Australia	Canada
Austria	Norway	Canada	Japan
Belgium	Switzerland	Japan	France
Denmark		New Zealand	Germany
Finland		United States	Italy
France			United Kingdom
Germany			United States
Greece			
Ireland			
Italy			
Luxembourg			
Netherlands			
Portugal			
Spain			
Sweden			
United Kingdom			
New EU member States			
Bulgaria			
Croatia			
Cyprus			
Czech Republic			
Estonia			
Hungary			
Latvia			
Lithuania			
Malta			
Poland			
Romania			
Slovakia			
Slovenia			

Table B
Economies in transition

South-Eastern Europe	Commonwealth of Independent States and Georgia[a]	
Albania	Armenia	Republic of Moldova
Bosnia and Herzegovina	Azerbaijan	Russian Federation
Montenegro	Belarus	Tajikistan
Serbia	Georgia[a]	Turkmenistan
The former Yugoslav Republic of Macedonia	Kazakhstan	Ukraine
	Kyrgyzstan	Uzbekistan

Table C
Developing economies by region[a]

Africa		Asia	Latin America and the Caribbean
North Africa	Southern Africa	East Asia	Caribbean
Algeria	Angola	Brunei Darussalam	Barbados
Egypt	Botswana	China	Cuba
Libya	Lesotho	Hong Kong SAR[b]	Dominican Republic
Mauritania	Malawi	Indonesia	Guyana
Morocco	Mauritius	Malaysia	Haiti
Sudan	Mozambique	Myanmar	Jamaica
Tunisia	Namibia	Papua New Guinea	Trinidad and Tobago
Central Africa	South Africa	Philippines	
	Zambia	Republic of Korea	**Mexico and Central America**
Cameroon	Zimbabwe	Singapore	
Central African Republic		Taiwan Province of China	Costa Rica
Chad	**West Africa**	Thailand	El Salvador
Congo		Viet Nam	Guatemala
Equatorial Guinea	Benin		Honduras
Gabon	Burkina Faso	**South Asia**	Mexico
Sao Tome and Prinicipe	Cabo Verde		Nicaragua
	Côte d'Ivoire	Bangladesh	Panama
East Africa	Gambia	India	
	Ghana	Iran (Islamic Republic of)	**South America**
Burundi	Guinea	Nepal	
Comoros	Guinea-Bissau	Pakistan	Argentina
Democratic Republic of the Congo	Liberia	Sri Lanka	Bolivia (Plurinational State of)
Djibouti	Mali	**Western Asia**	Brazil
Eritrea	Niger		Chile
Ethiopia	Nigeria	Bahrain	Colombia
Kenya	Senegal	Iraq	Ecuador
Madagascar	Sierra Leone	Israel	Paraguay
Rwanda	Togo	Jordan	Peru
Somalia		Kuwait	Uruguay
Uganda		Lebanon	Venezuela (Bolivarian Republic of)
United Republic of Tanzania		Oman	
		Qatar	
		Saudi Arabia	
		Syrian Arab Republic	
		Turkey	
		United Arab Emirates	
		Yemen	

Table D
Fuel-exporting countries

	Developing countries				
Economies in transition	Latin America and the Caribbean	Africa	East Asia	South Asia	Western Asia
Azerbaijan	Bolivia (Plurinational State of)	Algeria	Brunei Darussalam	Iran (Islamic Republic of)	Bahrain
Kazakhstan		Angola	Indonesia		Iraq
Russian Federation	Colombia	Cameroon	Viet Nam		Kuwait
Turkmenistan	Ecuador	Chad			Oman
Uzbekistan	Trinidad and Tobago	Congo			Qatar
	Venezuela (Bolivarian Republic of)	Côte d'Ivoire			Saudi Arabia
		Egypt			United Arab Emirates
		Equatorial Guinea			Yemen
		Gabon			
		Libya			
		Nigeria			
		Sudan			

Table E
Economies by per capita GNI in 2013[a]

High-income		Upper middle income		Lower middle income	Low-income
Australia	Lithuania	Albania	Jordan	Armenia	Bangladesh
Austria	Luxembourg	Algeria	Kazakhstan	Bolivia (Plurinational	Benin
Bahrain	Malta	Angola	Lebanon	State of)	Burkina Faso
Barbados	Netherlands	Argentina	Libya	Cameroon	Burundi
Belgium	New Zealand	Azerbaijan	Malaysia	Cabo Verde	Central African
Brunei	Norway	Belarus	Mauritius	Congo	Republic
Darussalam	Oman	Bosnia and	Mexico	Côte d'Ivoire	Chad
Canada	Poland	Herzegovina	Montenegro	Djibouti	Comoros
Chile	Portugal	Botswana	Namibia	Egypt	Democratic Republic
Croatia	Qatar	Brazil	Panama	El Salvador	of the Congo
Cyprus	Republic	Bulgaria	Peru	Georgia	Eritrea
Czech	of Korea	China	Romania	Ghana	Ethiopia
Republic	Russian Federation	Colombia	Serbia	Guatemala	Gambia
Denmark	Saudi Arabia	Costa Rica	South Africa	Guyana	Guinea
Equatorial	Singapore	Cuba	Thailand	Honduras	Guinea-Bissau
Guinea	Slovak	Dominican	The former	India	Haiti
Estonia	Republic	Republic	Yugoslav	Indonesia	Kenya
Finland	Slovenia	Ecuador	Republic of	Kyrgyz Republic[c]	Liberia
France	Spain	Gabon	Macedonia	Lesotho	Madagascar
Germany	Sweden	Hungary	Tunisia	Mauritania	Malawi
Greece	Switzerland	Iran (Islamic	Turkey	Morocco	Mali
Hong Kong	Taiwan Province	Republic of)	Turkmenistan	Nicaragua	Mozambique
SAR[b]	of China	Iraq	Venezuela	Nigeria	Myanmar
Iceland	Trinidad and	Jamaica	(Bolivarian	Pakistan	Nepal
Ireland	Tobago		Republic of)	Papua New Guinea	Niger
Israel	United Arab			Paraguay	Rwanda
Italy	Emirates			Philippines	Sierra Leone
Japan	United Kingdom			Republic of Moldova	Somalia
Kuwait	United States			São Tomé and	Tajikistan
Latvia	Uruguay			Principe	Togo
				Senegal	Uganda
				Sri Lanka	United Republic
				Sudan	of Tanzania
				Syrian Arab Republic	Zimbabwe
				Ukraine	
				Uzbekistan	
				Viet Nam	
				Yemen	
				Zambia	

a Economies systematically monitored for the World Economic Situation and Prospects report and included in the United Nations' global economic forecast.
b Special Administrative Region of China.
c Indicates the country has been shifted upward by one category from previous year's classification.

Table F
Least developed countries (*as of November 2014*)

Africa		East Asia	South Asia	Western Asia	Latin America and the Caribbean
Angola	Madagascar	Cambodia[a]	Afghanistan[a]	Yemen	Haiti
Benin	Malawi	Kiribati[a]	Bangladesh		
Burkina Faso	Mali	Lao People's Democratic Republic[a]	Bhutan[a]		
Burundi	Mauritania		Nepal		
Central African Republic	Mozambique	Myanmar			
Chad	Niger	Solomon Islands[a]			
Comoros	Rwanda	Timor Leste[a]			
Democratic Republic of the Congo	Sao Tome and Principe	Tuvalu[a]			
Djibouti	Senegal	Vanuatu[a]			
Equatorial Guinea	Sierra Leone				
Eritrea	Somalia				
Ethiopia	South Sudan[a]				
Gambia	Sudan				
Guinea	Togo				
Guinea-Bissau	Uganda				
Lesotho	United Republic of Tanzania				
Liberia	Zambia				

a Not included in the WESP discussion because of insufficient data.

Table G
Heavily indebted poor countries (*as of September 2014*)

Post-completion point HIPCs[a]		Interim HIPCs[b]	Pre-decision point HIPCs[c]
Afghanistan	Honduras	Chad	Eritrea
Benin	Liberia		Somalia
Bolivia	Madagascar		Sudan
Burkina Faso	Malawi		
Burundi	Mali		
Cameroon	Mauritania		
Central African Republic	Mozambique		
Comoros	Nicaragua		
Congo	Niger		
Côte D'Ivoire	Rwanda		
Democratic Republic of the Congo	São Tomé and Principe		
Ethiopia	Senegal		
Gambia	Sierra Leone		
Ghana	Togo		
Guinea	Uganda		
Guinea-Bissau	United Republic of Tanzania		
Guyana	Zambia		
Haiti			

a Countries that have qualified for irrevocable debt relief under the HIPC Initiative.

b Countries that have qualified for assistance under the HIPC Initiative (that is to say, have reached decision point), but have not yet reached completion point.

c Countries that are potentially eligible and may wish to avail themselves of the HIPC Initiative or the Multilateral Debt Relief Initiative (MDRI).

Table H
Small island developing States

United Nations members		Non-UN members/Associate members of the Regional Commissions
Antigua and Barbuda	Marshall Islands	American Samoa
Bahamas	Mauritius	Anguilla
Bahrain	Nauru	Aruba
Barbados	Palau	Bermuda
Belize	Papua New Guinea	British Virgin Islands
Cabo Verde	Saint Kitts and Nevis	Cayman Islands
Comoros	Saint Lucia	Commonwealth of Northern Marianas
Cuba	Saint Vincent and the Grenadines	Cook Islands
Dominica		Curaçao
Dominican Republic	Samoa	French Polynesia
Federated States of Micronesia	São Tomé and Príncipe	Guadeloupe
Fiji	Seychelles	Guam
Grenada	Singapore	Martinique
Guinea-Bissau	Solomon Islands	Montserrat
Guyana	Suriname	New Caledonia
Haiti	Timor-Leste	Niue
Jamaica	Tonga	Puerto Rico
Kiribati	Trinidad and Tobago	Turks and Caicos Islands
Maldives	Tuvalu	U.S. Virgin Islands
	Vanuatu	

Table I
Landlocked developing countries

Landlocked developing countries		
Afghanistan	Kyrgystan	South Sudan
Armenia	Lao People's Democratic Republic	Swaziland
Azerbaijan		Tajikistan
Bhutan	Lesotho	The former Yugoslav Republic of Macedonia
Bolivia (Plurinational State of)	Malawi	
Botswana	Mali	Turkmenistan
Burkina Faso	Mongolia	Uganda
Burundi	Nepal	Uzbekistan
Central African Republic	Niger	Zambia
Chad	Paraguay	Zimbabwe
Ethiopia	Republic of Moldova	
Kazakhstan	Rwanda	

Annex tables

Table A.1
Developed economies: rates of growth of real GDP, 2006–2016

Annual percentage change

	2006-2013[a]	2006	2007	2008	2009	2010	2011	2012	2013	2014[b]	2015[c]	2016[c]
Developed economies	1.0	2.9	2.5	0.1	-3.7	2.6	1.5	1.1	1.2	1.6	2.1	2.3
United States	1.2	2.7	1.8	-0.3	-2.8	2.5	1.6	2.3	2.2	2.3	2.8	3.1
Canada	1.6	2.6	2.0	1.2	-2.7	3.4	2.5	1.7	2.0	2.3	2.6	2.8
Japan	0.5	1.7	2.2	-1.0	-5.5	4.7	-0.5	1.5	1.5	0.4	1.2	1.1
Australia	2.8	2.6	4.7	2.5	1.6	2.3	2.6	3.6	2.4	3.0	2.4	2.3
New Zealand	1.7	2.3	3.4	-0.7	0.6	1.8	1.2	2.6	2.5	3.0	3.3	3.0
European Union	0.7	3.4	3.1	0.5	-4.5	2.0	1.8	-0.4	0.0	1.3	1.7	2.0
EU-15	0.6	3.2	2.8	0.2	-4.5	2.1	1.7	-0.5	-0.1	1.2	1.5	1.9
Austria	1.3	3.4	3.6	1.5	-3.8	1.9	3.1	0.9	0.2	0.8	1.6	2.2
Belgium	1.0	2.6	3.0	1.0	-2.6	2.5	1.6	0.1	0.3	0.9	1.2	1.3
Denmark	0.1	3.4	1.6	-0.8	-5.7	1.4	1.1	-0.4	0.4	1.3	2.1	2.1
Finland	0.5	4.1	5.2	0.7	-8.3	3.0	2.6	-1.5	-1.2	-0.1	1.5	1.5
France	0.7	2.5	2.3	-0.1	-3.1	1.7	2.0	0.0	0.2	0.3	0.8	1.3
Germany	1.3	3.7	3.3	1.1	-5.6	4.1	3.6	0.4	0.1	1.4	1.4	1.7
Greece	-2.2	5.5	3.5	-0.2	-3.1	-4.9	-7.1	-7.0	-3.9	0.4	2.3	2.9
Ireland	0.4	5.5	4.9	-2.6	-6.4	-0.3	2.8	-0.3	0.2	4.4	3.5	3.4
Italy	-0.6	2.0	1.5	-1.0	-5.5	1.7	0.6	-2.3	-1.9	-0.4	0.5	1.1
Luxembourg	1.5	4.9	6.6	-0.7	-5.6	3.1	1.9	-0.2	2.1	2.4	2.1	2.1
Netherlands	0.9	3.8	4.2	2.1	-3.3	1.1	1.7	-1.6	-0.7	0.7	1.3	1.6
Portugal	-0.4	1.4	2.4	0.0	-2.9	1.9	-1.3	-3.2	-1.4	0.6	0.8	1.1
Spain	0.2	4.1	3.5	0.9	-3.8	-0.2	0.0	-1.6	-1.2	1.2	2.1	2.5
Sweden	1.5	4.7	3.4	-0.6	-5.2	6.0	2.7	-0.3	1.5	1.7	3.2	3.4
United Kingdom	0.8	3.0	2.6	-0.3	-4.3	1.9	1.6	0.7	1.7	3.1	2.6	2.5
New EU member States	2.4	6.5	6.1	4.0	-4.0	2.0	3.1	0.7	1.1	2.6	2.9	3.3
Bulgaria	2.1	6.5	6.4	6.2	-5.5	0.4	1.8	0.6	0.9	1.3	2.5	2.9
Croatia	-0.1	4.9	5.1	2.1	-6.9	-2.3	-0.2	-2.2	-0.9	-0.5	0.7	2.5
Cyprus	0.6	4.1	5.1	3.6	-1.9	1.3	0.4	-2.4	-5.4	-3.7	0.9	1.0
Czech Republic	1.6	6.9	5.5	2.7	-4.8	2.3	2.0	-0.8	-0.7	2.5	2.5	2.9
Estonia	1.7	10.1	7.5	-4.2	-14.1	2.6	9.6	3.9	0.8	1.6	2.7	3.0
Hungary	0.0	3.9	0.1	0.9	-6.8	1.1	1.6	-1.7	1.1	2.8	2.8	3.2
Latvia	1.3	11.0	10.0	-2.8	-17.7	-1.3	5.3	5.2	4.1	2.6	3.5	4.0
Lithuania	2.4	7.4	11.1	2.6	-14.8	1.6	6.1	3.8	3.3	2.7	3.0	3.0
Malta	2.0	2.6	4.1	3.9	-2.8	4.1	1.6	0.6	2.4	2.0	2.1	2.2
Poland	3.9	6.2	6.8	5.1	1.6	3.9	4.5	2.0	1.6	3.4	3.5	3.6
Romania	2.4	7.9	6.3	7.3	-6.6	-1.1	2.3	0.6	3.5	3.1	3.0	3.9
Slovakia	3.6	8.3	10.5	5.8	-4.9	4.4	3.0	1.8	0.9	2.4	2.7	2.6
Slovenia	0.7	5.7	6.9	3.3	-7.8	1.2	0.6	-2.6	-1.0	2.0	3.0	3.5
Other Europe	1.6	3.3	3.5	1.3	-2.0	1.8	1.6	1.9	1.4	1.4	2.2	2.3
Iceland	1.0	4.7	6.0	1.2	-6.6	-4.1	2.7	1.5	3.3	2.2	1.0	0.3
Norway	1.1	2.3	2.7	0.1	-1.6	0.5	1.3	2.9	0.6	1.9	1.7	2.4
Switzerland	2.0	4.0	4.1	2.3	-2.1	3.0	1.8	1.1	1.9	1.0	2.6	2.3
Memorandum items												
North America	1.3	2.7	1.8	-0.2	-2.8	2.6	1.7	2.3	2.2	2.3	2.8	3.0
Western Europe	0.8	3.4	3.1	0.5	-4.3	2.0	1.8	-0.3	0.1	1.3	1.7	2.0
Asia and Oceania	0.9	1.9	2.6	-0.4	-4.2	4.1	0.1	1.9	1.7	1.0	1.5	1.4
Major developed economies	0.9	2.6	2.1	-0.2	-3.9	2.9	1.5	1.4	1.4	1.6	2.1	2.3
Euro area	0.5	3.2	3.0	0.4	-4.6	2.0	1.7	-0.8	-0.5	0.8	1.3	1.7

Sources: UN/DESA, based on data of the United Nations Statistics Division and individual national sources.

Note: Country groups are calculated as a weighted average of individual country growth rates of gross domestic product (GDP), where weights are based on GDP in 2010 prices and exchange rates.

a Average percentage change.

b Partly estimated.

c Baseline scenario forecasts, based in part on Project LINK and UN/DESA World Economic Forecasting Model.

Table A.2
Economies in transition: rates of growth of real GDP, 2006–2016

Annual percentage change

	2006–2013[a]	2006	2007	2008	2009	2010	2011	2012	2013	2014[b]	2015[c]	2016[c]
Economies in transition	3.7	8.6	8.8	5.3	-6.6	4.8	4.5	3.3	2.0	0.8	1.1	2.1
South-Eastern Europe	2.3	4.7	6.0	5.1	-2.1	1.7	1.8	-0.9	2.4	0.7	2.7	3.0
Albania	3.9	5.4	5.9	7.5	3.4	3.7	2.5	1.6	1.3	1.5	3.0	4.0
Bosnia and Herzegovina	2.2	5.7	6.0	5.6	-2.7	0.8	1.0	-1.2	2.5	1.5	2.6	2.5
Montenegro	3.3	8.6	10.7	6.9	-5.7	2.5	3.2	-2.5	3.4	2.3	2.7	3.0
Serbia	1.6	3.6	5.4	3.8	-3.5	1.0	1.6	-1.5	2.5	-0.8	2.5	3.0
The former Yugoslav Republic of Macedonia	3.1	5.1	6.5	5.5	-0.4	3.4	2.3	-0.5	2.7	3.5	3.5	3.0
Commonwealth of Independent States and Georgia[d]	3.8	8.7	8.9	5.3	-6.7	4.9	4.7	3.5	2.0	0.8	1.1	2.1
Net fuel exporters	3.9	8.8	9.0	5.4	-6.3	4.9	4.6	3.7	2.1	1.2	1.1	2.0
Azerbaijan	10.8	34.5	25.5	10.6	9.4	4.6	-1.6	2.1	6.0	2.7	4.2	3.5
Kazakhstan	6.2	10.7	8.9	3.3	1.2	7.3	7.5	5.0	6.0	4.0	4.8	6.0
Russian Federation	3.3	8.2	8.5	5.2	-7.8	4.5	4.3	3.4	1.3	0.5	0.2	1.2
Turkmenistan	10.9	11.0	11.0	14.7	6.1	9.2	14.1	11.1	10.2	10.3	9.5	8.9
Uzbekistan	8.2	7.3	9.5	9.0	8.1	8.5	8.3	8.2	7.0	7.5	7.0	6.9
Net fuel importers	2.8	8.0	8.4	4.4	-10.1	5.0	5.3	1.4	1.1	-2.6	1.0	2.7
Armenia	4.3	13.2	13.7	6.9	-14.1	2.2	4.7	7.2	3.5	4.0	4.0	4.2
Belarus	5.5	10.0	8.6	10.2	0.2	7.7	5.5	1.7	0.9	1.5	2.5	3.5
Georgia	5.3	9.4	12.3	2.3	-3.8	6.3	7.2	6.2	3.2	5.0	4.8	4.0
Kyrgyzstan	4.8	3.1	8.5	8.4	2.9	-0.5	6.0	-0.1	10.5	3.8	5.0	6.0
Republic of Moldova	3.8	4.8	3.0	7.8	-6.0	7.1	6.8	-0.7	8.9	3.0	3.5	3.5
Tajikistan	6.2	6.6	7.6	7.6	4.0	6.5	2.4	7.5	7.4	5.8	5.2	5.0
Ukraine	1.3	7.3	7.9	2.3	-14.8	4.2	5.2	0.3	0.0	-6.5	-0.8	1.8

Sources: UN/DESA, based on data of the United Nations Statistics Division and individual national sources.

Note: Country groups are calculated as a weighted average of individual country growth rates of gross domestic product (GDP), where weights are based on GDP in 2010 prices and exchange rates.

a Average percentage change.

b Partly estimated.

c Baseline scenario forecasts, based in part on Project LINK and the UN/DESA World Economic Forecasting Model.

d Georgia officially left the Commonwealth of Independent States on 18 August 2009. However, its performance is discussed in the context of this group of countries for reasons of geographic proximity and similarities in economic structure.

Table A.3
Developing economies: rates of growth of real GDP, 2006–2016

Annual percentage change

	2006–2013[a]	2006	2007	2008	2009	2010	2011	2012	2013	2014[b]	2015[c]	2016[c]
Developing countries[d]	6.0	7.8	8.2	5.4	3.2	7.8	5.9	4.8	4.8	4.3	4.8	5.1
Africa	4.5	6.7	6.5	5.3	2.9	4.9	0.8	5.6	3.5	3.5	4.6	4.9
North Africa	3.4	7.1	5.4	5.0	3.5	4.2	-5.3	6.6	1.4	1.6	3.9	4.3
East Africa	6.5	6.9	7.6	6.5	4.5	7.2	6.6	6.1	6.3	6.5	6.8	6.6
Central Africa	3.8	2.1	5.3	3.5	2.9	5.9	3.3	5.3	2.2	4.3	4.7	5.0
West Africa	6.2	6.1	6.4	6.0	5.7	7.0	4.8	6.9	7.0	5.9	6.2	6.1
Southern Africa	4.3	7.1	7.8	5.2	0.1	3.8	4.1	3.4	3.0	2.9	3.6	4.1
Net fuel exporters	4.7	7.3	7.3	5.9	4.1	5.3	-2.5	7.0	3.3	3.2	4.8	5.0
Net fuel importers	4.4	6.0	5.5	4.7	1.6	4.6	4.7	4.1	3.7	3.7	4.4	4.7
East and South Asia	7.5	9.3	10.4	6.3	6.1	9.3	7.1	5.6	5.9	5.9	6.0	6.0
East Asia	7.8	9.6	10.8	7.0	5.9	9.4	7.5	6.3	6.4	6.1	6.1	6.0
South Asia	6.1	8.2	8.9	3.5	7.0	8.7	5.5	2.9	4.1	4.9	5.4	5.7
Net fuel exporters	4.8	5.9	7.1	4.5	4.4	6.1	5.1	1.9	3.4	4.2	4.6	5.0
Net fuel importers	7.8	9.7	10.8	6.5	6.3	9.6	7.3	6.1	6.2	6.1	6.1	6.1
Western Asia	4.8	7.5	5.4	4.6	-0.7	6.3	7.2	4.5	4.0	2.9	3.7	4.3
Net fuel exporters	5.5	8.4	5.5	6.8	0.6	5.1	7.5	6.2	4.2	3.5	4.2	4.7
Net fuel importers	4.0	6.4	5.4	2.0	-2.3	7.9	6.9	2.4	3.8	2.1	3.1	3.7
Latin America and the Caribbean	3.7	5.5	5.8	4.1	-1.3	6.0	4.2	2.7	2.6	1.3	2.4	3.1
South America	4.0	5.4	6.5	4.9	-0.3	6.5	4.3	2.2	2.8	0.7	1.9	2.8
Mexico and Central America	2.6	5.1	3.7	1.7	-4.2	5.1	4.1	4.2	1.8	2.6	3.5	3.8
Caribbean	4.0	10.1	6.3	3.5	1.1	2.7	2.8	2.8	3.0	3.8	3.8	3.8
Net fuel exporters	4.2	8.0	7.1	4.6	-0.7	1.3	5.4	4.8	3.0	1.4	2.4	3.2
Net fuel importers	3.6	5.1	5.6	4.0	-1.4	6.8	4.0	2.4	2.5	1.3	2.3	3.1
Memorandum items:												
Least developed countries	6.2	8.2	9.2	7.8	5.2	5.9	3.5	5.0	5.3	5.3	5.7	5.9
Africa (excluding Libya)	4.7	6.1	6.6	5.4	3.1	5.0	3.6	4.0	4.0	3.9	4.5	4.8
North Africa (excluding Libya)	3.9	5.6	5.5	5.3	4.1	4.2	1.8	2.1	2.8	2.7	3.6	4.0
East Asia (excluding China)	4.5	5.8	6.2	3.4	0.9	7.7	4.5	4.0	4.0	3.9	4.3	4.5
South Asia (excluding India)	3.6	6.2	7.0	2.6	3.9	4.9	3.5	-1.2	2.0	3.7	4.0	4.2
Western Asia (excluding Israel and Turkey)	5.4	8.1	5.6	6.7	1.1	5.1	6.9	5.9	4.0	3.0	4.0	4.5
Arab States[e]	4.8	7.8	5.5	6.2	1.8	4.8	3.1	6.1	3.3	2.6	3.9	4.5
Landlocked developing economies	6.8	9.8	9.2	6.4	3.7	7.4	6.0	5.3	6.3	5.2	5.5	5.8
Small island developing economies	4.7	8.6	7.5	3.0	0.3	8.6	4.4	2.2	3.3	3.0	3.6	3.6
Major developing economies												
Argentina	5.1	8.4	8.0	3.1	0.1	9.1	8.6	0.9	2.9	-0.3	0.8	2.5
Brazil	3.5	4.0	6.1	5.2	-0.3	7.5	2.7	1.0	2.3	0.3	1.5	2.4
Chile	4.2	5.7	5.2	3.3	-1.0	5.8	5.8	5.4	4.1	1.9	3.0	3.5
China	10.1	12.7	14.2	9.6	9.2	10.4	9.3	7.7	7.7	7.3	7.0	6.8
Colombia	4.7	6.7	6.9	3.5	1.7	4.0	6.6	4.0	4.3	4.8	4.5	4.7
Egypt	4.6	6.8	7.1	7.2	4.7	5.1	1.8	2.2	2.1	2.2	3.5	4.0
Hong Kong SAR[f]	3.6	7.0	6.5	2.1	-2.5	6.8	4.8	1.5	2.9	2.2	2.5	2.8
India	7.2	9.3	9.8	3.9	8.5	10.5	6.4	4.7	5.0	5.4	5.9	6.3
Indonesia	5.9	5.5	6.3	6.0	4.6	6.2	6.5	6.3	5.8	5.1	5.4	5.7

Table A.3
Developing economies: rates of growth of real GDP, 2006–2016 (*continued*)

Annual percentage change

	2006–2013ᵃ	2006	2007	2008	2009	2010	2011	2012	2013	2014ᵇ	2015ᶜ	2016ᶜ
Iran (Islamic Republic of)	2.4	6.1	8.3	1.7	4.0	5.8	2.5	-6.6	-1.9	2.0	2.5	2.8
Israel	4.4	5.8	6.9	4.5	1.2	5.7	4.6	3.4	3.3	2.7	2.9	3.3
Republic of Korea	3.7	5.2	5.5	2.8	0.7	6.5	3.7	2.3	3.0	3.4	3.6	3.7
Malaysia	4.7	5.6	6.3	4.8	-1.5	7.4	5.1	5.6	4.7	5.7	5.3	5.5
Mexico	2.4	5.0	3.2	1.4	-4.7	5.2	3.9	4.0	1.4	2.4	3.4	3.8
Nigeria	6.8	7.5	7.5	6.3	6.9	7.8	4.7	6.7	7.3	5.8	6.1	5.9
Pakistan	3.7	6.2	4.8	1.7	2.8	1.6	2.8	4.0	6.1	4.2	4.1	4.3
Peru	6.6	7.5	8.5	9.1	1.0	8.5	6.5	6.0	5.6	3.2	4.9	5.0
Philippines	5.3	5.2	6.6	4.2	1.1	7.6	3.6	6.8	7.2	6.4	6.1	6.0
Saudi Arabia	5.9	5.6	6.0	8.4	1.8	7.4	8.6	5.8	4.0	4.0	4.2	4.2
Singapore	5.7	8.9	9.0	1.9	-0.6	15.1	6.0	1.9	4.1	2.8	3.3	3.6
South Africa	3.0	5.6	5.5	3.6	-1.5	3.1	3.6	2.5	1.9	2.0	2.7	3.3
Taiwan Province of China	3.5	5.4	6.0	0.7	-1.8	10.8	4.2	1.5	2.1	3.5	3.4	3.1
Thailand	3.6	4.9	5.4	1.7	-0.9	7.4	0.6	7.1	2.9	1.1	3.9	4.2
Turkey	3.9	6.9	4.7	0.7	-4.8	9.2	8.8	2.1	4.1	2.7	3.3	4.0
Venezuela (Bolivarian Republic of)	3.7	9.9	8.8	5.3	-3.2	-1.5	4.2	5.6	1.3	-3.0	-0.5	1.0

Sources: UN/DESA, based on data of the United Nations Statistics Division and individual national sources.

Note: Country groups are calculated as a weighted average of individual country growth rates of gross domestic product (GDP), where weights are based on GDP in 2005 prices and exchange rates.

a Average percentage change.

b Partly estimated.

c Baseline scenario forecasts, based in part on Project LINK and the UN/DESA World Economic Forecasting Model.

d Covering countries that account for 98 per cent of the population of all developing countries.

e Currently includes data for Algeria, Bahrain, Comoros, Djibouti, Egypt, Iraq, Jordan, Kuwait, Lebanon, Libya, Mauritania, Morocco, Oman, Qatar, Saudi Arabia, Somalia, Sudan, Syrian Arab Republic, Tunisia, United Arab Emirates and Yemen.

f Special Administrative Region of China.

Table A.4
Developed economies: consumer price inflation, 2006–2016

Annual percentage change[a]

	2006	2007	2008	2009	2010	2011	2012	2013	2014[b]	2015[c]	2016[c]
Developed economies	2.3	2.2	3.3	0.1	1.5	2.6	1.9	1.3	1.5	1.4	1.7
United States	3.1	2.9	3.8	-0.3	1.6	3.2	2.0	1.4	1.9	1.6	1.6
Canada	2.0	2.1	2.4	0.3	1.8	2.9	1.5	1.0	2.0	1.5	2.0
Japan	0.2	0.1	1.4	-1.3	-0.7	-0.3	0.0	0.4	2.7	1.3	1.5
Australia	3.6	2.3	4.4	1.8	2.9	3.3	1.8	2.5	2.7	1.6	2.2
New Zealand	3.4	2.4	4.0	2.1	2.3	4.0	1.1	1.2	1.6	1.9	2.0
European Union	2.2	2.3	3.5	0.8	1.9	3.0	2.6	1.5	0.7	1.2	1.7
EU-15	2.2	2.1	3.3	0.6	1.9	2.9	2.5	1.5	0.7	1.2	1.7
Austria	1.7	2.2	3.2	0.4	1.7	3.5	2.6	2.2	1.5	1.8	1.9
Belgium	2.3	1.8	4.5	0.0	2.3	3.4	2.6	1.2	0.7	1.2	2.2
Denmark	1.8	1.7	3.6	1.1	2.2	2.7	2.4	0.6	0.4	1.3	1.9
Finland	1.3	1.6	3.9	1.6	1.7	3.3	3.2	2.3	1.2	1.3	1.5
France	1.9	1.6	3.2	0.1	1.7	2.3	2.2	1.0	0.7	0.8	1.2
Germany	1.8	2.3	2.8	0.2	1.2	2.5	2.1	1.6	1.0	1.6	2.1
Greece	3.3	3.0	4.2	1.3	4.7	3.1	1.0	-0.8	-1.2	0.2	0.8
Ireland	2.7	2.9	3.1	-1.7	-1.6	1.2	1.9	0.6	0.6	1.2	1.3
Italy	2.2	2.0	3.5	0.8	1.6	2.9	3.3	1.3	0.3	0.7	1.5
Luxembourg	2.7	2.3	3.4	0.4	2.3	3.4	2.7	1.7	0.9	2.1	2.1
Netherlands	1.6	1.6	2.2	1.0	0.9	2.5	2.8	2.6	0.5	1.0	1.1
Portugal	3.0	2.4	2.7	-0.9	1.4	3.6	2.8	0.5	-0.2	0.5	0.7
Spain	3.6	2.8	4.1	-0.2	2.0	3.0	2.4	1.5	0.0	1.0	1.6
Sweden	1.5	1.7	3.3	1.9	1.9	1.4	0.9	0.5	0.2	1.1	2.2
United Kingdom	2.3	2.3	3.6	2.2	3.3	4.5	2.8	2.6	1.7	1.8	1.9
New EU member States	3.1	3.9	6.1	3.1	2.7	3.8	3.7	1.4	0.4	1.5	2.5
Bulgaria	7.3	8.4	12.3	2.8	2.5	4.2	2.9	0.7	-0.5	1.5	2.0
Croatia	3.2	2.9	6.0	2.4	1.0	2.3	3.4	2.1	-0.1	1.5	2.3
Cyprus	2.5	2.3	4.7	0.4	2.5	3.3	2.4	-0.4	-0.7	1.4	1.8
Czech Republic	2.1	3.0	6.3	0.6	1.2	2.1	3.5	1.4	0.5	1.5	2.0
Estonia	4.4	6.7	10.6	0.2	2.7	5.1	4.2	3.3	0.9	2.0	3.0
Hungary	4.0	7.9	6.0	4.0	4.7	3.9	5.7	1.7	0.5	2.3	2.9
Latvia	6.5	10.1	15.4	3.5	-1.1	4.4	2.3	0.0	0.5	1.5	2.5
Lithuania	3.8	5.7	10.9	4.4	1.3	4.1	3.1	1.0	0.5	1.5	2.5
Malta	2.8	1.3	4.2	2.1	1.4	2.8	2.4	1.4	1.1	1.8	1.8
Poland	1.3	2.6	4.2	4.0	2.7	3.9	3.7	0.8	0.2	1.0	2.5
Romania	6.6	4.8	7.9	5.6	6.1	5.8	3.4	3.2	1.2	2.3	3.0
Slovakia	4.3	1.9	3.9	0.9	0.7	4.1	3.7	1.5	0.1	1.9	2.5
Slovenia	2.5	3.8	5.5	0.9	2.1	2.1	2.8	1.9	0.4	1.2	2.0
Other Europe	1.7	0.8	2.9	0.7	1.4	0.7	-0.2	1.0	0.9	1.3	1.5
Iceland	6.7	5.0	12.7	12.0	5.4	4.0	5.2	3.9	2.8	2.6	2.5
Norway	2.5	0.7	3.4	2.3	2.3	1.3	0.4	2.0	1.9	1.7	1.7
Switzerland	1.0	0.8	2.3	-0.7	0.6	0.1	-0.7	0.2	0.1	0.9	1.3
Memorandum items											
North America	3.0	2.8	3.7	-0.2	1.6	3.2	2.0	1.4	1.9	1.6	1.6
Western Europe	2.2	2.2	3.5	0.8	1.9	2.9	2.4	1.5	0.7	1.2	1.7
Asia and Oceania	0.9	0.5	2.0	-0.7	0.0	0.4	0.3	0.8	2.7	1.4	1.6
Major developed economies	2.2	2.1	3.1	-0.1	1.3	2.5	1.8	1.3	1.7	1.4	1.6
Euro area	2.2	2.1	3.3	0.3	1.6	2.7	2.5	1.4	0.6	1.1	1.6

Sources: UN/DESA, based on OECD, Main Economic Indicators; Eurostat; and individual national sources.

a Data for country groups are weighted averages, where weights for each year are based on 2010 GDP in United States dollars.

b Partly estimated.

c Baseline scenario forecasts, based in part on Project LINK and the UN/DESA World Economic Forecasting Model.

Table A.5
Economies in transition: consumer price inflation, 2006–2016

Annual percentage change[a]

	2006	2007	2008	2009	2010	2011	2012	2013	2014[b]	2015[c]	2016[c]
Economies in Transition	9.4	9.4	14.9	10.9	7.0	9.5	6.1	6.3	8.1	7.4	5.7
South-Eastern Europe	6.6	4.0	8.3	4.7	4.7	5.5	4.6	4.3	1.2	2.3	2.6
Albania	2.4	2.9	3.3	2.3	3.6	3.4	2.1	1.9	1.5	2.1	2.5
Bosnia and Herzegovina	4.7	0.0	6.7	0.8	1.9	3.0	4.3	-0.1	-0.8	1.2	2.0
Montenegro	2.9	4.4	8.8	3.4	0.7	3.2	3.6	2.3	-0.5	1.5	2.5
Serbia	10.2	6.6	10.5	8.9	7.5	8.1	6.8	7.6	2.7	3.0	3.0
The former Yugoslav Republic of Macedonia	3.2	2.3	8.4	-0.8	1.5	3.1	-0.3	3.0	-0.5	2.0	2.5
Commonwealth of Independent States and Georgia[d]	9.5	9.6	15.2	11.2	7.1	9.7	6.2	6.4	8.4	7.6	5.8
Net fuel exporters	9.6	9.4	14.4	10.9	6.9	8.4	5.1	6.7	7.8	7.3	5.9
Azerbaijan	8.2	16.6	20.8	1.4	5.6	7.8	1.0	2.5	1.9	3.0	3.5
Kazakhstan	8.6	10.8	17.1	7.3	7.2	8.3	5.1	5.5	7.0	6.5	4.5
Russian Federation	9.7	9.0	14.0	11.7	6.9	8.4	5.0	6.8	8.0	7.5	6.0
Turkmenistan	8.2	6.3	14.5	-2.7	4.5	8.0	8.0	9.0	9.5	9.0	9.5
Uzbekistan	14.2	12.3	12.7	14.1	9.4	12.0	11.0	10.0	11.0	8.8	8.5
Net fuel importers	8.3	11.2	20.9	13.1	8.8	19.2	15.0	4.5	12.6	9.4	5.3
Armenia	2.9	4.4	8.9	3.4	8.2	7.7	2.6	6.0	3.5	4.0	2.9
Belarus	7.0	8.2	14.9	12.9	7.7	53.4	59.1	18.3	18.0	15.0	8.3
Georgia	9.1	9.3	10.0	1.7	7.1	8.5	-0.9	-0.5	3.5	4.5	3.0
Kyrgyzstan	5.6	10.1	24.5	6.9	8.0	16.4	2.7	6.9	6.8	6.5	4.5
Republic of Moldova	10.8	14.8	10.8	0.6	13.3	8.1	5.8	4.6	5.6	5.0	4.8
Tajikistan	10.0	13.4	20.9	6.4	6.4	12.4	5.8	5.6	6.0	6.5	5.5
Ukraine	9.1	12.8	25.3	15.8	9.4	7.9	0.6	-0.9	12.5	8.3	4.5

Source: UN/DESA, based on data of the Economic Commission for Europe.

a Data for country groups are weighted averages, where weights for each year are based on 2010 GDP in United States dollars.

b Partly estimated.

c Baseline scenario forecasts, based in part on Project LINK and the UN/DESA World Economic Forecasting Model.

d Georgia officially left the Commonwealth of Independent States on 18 August 2009. However, its performance is discussed in the context of this group of countries for reasons of geographic proximity and similarities in economic structure.

Table A.6
Developing economies: consumer price inflation, 2006–2016

Annual percentage change[a]

	2006	2007	2008	2009	2010	2011	2012	2013	2014[b]	2015[c]	2016[c]
Developing countries by region	4.8	5.7	8.3	3.9	5.5	6.7	5.6	5.8	5.7	5.3	5.0
Africa	6.1	6.6	11.7	8.1	7.2	8.5	8.9	7.2	6.9	6.9	6.8
North Africa	4.8	6.0	10.8	7.1	6.9	8.3	9.4	8.6	7.5	7.2	7.1
East Africa	11.1	11.4	22.7	9.5	6.1	17.7	13.6	5.9	5.9	6.2	6.0
Central Africa	4.4	0.9	6.7	4.5	2.5	2.0	5.2	2.7	3.6	2.8	2.9
West Africa	7.6	5.5	11.4	9.9	10.8	9.3	9.9	7.4	7.9	8.8	8.5
Southern Africa	5.7	7.4	10.6	8.4	6.1	6.7	6.7	6.3	6.2	6.0	5.9
Net fuel exporters	6.4	6.4	11.7	9.2	9.5	9.8	10.6	8.8	8.1	8.2	8.1
Net fuel importers	5.7	6.7	11.6	6.9	4.5	7.1	6.8	5.4	5.6	5.4	5.2
East and South Asia	3.7	5.3	7.6	2.6	5.0	6.4	4.8	5.3	3.8	3.7	3.8
East Asia	2.7	4.4	6.4	0.4	3.3	5.2	2.8	2.8	2.4	2.7	2.9
South Asia	7.1	8.6	12.5	11.2	11.5	11.1	12.2	14.7	9.2	7.8	7.2
Net fuel exporters	12.1	10.1	16.4	7.7	7.1	11.6	12.4	17.4	9.7	8.0	7.5
Net fuel importers	2.7	4.7	6.6	2.0	4.8	5.8	3.9	3.8	3.1	3.2	3.4
Western Asia	9.2	8.2	10.1	3.5	5.7	6.5	6.3	4.4	4.7	4.9	5.3
Net fuel exporters	10.4	9.7	10.4	2.2	4.9	7.1	4.4	2.8	3.2	3.9	4.1
Net fuel importers	7.8	6.5	9.6	5.1	6.7	5.7	8.7	6.3	6.4	6.1	6.7
Latin America and the Caribbean	5.1	5.1	7.8	5.9	6.1	6.8	6.0	7.2	10.2	8.8	7.0
South America	5.5	5.4	8.4	6.4	6.9	7.9	6.8	8.5	12.7	10.8	8.3
Mexico and Central America	4.0	4.4	5.9	5.1	4.2	3.7	4.1	3.9	3.8	3.7	3.8
Caribbean	5.0	4.3	7.6	2.2	4.8	4.6	3.3	3.2	2.5	2.8	3.1
Net fuel exporters	7.9	10.2	17.2	14.1	13.7	13.4	11.3	18.7	30.9	24.9	15.2
Net fuel importers	4.7	4.3	6.2	4.6	4.9	5.7	5.2	5.3	6.9	6.3	5.7
Memorandum items											
Least developed countries	9.8	11.1	14.8	7.7	8.9	12.0	12.2	10.1	8.5	7.4	7.3
Africa (excluding Libya)	6.3	6.6	11.7	8.4	7.4	8.2	9.0	7.4	7.0	6.9	6.8
North Africa (excluding Libya)	5.2	6.0	10.8	7.7	7.4	7.4	9.8	9.4	7.9	7.4	7.4
East Asia (excluding China)	5.0	3.7	7.0	2.1	3.3	4.6	3.2	3.0	3.0	3.1	3.3
South Asia (excluding India)	10.0	13.5	21.5	11.7	10.4	16.1	18.7	24.9	12.9	10.5	9.6
Western Asia (excluding Israel and Turkey)	10.2	9.2	10.8	2.2	4.7	7.0	5.7	3.2	3.1	3.8	4.2
Arab States[d]	8.5	8.2	10.8	3.7	5.4	7.4	6.9	4.9	4.5	4.9	5.1
Landlocked developing economies	8.5	9.8	16.6	6.5	6.2	9.9	7.1	5.7	6.1	5.9	5.3
Small island developing economies	2.7	3.0	6.8	1.5	3.5	4.7	3.8	2.6	1.8	2.4	2.6
Major developing economies	8.5	9.8	16.6	6.5	6.2	9.9	7.1	5.7	6.1	5.9	5.3
Argentina	10.9	8.9	8.5	6.2	10.5	9.8	10.0	10.9	25.0	19.0	15.3
Brazil	4.3	3.6	5.7	4.8	5.0	6.6	5.4	5.9	6.3	6.3	5.8
Chile	3.4	4.4	8.7	0.4	1.4	3.3	3.0	1.9	4.2	3.2	3.0
China	1.4	4.8	6.0	-0.7	3.3	5.5	2.6	2.7	2.1	2.4	2.7
Colombia	4.3	5.5	7.0	4.2	2.3	3.4	3.2	2.0	2.9	3.4	3.3
Egypt	7.6	9.3	18.3	11.8	11.3	10.1	7.1	9.5	10.0	10.1	9.9
Hong Kong SAR[e]	2.1	2.0	4.3	0.6	2.3	5.3	4.1	4.3	4.2	4.2	4.1
India	5.8	6.4	8.4	10.9	12.0	8.9	9.3	10.1	7.5	6.6	6.2

Table A.6
Developing economies: consumer price inflation, 2006–2016 (*continued*)

Annual percentage change[a]

	2006	2007	2008	2009	2010	2011	2012	2013	2014[b]	2015[c]	2016[c]
Indonesia	13.1	6.4	10.2	4.4	5.2	5.4	4.3	6.4	6.0	5.1	5.3
Iran (Islamic Republic of)	11.9	17.2	25.5	13.5	10.1	20.6	27.4	39.3	17.8	14.0	12.0
Israel	2.1	0.5	4.6	3.3	2.7	3.5	1.7	1.5	0.7	1.5	2.1
Republic of Korea	2.2	2.5	4.7	2.8	2.9	4.0	2.2	1.3	1.4	2.0	2.3
Malaysia	3.6	2.0	5.4	0.6	1.7	3.2	1.7	2.1	3.2	4.2	3.7
Mexico	3.6	4.0	5.1	5.3	4.2	3.4	4.1	3.8	3.8	3.6	3.7
Nigeria	8.2	5.4	11.6	11.5	13.7	10.8	12.2	8.5	8.5	10.2	9.9
Pakistan	7.9	7.6	20.3	13.6	13.9	11.9	9.7	7.7	7.7	6.8	7.2
Peru	2.0	1.8	5.8	2.9	1.5	3.4	3.7	2.8	3.4	2.7	3.0
Philippines	5.5	2.9	8.3	4.2	3.8	4.6	3.2	3.0	4.3	3.9	3.6
Saudi Arabia	2.3	4.1	10.0	5.0	5.4	5.8	2.9	3.5	3.0	3.7	4.0
Singapore	1.0	2.1	6.5	0.6	2.8	5.3	4.5	2.4	1.3	2.0	2.1
South Africa	3.2	6.1	10.1	7.3	4.1	5.0	5.8	5.7	5.9	5.7	5.6
Taiwan Province of China	0.6	1.8	3.5	-0.9	1.0	1.4	1.9	0.8	1.2	1.6	1.9
Thailand	4.6	2.2	5.5	-0.8	3.3	3.8	3.0	2.2	2.0	2.2	2.5
Turkey	9.6	8.8	10.4	6.3	8.6	6.5	8.9	7.5	8.9	8.2	8.5
Venezuela (Bolivarian Republic of)	12.8	16.9	29.8	27.1	28.2	26.1	21.1	40.6	68.0	53.2	30.6

Source:　UN/DESA, based on IMF, International Financial Statistics.

a Data for country groups are weighted averages, where weights are based on GDP in 2010 prices and exchange rates.

b Partly estimated.

c Baseline scenario forecasts, based in part on Project LINK and the UN/DESA World Economic Forecasting Model.

d Currently includes data for Algeria, Bahrain, Comoros, Djibouti, Egypt, Iraq, Jordan, Kuwait, Lebanon, Libya, Mauritania, Morocco, Oman, Qatar, Saudi Arabia, Somalia, Sudan, Syrian Arab Republic, Tunisia, United Arab Emirates and Yemen.

e Special Administrative Region of China.

Table A.7
Developed economies: unemployment rates,[a,b] 2006–2016

Percentage of labour force

	2006	2007	2008	2009	2010	2011	2012	2013	2014[c]	2015[d]	2016[d]
Developed economies	6.3	5.8	6.1	8.3	8.8	8.5	8.5	8.5	7.8	7.5	7.2
United States	4.6	4.6	5.8	9.3	9.6	8.9	8.1	7.4	6.2	5.8	5.5
Canada	6.3	6.0	6.1	8.3	8.0	7.5	7.1	7.0	6.9	6.7	6.4
Japan	4.1	3.8	4.0	5.1	5.1	4.6	4.4	4.0	3.5	3.3	3.5
Australia	4.8	4.4	4.2	5.6	5.2	5.1	5.2	5.7	6.8	6.6	6.1
New Zealand	3.9	3.7	4.2	6.1	6.5	6.5	6.9	6.1	5.7	5.3	5.1
European Union	8.3	7.2	7.0	8.9	9.6	9.6	10.4	10.8	10.3	10.0	9.6
EU-15	7.8	7.1	7.2	9.1	9.5	9.6	10.5	11.0	10.5	10.2	9.9
Austria	4.8	4.4	3.8	4.8	4.4	4.1	4.4	4.9	5.0	5.0	5.0
Belgium	8.3	7.5	7.0	7.9	8.3	7.2	7.6	8.5	8.6	8.4	8.1
Denmark	3.9	3.8	3.5	6.0	7.5	7.6	7.5	6.9	6.3	5.9	5.6
Finland	7.7	6.9	6.4	8.2	8.4	7.8	7.6	8.1	8.5	8.2	7.7
France	8.9	8.0	7.5	9.1	9.3	9.2	9.8	10.3	10.2	10.2	9.9
Germany	10.3	8.7	7.5	7.8	7.1	6.0	5.5	5.3	5.1	5.2	5.1
Greece	9.0	8.4	7.8	9.6	12.8	17.9	24.5	27.5	26.8	25.9	24.3
Ireland	4.5	4.7	6.4	12.0	13.9	14.6	14.6	13.0	11.4	10.2	10.1
Italy	6.8	6.1	6.7	7.8	8.4	8.4	10.7	12.2	12.6	12.9	12.7
Luxembourg	4.3	4.2	5.4	5.1	4.2	5.0	5.2	6.0	6.2	6.3	6.1
Netherlands	4.3	3.6	3.1	3.7	4.5	4.5	5.3	6.7	7.0	6.7	6.5
Portugal	8.6	8.9	8.5	10.6	12.0	12.9	15.8	16.4	14.4	13.3	12.9
Spain	8.5	8.2	11.3	17.9	19.9	21.4	24.8	26.1	24.6	23.1	21.6
Sweden	7.0	6.1	6.2	8.3	8.6	7.8	8.0	8.0	7.9	7.5	7.2
United Kingdom	5.4	5.3	5.7	7.6	7.8	8.0	7.9	7.5	6.4	6.0	6.0
New EU member States	10.1	7.7	6.5	8.4	9.9	9.8	9.9	10.1	9.4	9.0	8.5
Bulgaria	8.9	6.9	5.6	6.8	10.2	11.3	12.3	12.9	12.0	11.4	10.1
Croatia	11.1	9.6	8.4	9.1	11.8	13.4	15.8	17.7	17.5	16.8	15.5
Cyprus	4.5	3.8	3.6	5.4	6.3	8.0	11.8	15.9	16.5	16.2	15.9
Czech Republic	7.1	5.3	4.4	6.7	7.3	6.7	7.0	7.0	6.5	6.1	5.6
Estonia	5.9	4.6	5.5	13.6	16.7	12.4	10.0	08.6	7.8	7.0	6.5
Hungary	7.5	7.4	7.8	10.0	11.2	11.0	10.9	10.2	8.0	7.6	7.5
Latvia	6.8	6.0	7.4	17.1	18.7	16.2	14.9	11.1	11.0	10.5	10.3
Lithuania	5.7	4.3	5.7	13.6	17.8	15.2	13.2	11.8	11.0	10.4	10.2
Malta	6.5	6.3	5.7	6.7	6.6	6.5	6.3	6.3	4.6	4.5	4.5
Poland	14.0	9.6	7.0	8.1	9.7	9.7	10.1	10.3	9.9	9.5	9.0
Romania	7.3	6.4	5.8	6.9	7.3	7.4	7.0	7.3	6.8	6.5	6.4
Slovakia	13.5	11.2	9.6	12.1	14.5	13.7	14.0	14.2	13.5	13.1	12.6
Slovenia	6.0	4.9	4.4	5.9	7.3	8.2	8.9	10.1	8.6	8.0	7.5
Other Europe	3.7	3.2	3.1	3.9	4.2	3.8	3.8	4.0	3.9	3.9	3.8
Iceland[e]	2.8	2.2	3.2	7.1	7.5	6.9	5.8	5.2	3.5	3.6	3.7
Norway	3.4	2.5	2.6	3.2	3.6	3.3	3.2	3.5	3.4	3.7	3.6
Switzerland	3.9	3.6	3.3	4.2	4.4	3.9	4.0	4.2	4.2	4.0	3.9
Memorandum items											
Major developed economies	5.8	5.4	5.9	8.0	8.2	7.6	7.4	7.1	6.4	6.2	6.0
Euro area	8.4	7.5	7.6	9.6	10.1	10.1	11.3	11.9	11.6	11.3	10.9

Source: UN/DESA, based on data of the OECD and Eurostat.

a Unemployment data are standardized by the OECD and Eurostat for comparability among countries and over time, in conformity with the definitions of the International Labour Organization (see OECD, Standardized Unemployment Rates: Sources and Methods (Paris, 1985)).

b Data for country groups are weighted averages, where labour force is used for weights.

c Partly estimated.

d Baseline scenario forecasts, based in part on Project LINK and the UN/DESA World Economic Forecasting Model.

e Not standardized.

Table A.8
Economies in transition and developing economies: unemployment rates,[a] 2005–2014

Percentage of labour force

	2005	2006	2007	2008	2009	2010	2011	2012	2013	2014[b]
South-Eastern Europe										
Albania[c]	14.1	13.8	13.4	13.1	13.8	14.0	14.0	13.3	15.6	17.7
Bosnia and Herzegovina	..	31.1	29.0	23.4	24.1	27.2	27.6	28.0	27.5	27.5
Montenegro	30.3	29.6	19.4	16.8	19.1	19.7	19.7	19.7	19.5	18.8
Serbia	20.8	20.9	18.1	13.6	16.1	19.2	23.0	23.9	22.1	20.5
The former Yugoslav Republic of Macedonia	37.3	36.0	34.9	33.8	32.2	32.1	31.4	31.0	29.0	28.3
Commonwealth of Independent States and Georgia[d]										
Armenia	31.2	27.8	28.7	16.4	18.7	19.0	18.4	17.3	16.5	17.4
Azerbaijan	7.6	6.8	6.5	6.0	5.9	5.6	5.4	5.4	5.5	5.2
Belarus[c]	1.5	1.1	1.0	0.8	0.9	0.7	0.6	0.5	0.5	0.5
Georgia	13.8	13.6	13.3	16.5	16.9	16.3	15.1	15.0	14.6	..
Kazakhstan	8.1	7.8	7.3	6.6	6.6	5.8	5.4	5.3	5.2	5.0
Kyrgyzstan	3.3	3.5	3.3	2.8	2.8	2.5	2.6	2.5	2.5	2.5
Republic of Moldova	7.3	7.6	5.1	4.0	6.4	7.5	6.8	5.6	5.2	4.4
Russian Federation	7.1	7.0	6.0	6.2	8.2	7.3	6.5	5.5	5.5	5.1
Tajikistan[c]	2.1	2.3	2.5	2.1	2.1	2.2	2.1	2.6	2.5	2.5
Turkmenistan[c]	3.7	..	3.6	2.5	2.2	2.0	2.3	2.1	2.0	2.0
Ukraine	7.2	7.4	6.6	6.4	8.8	8.1	8.0	7.7	8.0	9.2
Uzbekistan[c]	0.3	0.3	0.2	0.2	0.2	0.2	0.2	0.2	0.2	0.2
Africa										
Algeria	15.3	12.3	13.8	11.3	10.2	10.0	10.0	11.0	9.8	9.8
Botswana	..	17.6	20.2	..	..	17.8	..	..	..	..
Egypt	11.2	10.7	8.9	8.7	9.4	9.0	12.0	12.6	13.3	13.2
Mauritius	9.6	9.1	8.5	7.2	7.3	7.8	7.9	8.0	8.3	..
Morocco	11.1	9.7	9.8	9.6	9.1	9.1	8.9	9.0	9.2	9.7
South Africa	26.6	25.5	23.3	22.9	24.0	24.9	24.9	24.9	24.7	25.4
Tunisia	12.9	12.5	12.4	12.4	13.3	13.0	18.3	16.9	15.8	15.3
Developing America										
Argentina[e]	11.6	10.2	8.5	7.9	8.7	7.7	7.2	7.6	6.8	7.5
Barbados	9.1	8.7	7.4	8.1	10.0	10.7	11.2	11.6	11.6	..
Bolivia[e] (Plurinational State of)	8.1	8.0	7.7	6.7	7.9	6.1	5.8	..	..	..
Brazil[f]	9.8	10.0	9.3	7.9	8.1	6.7	6.0	5.5	5.4	4.9
Chile	9.2	7.8	7.1	7.8	9.7	8.3	7.2	6.5	6.0	6.4
Colombia[g]	13.9	12.9	11.4	11.5	13.0	12.4	11.5	10.4	9.6	9.4
Costa Rica	6.9	6.0	4.8	4.8	8.5	7.1	7.7	7.8	9.2	9.7
Dominican Republic	17.9	16.2	15.6	14.1	14.9	14.3	14.6	14.7	15.0	..
Ecuador[h]	8.5	8.1	7.3	6.9	8.5	7.6	6.0	4.9	4.7	5.7
El Salvador	7.3	5.7	5.8	5.5	7.3	7.0	6.6	6.2	..	..
Guatemala	..	..	..	..	..	4.8	3.1	4.0	..	..
Honduras	6.1	4.6	3.9	4.2	4.9	6.4	6.8	5.6	3.6	..
Jamaica	11.2	10.3	9.8	10.6	11.4	12.4	12.6	13.9	15.5	13.6
Mexico	4.7	4.6	4.8	4.9	6.6	6.4	6.0	4.9	4.9	5.0
Nicaragua[i]	5.6	5.2	5.9	6.1	8.2	7.8	5.9	5.9	5.9	..

Table A.8

Economies in transition and developing economies: unemployment rates,[a] 2005–2014 (*continued*)

Percentage of labour force

	2005	2006	2007	2008	2009	2010	2011	2012	2013	2014[b]
Panama	12.1	10.4	7.8	6.5	7.9	7.7	5.4	4.8	5.1	3.1
Paraguay[f]	7.6	8.9	7.2	7.4	8.2	7.2	7.1	8.0	8.1	8.8
Peru[j]	9.6	8.5	8.4	8.4	8.4	7.9	7.7	6.8	5.9	6.0
Trinidad and Tobago	8.0	6.2	5.5	4.6	5.3	5.9	5.1	5.2	3.8	..
Uruguay[e]	12.2	10.8	9.4	8.0	7.7	7.2	6.3	6.5	6.5	6.6
Venezuela (Bolivarian Republic of)	12.3	10.6	8.4	7.3	7.9	8.7	8.3	8.1	8.1	..
Developing Asia										
China	4.2	4.1	4.0	4.2	4.3	4.1	4.1	4.1	4.1	4.1
Hong Kong SAR[k]	5.6	4.8	4.0	3.5	5.3	4.3	3.4	3.3	3.4	3.3
India[l]	..	..	..	..	9.4	..	3.8	4.7	..	..
Indonesia	10.8	10.4	9.4	8.4	8.0	7.3	6.7	6.2	6.0	5.8
Iran (Islamic Republic of)	11.5	11.3	10.6	10.5	12.0	13.5	12.3	12.1	10.4	..
Israel	9.0	8.4	7.3	6.1	7.6	6.6	5.6	6.9	6.2	5.9
Jordan	14.8	14.0	13.1	12.7	12.9	12.5	12.9	12.2	12.6	11.7
Republic of Korea	3.7	3.5	3.2	3.2	3.6	3.7	3.4	3.2	3.1	3.6
Malaysia	3.5	3.3	3.2	3.3	3.7	3.3	3.1	3.0	3.1	2.9
Pakistan	..	6.1	5.1	5.0	5.2	5.3	5.7	..	6.0	..
Philippines[m]	9.8	7.9	7.3	7.4	7.5	7.3	7.0	7.0	7.1	7.1
Saudi Arabia	6.1	6.3	6.1	6.3	6.3	6.2	5.9	5.6	5.6	6.0
Singapore	3.1	2.7	2.1	2.2	3.0	2.2	2.0	2.0	1.9	2.0
Sri Lanka[n]	7.2	6.5	6.0	5.2	5.7	4.9	4.0	4.0	4.4	4.1
Taiwan Province of China	4.1	3.9	3.9	4.1	5.9	5.2	4.4	4.2	4.2	4.0
Thailand	1.8	1.5	1.4	1.4	1.5	1.1	0.7	0.7	0.7	0.9
Turkey[o]	9.5	9.0	9.2	10.0	13.1	11.1	9.1	8.4	9.0	9.6
Viet Nam[e]	5.3	4.8	4.6	4.7	4.6	4.3	6.6	3.2	3.6	3.6

Sources: UN/DESA, based on data of the Economic Commission for Europe (ECE); ILO LABORSTAT database and KILM 8th edition; Economic Commission for Latin America and the Caribbean (ECLAC); and national sources.

a As a percentage of labour force. Reflects national definitions and coverage. Not comparable across economies.

b Partly estimated.

c End-of-period registered unemployment data (as a percentage of labour force).

d Georgia officially left the Commonwealth of Independent States on 18 August 2009. However, its performance is discussed in the context of this group of countries for reasons of geographic proximity and similarities in economic structure.

e Urban areas.

f Six main cities.

g Thirteen main cities.

h Covers Quito, Guayaquil and Cuenca.

i Break in series; new methology starting in 2010.

j Metropolitan Lima.

k Special Administrative Region of China.

l Data for 2011 and 2012 refer to the fiscal year.

m Partly adopts the ILO definition; that is to say, it does not include one ILO criterion, namely, "currently available for work".

n Excluding Northern and Eastern provinces.

o Data based on a new methodology starting from February 2014 onward.

Table A.9
Major developed economies: quarterly indicators of growth, unemployment and inflation, 2012–2014

Percentage

	2012				2013				2014		
	I	II	III	IV	I	II	III	IV	I	II	III
Growth of gross domestic product[a] (*percentage change in seasonally adjusted data from preceding quarter*)											
Canada	0.9	1.7	0.7	0.7	3.2	2.0	2.7	2.9	1.0	3.6	2.8
France	0.9	-1.0	1.0	-1.0	0.0	2.7	-0.4	0.8	0.1	-0.4	1.1
Germany	1.3	0.5	0.3	-1.6	-1.6	3.2	1.2	1.8	3.1	-0.3	0.3
Italy	-3.4	-1.7	-1.6	-3.1	-3.4	-0.8	-0.1	-0.5	0.1	-0.9	-0.4
Japan	4.5	-2.4	-2.2	-1.2	5.6	3.2	2.4	-1.6	6.7	-7.3	-1.6
United Kingdom	0.3	-0.7	3.4	-1.3	2.1	2.7	3.5	2.5	3.0	3.7	2.8
United States	2.2	1.6	2.5	0.1	2.7	1.8	4.5	3.5	-2.1	4.6	3.9
Major developed economies[b]	1.8	0.3	1.1	-0.7	2.1	2.1	3.0	1.9	0.7	1.2	2.0
Euro area	-0.4	-1.0	-0.4	-1.9	-1.3	1.3	0.6	1.0	1.2	0.3	0.6
Unemployment rate[c] (*percentage of total labour force*)											
Canada	7.4	7.3	7.3	7.2	7.1	7.1	7.1	7.0	7.0	7.0	6.9
France	9.5	9.7	9.8	10.2	10.3	10.3	10.3	10.2	10.1	10.2	10.5
Germany	5.5	5.5	5.4	5.4	5.4	5.3	5.3	5.2	5.1	5.1	5.0
Italy	10.0	10.6	10.8	11.3	11.9	12.2	12.3	12.5	12.6	12.5	12.6
Japan	4.5	4.4	4.3	4.2	4.2	4.0	4.0	3.9	3.6	3.6	3.6
United Kingdom	8.2	7.9	7.8	7.7	7.8	7.7	7.6	7.1	6.7	6.3	
United States	8.2	8.2	8.0	7.8	7.7	7.5	7.2	7.0	6.7	6.2	6.1
Major developed economies[d]	7.4	7.4	7.3	7.3	7.3	7.2	7.0	6.9	6.6	6.4	
Euro area	10.8	11.2	11.4	11.7	12.0	12.0	12.0	11.9	11.7	11.6	11.5
Change in consumer prices (*percentage change from one year ago*)											
Canada	2.3	1.6	1.2	0.9	0.9	0.8	1.1	0.9	1.4	2.2	2.1
France	2.6	2.3	2.3	1.7	1.2	0.9	1.1	0.8	0.9	0.8	0.5
Germany	2.4	2.1	2.1	2.0	1.8	1.5	1.7	1.3	1.0	0.9	0.8
Italy	3.6	3.6	3.4	2.6	2.1	1.3	1.1	0.7	0.5	0.4	-0.1
Japan	0.3	0.2	-0.4	-0.2	-0.6	-0.3	0.9	1.4	1.5	3.6	3.3
United Kingdom	3.5	2.7	2.4	2.7	2.8	2.7	2.7	2.1	1.8	1.7	1.5
United States	2.8	1.9	1.7	1.9	1.7	1.4	1.6	1.2	1.4	2.1	1.8
Major developed economies[b]	2.4	1.8	1.6	1.6	1.3	1.1	1.4	1.3	1.3	2.0	1.7
Euro area	2.7	2.5	2.5	2.3	1.9	1.4	1.3	0.8	0.6	0.6	0.4

Source: UN/DESA, based on Eurostat, OECD and national sources.

a Expressed as an annualized rate.

b Calculated as a weighted average, where weights are based on 2010 GDP in United States dollars.

c Seasonally adjusted data as standardized by OECD.

d Calculated as a weighted average, where weights are based on labour force.

Table A.10
Selected economies in transition: quarterly indicators of growth and inflation, 2012–2014

Percentage

	2012				2013				2014		
	I	II	III	IV	I	II	III	IV	I	II	III
Rates of growth of gross domestic product[a]											
Armenia	5.2	7.2	9.1	6.3	7.9	0.8	1.5	5.1	3.1	2.3	..
Azerbaijan[b]	0.5	1.5	1.1	2.2	3.1	5.0	5.4	5.8	2.5	2.1	2.5
Belarus	3.0	2.5	2.6	-2.0	4.0	-0.5	0.8	0.0	0.7	1.6	2.0
Bosnia and Herzegovina	-1.5	-0.7	-1.5	-1.1	3.2	2.0	1.5	2.0	2.7	-1.2	..
Georgia	6.6	8.2	7.5	3.0	2.4	1.5	1.4	7.1	7.5	5.2	5.5
Kazakhstan[b]	5.6	5.6	5.2	5.0	4.7	5.1	5.7	5.9	3.8	3.9	..
Kyrgyzstan[b]	-8.4	-6.9	-5.6	-0.9	7.6	7.9	9.2	13.1	5.6	4.1	3.0
Republic of Moldova	1.0	0.7	-1.6	-2.4	3.0	6.0	12.9	11.3	3.6	4.2	..
Russian Federation	4.8	4.3	3.0	2.1	1.6	1.2	1.2	2.0	0.9	0.8	..
The former Yugoslav Republic of Macedonia	-1.3	-0.9	0.4	1.0	-0.5	1.3	2.9	4.5	3.5	4.3	
Ukraine	**2.5**	**3.1**	**-1.3**	**-2.3**	**-1.2**	**-1.3**	**-1.2**	**3.3**	**-1.2**	**-4.6**	**-5.1**
Change in consumer prices[a]											
Armenia	3.3	1.0	2.4	3.4	3.0	5.2	8.7	6.4	4.6	3.3	0.9
Azerbaijan	3.0	1.2	0.0	-0.2	1.1	2.7	3.0	2.9	2.0	1.3	1.5
Belarus	107.8	82.4	52.3	24.8	22.6	19.4	16.0	15.9	15.7	19.0	..
Bosnia and Herzegovina	2.3	2.1	1.8	2.0	0.8	0.4	0.0	-1.0	-1.6	-1.4	-0.5
Georgia	-1.3	-1.9	0.0	-0.6	-1.9	-0.5	-0.6	1.0	3.3	2.6	..
Kazakhstan	5.1	4.9	4.8	5.7	6.8	6.1	5.7	4.6	5.2	6.6	7.1
Kyrgyzstan	1.9	-0.3	2.1	7.1	7.7	7.9	6.7	4.2	4.7	8.0	7.6
Republic of Moldova	6.2	4.1	4.4	3.9	4.4	5.2	4.0	4.9	5.4	5.2	..
Russian Federation	3.9	3.8	6.0	6.5	7.1	7.2	6.4	6.4	6.4	7.5	7.7
The former Yugoslav Republic of Macedonia	2.4	2.2	3.7	4.9	3.5	3.6	2.8	1.3	0.6	-0.9	..
Ukraine	2.9	-0.4	0.0	-0.1	-0.5	-0.4	-0.3	0.2	1.7	9.9	..

Source: UN/DESA, based on data of the Economic Commission for Europe, European Bank for Reconstruction and Development and national sources.

a Percentage change from the corresponding period of the preceding year.

b Data reflect growth rate of cumulative GDP from the beginning of the year.

Table A.11

Major developing economies: quarterly indicators of growth, unemployment and inflation, 2012–2014

Percentage

	2012				2013				2014		
	I	II	III	IV	I	II	III	IV	I	II	III
Rates of growth of gross domestic product[a]											
Argentina	4.6	-1.5	0.2	0.9	1.5	5.5	3.4	1.3	0.3	0.0	..
Brazil	0.8	0.6	0.9	1.8	1.9	3.5	2.4	2.2	1.9	-0.9	-0.2
Chile	5.1	5.8	5.5	5.2	4.9	3.8	5.0	2.7	2.7	1.9	0.8
China	8.1	7.8	7.7	7.8	7.7	7.6	7.7	7.7	7.4	7.5	7.3
Colombia	6.0	5.1	2.5	2.7	3.0	4.5	5.8	5.4	6.5	4.3	..
Ecuador	6.7	5.6	4.3	4.3	3.6	4.2	5.6	5.2	4.6	3.5	..
Hong Kong SAR[b]	0.7	0.8	1.6	2.9	2.9	3.0	3.0	2.9	2.6	1.8	2.7
India	5.8	4.5	4.6	4.4	4.4	4.7	5.2	4.6	4.6	5.7	5.3
Indonesia	6.3	6.3	6.2	6.2	6.0	5.8	5.6	5.7	5.2	5.1	5.0
Israel	3.7	2.7	2.7	2.7	2.3	5.2	2.2	3.7	3.9	1.8	2.5
Republic of Korea	2.6	2.4	2.1	2.1	2.1	2.7	3.4	3.7	3.9	3.5	3.2
Malaysia	5.1	5.7	5.2	6.5	4.2	4.5	5.0	5.1	6.2	6.5	5.6
Mexico	4.8	4.5	3.2	3.6	1.0	1.8	1.6	1.1	1.9	1.6	2.2
Philippines	6.4	6.3	7.3	7.2	7.7	7.9	7.0	6.3	5.6	6.4	5.3
Singapore	1.5	2.3	0.0	1.5	0.3	4.2	5.0	4.9	4.8	2.4	2.4
South Africa	2.2	2.8	2.1	1.8	1.8	2.2	1.8	2.9	1.9	1.3	1.4
Taiwan Province of China	0.5	0.1	1.4	3.9	1.4	2.7	1.3	2.9	3.2	3.7	3.8
Thailand	0.4	4.4	3.1	19.1	5.4	2.9	2.7	0.6	-0.5	0.4	0.6
Turkey	3.1	2.7	1.5	1.3	3.1	4.6	4.2	4.5	4.7	2.1	..
Venezuela (Bolivarian Republic of)	5.9	5.6	5.5	5.5	0.8	2.6	1.1	1.0	..	..	..
Unemployment rate[c]											
Argentina	7.1	7.2	7.6	6.9	7.9	7.2	6.8	6.4	7.1	7.5	7.5
Brazil	5.8	5.9	5.4	4.9	5.6	5.9	5.4	4.7	5.0	4.9	4.9
Chile	6.5	6.6	6.5	6.3	6.1	6.3	5.7	5.7	6.2	6.3	6.6
Colombia	11.6	10.5	10.2	9.2	11.4	9.6	9.4	8.2	10.5	9.0	8.8
Ecuador	4.9	5.2	4.6	5.0	4.6	4.9	4.6	4.9	5.6	5.7	4.7
Hong Kong SAR[b]	3.3	3.3	3.5	3.1	3.5	3.4	3.5	3.1	3.1	3.3	3.4
Israel	6.9	6.8	6.8	6.9	6.6	6.7	5.9	5.8	5.8	6.1	6.4
Republic of Korea	3.8	3.3	3.0	2.8	3.6	3.1	3.0	2.8	4.0	3.7	3.3
Malaysia	3.0	3.0	3.0	3.1	3.1	3.0	3.1	3.2	3.1	2.7	2.7
Mexico	4.9	4.8	5.1	4.9	4.9	5.0	5.2	4.6	4.8	4.9	5.2
Philippines	7.2	6.9	7.0	6.8	7.1	7.5	7.3	6.5	7.5	7.0	6.7
Singapore	2.1	2.0	1.9	1.8	1.9	2.0	1.8	1.8	2.0	2.0	1.9
South Africa	25.0	24.8	25.2	24.5	25.0	25.3	24.5	24.1	25.2	25.5	25.4
Taiwan Province of China	4.2	4.1	4.3	4.3	4.2	4.1	4.3	4.2	4.0	3.9	4.0
Thailand	0.7	0.9	0.6	0.5	0.7	0.7	0.7	0.8	0.9	1.0	0.8
Turkey[d]	10.2	8.4	8.8	9.5	10.4	9.0	9.7	9.9	9.2	9.6	..
Uruguay	6.1	6.8	6.6	6.0	6.7	6.6	6.3	6.2	6.7	6.8	6.2

Table A.11

Major developing economies: quarterly indicators of growth, unemployment and inflation, 2012–2014 (*continued*)

Percentage

	2012				2013				2014		
	I	II	III	IV	I	II	III	IV	I	II	III
Venezuela (Bolivarian Republic of)	9.1	8.0	7.7	6.5	8.2	7.8	7.9	7.0	8.4	7.2	..
Change in consumer prices[a]											
Argentina[e]	..	..	..	..	..	..	..	..	10.0	15.0	19.8
Brazil	5.8	5.0	5.2	5.6	6.3	6.5	6.1	5.8	5.8	6.4	6.6
Chile	4.1	3.1	2.6	2.2	1.5	1.3	2.1	2.3	3.2	4.4	4.6
China	3.8	2.9	1.9	2.1	2.4	2.4	2.8	2.9	2.3	2.2	2.0
Colombia	3.5	3.4	3.1	2.8	1.9	2.1	2.3	1.8	2.3	2.8	2.9
Ecuador	5.6	5.1	5.1	4.6	3.5	2.9	2.1	2.3	3.0	3.4	4.2
Hong Kong SAR[b]	5.2	4.2	3.0	3.7	3.7	4.0	5.3	4.3	4.1	3.7	4.8
India[f]	8.6	10.2	9.9	10.1	10.7	9.5	9.7	10.4	8.4	8.1	7.4
Indonesia	3.7	4.5	4.5	4.4	5.3	5.6	8.6	8.4	7.8	7.1	4.4
Israel	1.8	1.6	1.8	1.6	1.4	1.2	1.6	1.9	1.3	0.8	0.0
Republic of Korea	3.0	2.4	1.6	1.7	1.6	1.2	1.4	1.1	1.1	1.6	1.4
Malaysia	2.3	1.7	1.3	1.3	1.5	1.8	2.2	3.0	3.4	3.3	3.0
Mexico	3.9	3.9	4.6	4.1	3.7	4.5	3.4	3.7	4.2	3.6	4.1
Philippines	3.1	2.9	3.5	2.9	3.2	2.7	2.4	3.4	4.1	4.3	4.7
Singapore	4.9	5.3	4.2	4.0	4.0	1.6	1.8	2.0	1.0	2.4	0.9
South Africa	5.8	5.4	4.9	5.4	5.5	5.2	5.9	5.3	5.8	6.3	6.2
Taiwan Province of China	1.3	1.6	2.9	1.8	1.8	0.8	0.0	0.5	0.8	1.6	1.5
Thailand	3.4	2.5	2.9	3.2	3.1	2.3	1.7	1.7	2.0	2.5	2.0
Turkey	10.5	9.4	9.0	6.8	7.2	7.0	8.3	7.5	8.0	9.4	9.2
Venezuela (Bolivarian Republic of)	25.3	22.6	18.5	18.7	23.4	34.8	45.8	56.2	57.7	61.0	..

Sources: IMF, International Financial Statistics, and national sources.

a Percentage change from the corresponding quarter of the previous year.

b Special Administrative Region of China.

c Reflects national definitions and coverage. Not comparable across economies.

d Data based on a new statistics available from 2011 onward.

e In December 2013, Argentina launched a new national consumer price index. The numbers reported correspond to the accumulated variation of the index since that date. No matching data for the period before December 2013 were released.

f Data based on new statistics available from 2011 onward.

Table A.12

Major developed economies: financial indicators, 2005–2014

Percentage

	2005	2006	2007	2008	2009	2010	2011	2012	2013	2014[a]
Short-term interest rates[b]										
Canada	2.8	4.2	4.6	3.3	0.7	0.8	1.2	1.2	1.2	1.2
France[c]	2.2	3.1	4.3	4.6	1.2	0.8	1.4	0.6	0.2	0.2
Germany[c]	2.2	3.1	4.3	4.6	1.2	0.8	1.4	0.6	0.2	0.2
Italy[c]	2.2	3.1	4.3	4.6	1.2	0.8	1.4	0.6	0.2	0.2
Japan	0.1	0.3	0.7	0.8	0.6	0.4	0.3	0.3	0.2	0.2
United Kingdom	4.7	4.8	6.0	5.5	1.2	0.7	0.9	0.8	0.5	0.5
United States	3.5	5.2	5.3	3.0	0.6	0.3	0.3	0.3	0.2	0.1
Long-term interest rates[d]										
Canada	4.1	4.2	4.3	3.6	3.2	3.2	2.8	1.9	2.3	2.3
France	3.4	3.8	4.3	4.2	3.6	3.1	3.3	2.5	2.2	1.8
Germany	3.4	3.8	4.2	4.0	3.2	2.7	2.6	1.5	1.6	1.3
Italy	3.6	4.0	4.5	4.7	4.3	4.0	5.4	5.5	4.3	3.0
Japan	1.4	1.7	1.7	1.5	1.3	1.1	1.1	0.8	0.7	0.6
United Kingdom	4.4	4.5	5.0	4.6	3.6	3.6	3.1	1.9	2.5	2.7
United States	4.3	4.8	4.6	3.7	3.3	3.2	2.8	1.8	2.4	2.6
General government financial balances[e]										
Canada	1.7	1.8	1.5	-0.3	-4.5	-4.9	-3.7	-3.4	-3.0	-2.1
France	-3.0	-2.4	-2.7	-3.3	-7.5	-7.0	-5.2	-4.9	-4.3	-3.8
Germany	-3.3	-1.7	0.2	-0.1	-3.1	-4.2	-0.8	0.1	0.0	-0.2
Italy	-4.5	-3.4	-1.6	-2.7	-5.4	-4.4	-3.6	-2.9	-2.8	-2.7
Japan	-4.8	-1.3	-2.1	-1.9	-8.8	-8.3	-8.8	-8.7	-9.3	-8.4
United Kingdom	-3.4	-2.9	-3.0	-5.1	-11.2	-10.0	-7.9	-6.3	-5.9	-5.3
United States	-4.2	-3.1	-3.7	-7.2	-12.8	-12.2	-10.7	-9.3	-6.4	-5.8

Sources: UN/DESA, based on OECD, Economic Outlook; OECD, Main Economic Indicators and Eurostat.

a Average for the first nine months for short- and long-term interest rates.

b Three-month Interbank Rate.

c Three-month Euro Interbank Offered Rate (EURIBOR).

d Yield on 10-year government bonds.

e Surplus (+) or deficit (-) as a percentage of nominal GDP. Estimates for 2014.

Table A.13
Selected economies: real effective exchange rates, broad measurement,[a, b] 2005–2014

	2005	2006	2007	2008	2009	2010	2011	2012	2013	2014[c]
Developed economies										
Australia	128.0	133.4	142.4	141.5	130.1	146.5	156.4	158.4	154.2	149.1
Bulgaria	116.6	126.8	133.6	143.7	140.2	143.5	151.3	152.7	153.1	152.7
Canada	108.0	111.6	112.4	103.2	95.0	101.7	100.3	98.0	95.0	88.4
Croatia	115.3	116.2	117.5	125.5	128.0	128.0	128.0	130.5	132.3	130.1
Czech Republic	129.5	133.7	139.3	157.4	149.4	150.1	156.1	151.2	150.0	142.1
Denmark	112.1	110.2	110.1	111.3	117.6	112.8	110.7	108.7	112.1	113.7
Euro area	119.6	120.6	125.3	130.6	125.6	118.1	120.2	114.8	120.2	120.7
Hungary	119.4	115.9	120.1	122.6	119.3	119.1	117.4	114.5	114.9	111.0
Japan	79.0	72.0	67.1	73.6	83.4	83.6	85.3	84.2	68.6	66.1
New Zealand	147.1	135.7	146.0	134.5	127.4	139.6	145.5	152.7	162.6	170.2
Norway	117.2	122.9	132.1	134.5	129.6	139.9	146.4	146.5	143.4	139.0
Poland	111.4	113.7	117.7	126.5	109.6	114.6	114.5	113.1	113.2	113.3
Romania	153.9	171.7	191.4	181.9	174.0	175.8	177.6	168.6	180.4	182.7
Slovakia	117.3	118.6	128.8	132.3	141.5	130.2	125.2	122.5	124.9	124.9
Sweden	93.4	94.3	97.7	92.0	89.4	92.4	92.4	90.6	91.4	90.0
Switzerland	106.1	101.5	96.6	98.8	107.1	110.0	118.3	114.1	114.1	115.6
United Kingdom	97.4	97.2	99.2	87.5	79.2	78.8	78.7	82.5	82.3	87.7
United States	89.2	86.7	82.6	79.3	87.7	83.2	78.3	82.2	85.9	88.8
Economies in transition										
Russian Federation	154.8	170.5	180.2	193.0	182.6	199.0	205.1	210.9	219.7	206.9
Developing economies										
Argentina	60.1	58.5	57.8	58.9	57.6	57.6	56.0	59.6	56.9	47.7
Brazil	129.7	140.8	155.6	175.2	168.3	192.9	207.9	190.1	188.4	187.9
Chile	111.7	117.9	117.2	122.7	126.9	126.4	127.7	132.6	128.2	113.9
China	98.2	101.1	103.3	112.3	112.5	113.6	116.6	119.6	126.0	125.0
Colombia	104.8	102.7	110.3	114.3	107.7	124.2	123.7	126.7	120.8	114.1
Ecuador	121.1	130.6	125.9	136.6	111.0	128.1	141.4	143.1	146.2	145.9
Egypt	72.2	74.3	76.6	86.9	85.6	92.5	92.8	96.3	87.3	89.2
Hong Kong SAR[d]	86.4	84.1	80.1	75.7	80.6	77.7	74.4	77.2	79.5	80.5
India	101.3	99.2	106.3	99.4	94.3	100.8	98.2	92.1	87.5	86.6
Indonesia	113.8	142.0	149.3	162.7	163.3	184.3	184.0	182.3	178.6	173.3
Israel	86.4	86.9	88.0	98.2	97.7	103.0	103.4	99.3	107.8	111.4
Republic of Korea	105.6	110.7	108.4	91.4	79.7	86.5	88.9	88.7	93.5	98.5
Kuwait	96.4	95.4	93.3	97.3	96.7	98.4	96.6	99.2	103.6	105.4
Malaysia	103.3	107.0	112.7	115.6	113.1	124.5	131.1	132.0	132.2	132.9
Mexico	104.6	108.0	108.6	110.0	94.1	102.5	105.7	103.8	108.1	106.2
Morocco	94.9	94.8	93.8	94.4	100.3	96.3	92.4	91.5	94.7	95.1
Nigeria	127.8	136.3	133.9	145.5	139.2	152.1	149.8	170.0	185.1	193.4
Pakistan	102.3	105.9	105.7	106.1	108.2	118.4	128.9	129.8	130.5	139.6
Peru	99.3	99.4	99.6	106.5	105.6	110.0	111.1	119.0	118.5	115.0

Table A.13

Selected economies: real effective exchange rates, broad measurement,[a, b] 2005–2014 (*continued*)

	2005	2006	2007	2008	2009	2010	2011	2012	2013	2014[c]
Developing economies (*continued*)										
Philippines	107.1	129.4	135.9	130.7	129.5	118.9	110.5	112.5	106.5	99.3
Saudi Arabia	85.0	84.1	81.9	83.3	92.2	93.3	91.3	95.7	101.6	104.2
Singapore	106.8	112.1	119.5	125.3	114.5	116.5	118.8	116.4	117.9	115.1
South Africa	117.7	113.6	109.4	100.3	105.2	118.7	116.5	109.8	97.3	89.0
Taiwan Province of China	89.1	88.9	87.7	84.6	76.6	79.7	79.8	78.7	79.6	78.8
Thailand	102.7	111.6	124.9	121.1	112.3	123.0	126.2	126.3	133.4	128.5
Turkey	120.5	116.7	123.8	122.2	112.3	117.1	106.1	106.0	103.6	96.6
Venezuela (Bolivarian Republic of)	99.2	107.8	119.6	138.4	189.3	117.3	133.4	156.6	152.2	214.0

Source: JPMorgan Chase.

a Year 2000=100.

b Indices based on a "broad" measure currency basket of 46 currencies (including the euro). The real effective exchange rate, which adjusts the nominal index for relative price changes, gauges the effect on international price competitiveness of the country's manufactures owing to currency changes and inflation differentials. A rise in the index implies a fall in competitiveness and vice versa. The relative price changes are based on indices most closely measuring the prices of domestically produced finished manufactured goods, excluding food and energy, at the first stage of manufacturing. The weights for currency indices are derived from 2000 bilateral trade patterns of the corresponding countries.

c Average for the first ten months.

d Special Administrative Region of China.

Table A.14
Indices of prices of primary commodities, 2005–2014

Index: Year 2000=100

	Non-fuel commodities					Combined index		Manufactured export prices	Real prices of non-fuel commodities[a]	Crude petroleum[b]
	Food	Tropical beverages	Vegetable oilseeds and oils	Agricultural raw materials	Minerals and metals	Dollar	SDR			
2005	127	126	141	129	173	140	126	121	116	183.5
2006	151	134	148	147	278	183	164	125	146	221.3
2007	164	148	226	164	313	207	178	135	153	250.4
2008	234	178	298	198	332	256	213	142	180	342.2
2009	220	181	213	163	232	213	182	134	159	221.2
2010	230	213	262	226	327	256	222	136	188	280.6
2011	265	270	333	289	375	302	253	148	204	389.3
2012	270	212	307	223	322	277	239	145	191	396.6
2013	255	174	269	206	306	258	225	153	169	383.6
2011										
I	274	278	364	315	406	321	271	144	223	365.9
II	261	283	345	303	393	308	255	150	205	407.1
III	270	274	324	290	382	306	254	150	204	393.2
IV	255	247	299	248	319	274	232	146	187	391.0
2012										
I	257	232	316	246	342	280	241	147	191	425.4
II	264	208	318	229	323	275	238	143	192	386.8
III	285	211	318	205	306	278	242	143	194	386.2
IV	276	198	277	211	319	274	236	146	188	388.6
2013										
I	266	186	280	216	332	273	237	152	180	397
II	260	176	262	202	297	259	228	153	169	366
III	251	169	258	202	296	252	220	152	166	387
IV	243	164	274	203	297	250	215	155	161	386
2014										
I	244	198	279	198	289	249	214	155	161	379.6
II	245	220	270	191	281	248	212	153	162	383.6
III	238	220	237	180	285	242	210	..	..	365.2

Sources: UNCTAD, Monthly Commodity Price Bulletin; United Nations, Monthly Bulletin of Statistics; and data from the Organization of the Petroleum Exporting Countries (OPEC) website, available from http://www.opec.org.

a Combined index of non-fuel commodity prices in dollars, deflated by manufactured export price index.

b The new OPEC reference basket, introduced on 16 June 2005, currently has 12 crudes.

Table A.15
World oil supply and demand, 2006–2015

	2006	2007	2008	2009	2010	2011	2012	2013	2014[a]	2015[b]
World oil supply[c, d] *(millions of barrels per day)*	85.5	85.8	86.8	85.6	87.4	88.6	90.8	91.3	92.9	93.7
Developed economies	16.1	16.0	15.6	15.8	15.9	15.9	16.9	18.0	19.5	20.4
Economies in transition	12.3	12.8	12.8	13.3	13.5	13.6	13.7	13.9	13.9	13.5
Developing economies	54.3	53.9	55.0	52.9	54.1	55.1	56.2	55.2	55.3	55.3
OPEC[e]	35.1	35.0	36.2	34.2	34.7	35.8	37.5	36.7	36.7	36.5
Non-OPEC	19.2	18.9	18.8	18.7	19.4	19.3	18.7	18.5	18.6	18.9
Processing gains[f]	2.0	2.0	2.0	2.0	2.1	2.1	2.1	2.2	2.2	2.2
Global biofuels[g]	0.8	1.1	1.4	1.6	1.8	1.9	1.9	2.0	2.0	2.2
World total demand[h]	85.6	87.0	86.3	85.5	88.3	89.5	90.5	91.8	92.4	93.5
Oil prices *(dollars per barrel)*										
OPEC basket[i]	61.1	69.1	94.5	61.1	77.5	107.5	109.5	105.9	101.2	..
Brent oil	65.4	72.7	97.6	61.9	79.6	111.6	112.0	108.5	102.0	92.0

Sources: United Nations, World Bank, International Energy Agency, U.S. Energy Information Administration, and OPEC.
a Partly estimated.
b Forecasts.
c Including global biofuels, crude oil, condensates, natural gas liquids (NGLs), oil from non-conventional sources and other sources of supply.
d Totals may not add up because of rounding.
e Includes Angola as of January 2007 and Ecuador as of December 2007.
f Net volume gains and losses in the refining process (excluding net gain/loss in the economies in transition and China) and marine transportation losses.
g Global biofuels comprise all world biofuel production including fuel ethanol from Brazil and the United States.
h Including deliveries from refineries/primary stocks and marine bunkers, and refinery fuel and non-conventional oils.
i The new OPEC reference basket, introduced on 16 June 2005, currently has 12 crudes.

Table A.16
World trade:ᵃ changes in value and volume of exports and imports, by major country group, 2006–2016

Annual percentage change

	2006	2007	2008	2009	2010	2011	2012	2013ᵇ	2014ᶜ	2015ᶜ	2016ᶜ
Dollar value of exports											
World	15.2	16.2	14.3	-19.6	19.3	17.9	1.0	3.5	2.5	2.6	5.4
Developed economies	12.4	15.4	11.2	-19.7	13.7	15.3	-1.8	2.8	3.1	1.4	4.3
North America	11.6	11.5	9.7	-16.7	17.4	14.3	3.3	2.6	3.5	7.3	7.2
EU plus other Europe	13.2	17.3	11.2	-20.0	10.2	16.3	-3.4	4.4	3.2	-0.7	3.1
Developed Asia	8.5	11.2	14.2	-23.2	31.1	11.6	-2.4	-6.5	1.2	1.8	5.1
Economies in transition	24.9	21.4	31.7	-32.3	27.7	31.2	3.6	5.4	-3.1	-1.0	0.9
South-Eastern Europe	25.6	22.6	22.7	-19.5	13.5	20.8	-6.3	14.3	5.1	5.6	4.1
Commonwealth of Independent States	24.8	21.4	32.0	-32.8	28.4	31.7	4.0	5.1	-3.4	-1.2	0.8
Developing economies	19.4	16.9	17.9	-18.1	27.2	20.3	4.5	4.1	2.3	4.4	7.1
Latin America and the Caribbean	18.6	13.3	15.4	-20.5	30.5	17.6	1.5	0.9	3.4	4.5	6.0
Africa	25.0	11.7	29.3	-27.2	27.4	16.9	2.3	2.6	0.3	3.4	5.9
Western Asia	19.9	15.7	29.8	-26.7	20.7	35.7	8.9	3.7	0.1	-0.3	4.1
East and South Asia	18.7	18.7	14.5	-14.2	27.8	18.3	4.5	5.0	2.8	5.6	8.1
Dollar value of imports											
World	14.5	16.0	14.3	-20.1	19.1	18.2	1.3	2.5	2.4	3.8	6.1
Developed economies	12.9	13.5	11.2	-22.2	14.4	16.0	-2.0	1.1	2.4	2.4	5.1
North America	10.8	6.6	7.6	-22.0	19.7	13.6	2.8	0.2	3.2	4.3	6.1
EU plus other Europe	14.2	17.1	11.4	-21.9	11.0	15.9	-5.3	2.7	2.2	1.3	4.9
Developed Asia	9.9	10.6	20.5	-24.7	24.1	23.1	5.5	-5.4	1.8	4.0	3.5
Economies in transition	24.5	34.5	29.3	-30.1	22.3	28.2	7.4	3.1	-6.1	-1.3	0.3
South-Eastern Europe	16.7	34.3	27.3	-27.1	2.4	18.5	-6.0	3.5	3.7	5.1	4.7
Commonwealth of Independent States	25.3	34.5	29.5	-30.4	24.2	29.0	8.4	3.1	-6.7	-1.8	-0.1
Developing economies	17.3	19.5	19.1	-15.2	26.8	20.7	5.7	4.4	3.1	5.9	7.9
Latin America and the Caribbean	18.1	19.2	20.9	-20.2	28.5	19.4	5.6	3.2	3.4	6.1	7.3
Africa	16.5	27.9	25.7	-10.0	11.8	15.3	8.0	5.6	6.9	7.4	8.4
Western Asia	21.8	29.1	22.3	-17.8	15.0	21.3	6.6	8.7	7.6	8.7	10.1
East and South Asia	16.4	16.8	17.1	-14.1	31.0	21.5	5.3	3.7	1.7	5.1	7.5
Volume of exports											
World	9.5	7.3	2.8	-9.9	12.0	6.4	2.5	3.1	3.5	4.4	4.8
Developed economies	8.6	6.5	1.8	-11.7	11.3	5.6	2.2	2.2	3.5	4.4	4.6
North America	6.9	7.2	3.3	-9.7	10.9	6.4	2.9	2.9	3.3	5.3	4.5
EU plus other Europe	9.2	6.1	1.4	-11.4	10.3	6.3	2.1	1.8	3.3	4.3	4.6
Developed Asia	8.1	7.4	1.6	-17.7	18.6	-0.2	1.4	2.8	5.0	2.8	4.1
Economies in transition	6.6	7.3	1.8	-6.6	6.8	3.2	1.1	2.8	0.1	0.9	1.9
South-Eastern Europe	14.9	5.9	5.8	-7.7	15.6	4.3	0.9	10.4	6.5	7.4	5.3
Commonwealth of Independent States	6.4	7.3	1.7	-6.6	6.4	3.1	1.1	2.5	-0.2	0.6	1.7
Developing economies	11.2	8.5	4.5	-7.3	13.5	7.8	3.1	4.5	3.9	4.6	5.5
Latin America and the Caribbean	5.0	3.5	1.0	-9.7	8.9	7.1	2.1	1.2	2.7	3.3	4.0
Africa	12.5	2.7	8.5	-14.4	10.0	2.4	0.9	1.1	2.0	4.6	5.0
Western Asia	8.2	5.3	3.8	-6.9	6.0	11.5	7.9	1.9	3.0	3.0	5.3
East and South Asia	13.5	11.5	5.0	-5.9	16.6	7.9	2.6	6.2	4.5	5.2	5.8

Table A.16

World trade[a]: changes in value and volume of exports and imports, by major country group, 2006–2016 (*continued*)

Annual percentage change

	2006	2007	2008	2009	2010	2011	2012	2013[b]	2014[c]	2015[c]	2016[c]
Volume of imports											
World	9.7	8.1	2.8	-11.1	13.1	7.0	2.6	2.9	3.3	4.7	5.0
Developed economies	**8.0**	**5.2**	**0.2**	**-12.4**	**10.8**	**5.0**	**1.0**	**1.2**	**3.3**	**4.6**	**4.5**
North America	6.2	3.0	-2.0	-13.5	12.9	5.5	2.5	1.1	3.3	4.9	4.9
EU plus other Europe	9.4	6.2	0.9	-11.7	9.8	4.4	-0.4	1.1	3.2	4.5	4.8
Developed Asia	5.0	4.6	2.5	-14.1	12.1	7.1	5.5	2.1	4.4	3.7	1.8
Economies in transition	**16.3**	**23.2**	**11.9**	**-26.4**	**16.7**	**16.6**	**8.1**	**2.2**	**-2.8**	**0.6**	**1.6**
South-Eastern Europe	11.1	19.7	8.7	-15.9	2.9	6.1	0.9	2.5	6.0	6.8	7.0
Commonwealth of Independent States	16.8	23.5	12.2	-27.3	18.0	17.5	8.7	2.2	-3.4	0.2	1.1
Developing economies	**12.4**	**12.3**	**6.6**	**-7.3**	**16.4**	**9.4**	**4.4**	**5.3**	**3.8**	**5.3**	**6.0**
Latin America and the Caribbean	13.6	13.1	8.6	-14.6	21.6	11.3	4.5	2.8	3.1	4.0	5.0
Africa	11.4	17.6	8.6	-5.1	7.2	5.8	2.5	3.7	5.4	6.7	7.0
Western Asia	14.8	20.0	8.2	-12.3	8.6	11.5	7.7	6.9	4.9	6.6	7.4
East and South Asia	11.8	10.0	5.5	-4.8	18.0	9.1	4.0	5.7	3.5	5.1	5.8
Western Asia	16.3	10.0	18.8	7.7	-13.8	8.8	9.0	4.1	4.6	4.8	6.0
East and South Asia	12.6	11.7	9.2	5.3	-1.6	20.7	10.0	4.6	4.8	6.2	6.6

Source: UN/DESA.

a Includes goods and non-factor services.

b Partly estimated.

c Baseline scenario forecasts, based in part on Project LINK.

Table A.17

Balance of payments on current accounts, by country or country group, summary table, 2005–2013

Billions of dollars

	2005	2006	2007	2008	2009	2010	2011	2012	2013
Developed economies	-500.8	-591.3	-548.6	-706.7	-236.2	-197.7	-257.0	-228.3	-24.3
Japan	170.1	174.5	212.1	142.6	145.3	217.6	126.5	58.7	33.6
United States	-745.4	-806.7	-718.6	-686.6	-380.8	-443.9	-459.3	-460.8	-400.3
Europe[a]	104.3	76.1	19.2	-102.8	88.0	133.1	174.4	310.9	456.8
EU-15	47.6	30.6	35.3	-59.4	47.7	50.2	111.3	195.5	296.5
New EU member States	-42.3	-63.7	-106.5	-119.2	-38.2	-45.1	-46.8	-26.9	-1.5
Economies in transition[b]	82.3	88.6	53.8	89.7	35.5	63.1	99.3	58.7	11.1
South-Eastern Europe	-5.1	-5.3	-11.5	-18.5	-7.3	-6.0	-8.5	-8.5	-5.9
Commonwealth of Independent States[c]	88.1	95.1	67.3	111.0	43.9	70.3	109.7	69.0	18.0
Developing economies	475.9	692.7	759.0	775.1	383.6	444.9	497.4	522.9	435.0
Net fuel exporters	290.0	383.5	334.9	435.4	76.3	223.7	495.5	474.1	375.7
Net fuel importers	185.9	309.2	424.1	339.7	307.3	221.2	1.9	48.9	59.3
Latin America and the Caribbean	34.1	48.4	8.1	-36.7	-28.0	-62.4	-79.5	-105.0	-149.7
Net fuel exporters	28.2	33.9	18.5	37.9	0.3	3.5	17.3	2.7	2.0
Net fuel importers	5.9	14.6	-10.5	-74.6	-28.3	-65.9	-96.8	-107.6	-151.8
Africa	60.2	85.1	69.3	62.8	-36.0	5.2	-7.4	-22.1	-56.0
Net fuel exporters	81.6	107.3	102.4	114.0	6.2	41.7	46.8	53.4	21.0
Net fuel importers	-21.4	-22.2	-33.1	-51.2	-42.2	-36.5	-54.2	-75.5	-77.0
Western Asia	136.1	178.8	138.7	221.2	40.9	98.9	284.2	344.5	271.6
Net fuel exporters	159.3	206.6	175.7	264.3	52.0	144.6	364.0	401.1	339.9
Net fuel importers	-23.2	-27.8	-37.0	-43.1	-11.1	-45.7	-79.8	-56.6	-68.3
East and South Asia	245.5	380.3	542.9	527.9	406.7	403.1	300.1	305.5	369.1
Net fuel exporters	20.9	35.7	38.3	19.2	17.8	33.9	67.4	16.8	12.9
Net fuel importers	224.5	344.6	504.6	508.7	388.9	369.2	232.7	288.7	356.2
World residual[d]	57.4	189.9	264.2	158.1	182.8	310.3	339.8	353.3	421.8

Sources: International Monetary Fund (IMF), World Economic Outlook, October 2014; and IMF, Balance of Payments Statistics.

a Europe consists of the EU-15, the new EU member States and Iceland, Norway and Switzerland.

b Includes Georgia.

c Excludes Georgia, which left the Commonwealth of Independent States on 18 August 2009.

d Statistical discrepancy.

Note: IMF World Economic Outlook has adopted the sixth edition of the Balance of Payments and International Investment Position Manual (BPM6).

Table A.18
Balance of payments on current accounts, by country or country group, 2005–2013

Billions of dollars

	2005	2006	2007	2008	2009	2010	2011	2012	2013
Developed economies									
Trade balance	-596.6	-728.8	-702.3	-824.5	-412.5	-508.8	-703.1	-658.5	-500.1
Services, net	173.8	220.6	302.0	329.6	307.9	347.9	432.7	423.9	494.0
Primary income	167.1	163.5	153.9	121.1	197.1	312.3	379.6	360.0	350.0
Secondary income	-245.1	-246.7	-302.2	-333.0	-328.8	-349.1	-366.2	-353.6	-368.2
Current-account balance	-500.8	-591.3	-548.6	-706.7	-236.2	-197.7	-257.0	-228.3	-24.3
Japan									
Trade balance	106.9	94.9	120.9	55.6	57.8	108.5	-4.5	-53.9	-90.0
Services, net	-37.1	-32.0	-37.0	-38.0	-34.9	-33.6	-38.4	-50.6	-35.7
Primary income	107.9	122.3	139.8	138.1	134.6	155.1	183.1	177.4	169.3
Secondary income	-7.6	-10.7	-11.5	-13.1	-12.3	-12.4	-13.8	-14.2	-10.0
Current-account balance	170.1	174.5	212.1	142.6	145.2	217.6	126.5	58.7	33.6
United States									
Trade balance	-782.8	-837.3	-821.2	-832.5	-509.7	-648.7	-740.6	-742.1	-701.7
Services, net	68.6	75.6	115.8	123.8	125.9	154.0	192.0	204.5	225.3
Primary income	67.6	43.3	100.6	146.1	123.6	177.7	221.0	203.0	199.7
Secondary income	-98.8	-88.3	-113.9	-124.1	-120.6	-126.9	-131.7	-126.1	-123.5
Current-account balance	-745.4	-806.7	-718.6	-686.6	-380.8	-443.9	-459.3	-460.8	-400.3
Europe[a]									
Trade balance	46.5	-13.5	-21.6	-79.0	49.5	27.4	16.9	161.6	293.1
Services, net	146.0	182.1	234.0	262.6	231.8	252.4	310.9	305.5	341.3
Primary income	48.8	53.4	-18.3	-90.9	-0.2	58.3	61.3	50.7	52.3
Secondary income	-137.0	-145.8	-174.9	-195.5	-193.0	-205.0	-214.8	-206.9	-229.8
Current-account balance	104.3	76.1	19.2	-102.8	88.0	133.1	174.4	310.9	456.9
EU-15									
Trade balance	40.0	-15.0	-4.7	-68.9	25.7	-19.1	-42.4	71.9	176.6
Services, net	99.5	129.8	171.7	192.3	170.2	191.7	245.9	243.4	275.7
Primary income	37.5	56.6	37.8	4.3	33.9	73.8	112.7	81.2	68.3
Secondary income	-129.3	-140.8	-169.5	-187.1	-182.1	-196.2	-204.9	-201.0	-224.1
Current-account balance	47.6	30.6	35.3	-59.4	47.7	50.2	111.3	195.5	296.5
New EU member States									
Trade balance	-51.8	-69.0	-97.3	-122.0	-39.8	-41.8	-43.6	-26.9	-5.5
Services, net	26.2	29.7	37.0	42.3	35.0	35.7	43.1	43.7	48.4
Primary income	-27.0	-36.3	-59.1	-53.7	-45.7	-54.1	-64.0	-59.0	-62.5
Secondary income	10.4	11.8	12.9	14.1	12.4	15.1	17.7	15.3	18.1
Current-account balance	-42.3	-63.7	-106.5	-119.2	-38.2	-45.1	-46.8	-26.9	-1.5
Economies in transition[b]									
Trade balance	113.4	133.3	114.0	176.4	105.2	155.3	222.1	205.2	183.9
Services, net	-16.5	-15.5	-23.8	-28.0	-24.2	-31.3	-36.9	-52.9	-65.7
Primary income	-26.6	-41.7	-48.1	-72.2	-59.0	-74.4	-100.4	-105.9	-116.8
Secondary income	12.1	12.6	11.8	13.6	13.4	13.6	14.6	12.3	9.8
Current-account balance	82.3	88.6	53.8	89.7	35.5	63.1	99.3	58.7	11.1

Table A.18

Balance of payments on current accounts, by country or country group, 2005–2013 (*continued*)

Billions of dollars

	2005	2006	2007	2008	2009	2010	2011	2012	2013
Economies in transition[b] (*continued*)									
South-Eastern Europe									
Trade balance	-14.0	-15.8	-22.6	-29.6	-19.6	-17.6	-20.6	-19.4	-17.0
Services, net	0.8	1.4	1.9	2.2	2.1	2.4	2.9	2.7	2.9
Primary income	0.0	0.2	-0.4	-0.6	-0.2	-0.9	-1.1	-1.5	-1.7
Secondary income	8.1	8.8	9.6	9.6	10.4	10.0	10.3	9.6	9.8
Current-account balance	-5.1	-5.3	-11.5	-18.5	-7.3	-6.0	-8.5	-8.5	-5.9
Commonwealth of Independent States[c]									
Trade balance	128.6	151.0	139.5	209.9	127.3	175.5	246.2	228.9	204.3
Services, net	-17.4	-17.1	-25.9	-30.2	-26.7	-34.3	-40.6	-56.8	-70.1
Primary income	-26.7	-42.2	-47.8	-71.5	-58.7	-73.3	-98.9	-104.3	-114.7
Secondary income	3.6	3.3	1.4	2.9	2.0	2.4	3.0	1.3	-1.5
Current-account balance	88.1	95.1	67.3	111.0	43.9	70.3	109.7	69.0	18.0
Developing economies									
Trade balance	597.0	784.4	835.9	897.6	565.8	718.6	891.2	906.7	924.2
Services, net	-90.2	-110.8	-126.4	-177.2	-182.6	-211.0	-261.1	-262.0	-306.9
Primary income	-192.6	-168.2	-164.0	-181.6	-206.7	-282.4	-355.0	-319.5	-370.0
Secondary income	161.7	187.2	213.5	236.3	207.1	219.8	222.3	197.8	187.8
Current-account balance	475.9	692.7	759.0	775.2	383.6	444.9	497.4	522.9	435.0
Net fuel exporters									
Trade balance	407.6	519.4	523.6	706.2	337.4	539.2	873.8	877.2	803.0
Services, net	-85.1	-113.7	-156.2	-211.0	-191.7	-208.4	-240.7	-252.4	-265.8
Primary income	-53.1	-36.2	-38.9	-64.1	-60.8	-93.3	-116.7	-122.5	-121.7
Secondary income	17.0	14.0	6.5	4.3	-8.6	-13.8	-20.9	-28.2	-39.7
Current-account balance	286.4	383.5	334.9	435.4	76.3	223.7	495.5	474.1	375.7
Net fuel importers									
Trade balance	189.4	265.1	312.3	191.4	228.4	179.4	17.4	29.5	121.2
Services, net	-5.1	2.9	29.8	33.8	9.2	-2.6	-20.4	-9.6	-41.1
Primary income	-139.5	-132.0	-125.1	-117.4	-145.9	-189.1	-238.3	-197.0	-248.3
Secondary income	144.7	173.3	207.1	232.0	215.6	233.6	243.2	226.0	227.5
Current-account balance	189.5	309.2	424.1	339.7	307.3	221.2	1.9	48.9	59.3
Latin America and the Caribbean									
Trade balance	81.2	99.0	69.0	39.9	50.7	47.7	70.3	41.4	9.9
Services, net	-16.7	-17.2	-24.8	-31.9	-33.4	-49.3	-64.7	-68.7	-72.6
Primary income	-83.5	-97.2	-103.0	-111.7	-102.7	-122.2	-148.2	-139.7	-149.7
Secondary income	53.1	63.9	66.8	67.0	57.4	61.4	63.1	62.0	62.7
Current-account balance	34.1	48.4	8.1	-36.7	-28.0	-62.4	-79.5	-105.0	-149.7
Africa									
Trade balance	64.5	90.5	92.5	111.2	-3.1	54.4	58.2	45.8	9.8
Services, net	-11.8	-21.6	-34.3	-56.0	-49.7	-54.7	-65.6	-64.3	-64.0
Primary income	-34.6	-33.2	-46.4	-58.2	-44.3	-62.4	-74.5	-80.0	-82.5

Table A.18

Balance of payments on current accounts, by country or country group, 2005–2013 (continued)

Billions of dollars

	2005	2006	2007	2008	2009	2010	2011	2012	2013
Developing economies (continued)									
Secondary income	42.1	49.5	57.6	65.8	61.0	67.9	74.5	76.5	80.6
Current-account balance	60.2	85.1	69.3	62.8	-36.0	5.2	-7.4	-22.1	-56.0
Western Asia									
Trade balance	185.0	236.2	222.2	343.2	169.5	253.2	466.8	538.7	489.3
Services, net	-26.9	-44.3	-64.6	-86.2	-76.1	-87.3	-106.2	-109.7	-119.8
Primary income	-13.8	2.1	7.9	-5.0	-12.1	-17.5	-16.4	-13.4	-17.3
Secondary income	-8.2	-15.2	-26.9	-30.8	-40.4	-49.5	-60.1	-71.1	-80.6
Current-account balance	136.1	178.8	138.7	221.2	40.9	98.9	284.2	344.5	271.6
East Asia									
Trade balance	303.8	410.8	523.9	519.9	471.1	484.5	452.9	483.5	565.4
Services, net	-51.6	-45.7	-27.8	-39.0	-44.5	-54.2	-76.0	-73.1	-112.7
Primary income	-50.8	-28.7	-13.5	5.4	-33.6	-58.2	-95.4	-59.8	-91.0
Secondary income	32.8	38.4	51.0	62.9	48.6	54.6	43.3	23.6	14.9
Current-account balance	234.2	374.8	533.7	549.2	441.7	426.6	324.8	374.2	376.6
South Asia									
Trade balance	-37.5	-52.1	-71.8	-116.6	-122.5	-121.2	-157.0	-202.6	-150.2
Services, net	16.8	18.1	25.1	35.9	21.2	34.5	51.3	53.8	62.1
Primary income	-9.8	-11.3	-9.2	-12.0	-14.1	-22.2	-20.5	-26.7	-29.6
Secondary income	41.9	50.8	65.0	71.4	80.5	85.4	101.5	106.9	110.2
Current-account balance	11.3	5.5	9.2	-21.3	-35.0	-23.5	-24.7	-68.7	-7.5
World residual[d]									
Trade balance	113.7	188.9	247.6	249.6	258.6	365.1	410.2	453.4	608.0
Services, net	67.0	94.3	151.7	124.4	101.1	105.6	134.7	108.9	121.3
Primary income	-52.0	-46.5	-58.2	-132.7	-68.6	-44.5	-75.8	-65.5	-136.7
Secondary income	-71.3	-46.8	-76.9	-83.1	-108.3	-115.8	-129.4	-143.5	-170.7
Current-account balance	57.4	189.9	264.2	158.2	182.8	310.3	339.8	353.3	421.8

Sources: International Monetary Fund (IMF), World Economic Outlook, October 2014; and IMF, Balance of Payments Statistics.

a Europe consists of EU-15, new EU member States plus Iceland, Norway and Switzerland.

b Includes Georgia.

c Excludes Georgia, which left the Commonwealth of Independent States on 18 August 2009.

d Statistical discrepancy.

Note: IMF World Economic Outlook has adopted the sixth edition of the Balance of Payments and International Investment Position Manual (BPM6).

Table A.19
Net ODA from major sources, by type, 1992–2013

Donor group or country	Growth rate of ODA (2012 prices and exchange rates)					ODA as a percentage of GNI	Total ODA (millions of dollars)	Percentage distribution of ODA by type, 2013			
								Bilateral	Multilateral		
	1992-2002	2002-2010	2011	2012	2013	2013	2013	Total	Total (United Nations & Other)	United Nations	Other
Total DAC countries	-0.5	5.3	-1.9	-3.4	6.1	0.30	134833	69.3	30.7	5.4	25.3
Total EU	0.0	5.6	-2.8	-6.8	5.2	0.42	70724	59.3	40.7	5.8	34.9
Austria	10.6	5.0	-14.1	5.7	0.7	0.28	1172	46.0	54.0	4.0	50.1
Belgium	1.6	6.4	-12.7	-12.5	-6.1	0.45	2281	57.7	42.3	5.4	36.9
Denmark	3.7	-0.8	-3.4	-3.0	3.8	0.85	2928	73.2	26.8	09.3	17.5
Finland	-4.2	8.2	-2.2	-1.3	3.5	0.55	1435	57.1	42.9	14.7	28.2
France[a]	-3.7	5.3	-5.4	-1.4	-9.8	0.41	11376	59.6	40.4	3.9	36.5
Germany	-1.7	5.7	2.1	-2.1	3.0	0.38	14059	65.3	34.7	3.3	31.4
Greece	..	3.9	-21.1	-15.9	-7.7	0.13	305	31.7	68.3	4.6	63.7
Ireland	16.2	9.5	-3.4	-4.9	-1.9	0.45	822	66.2	33.8	11.1	22.7
Italy	-5.0	1.9	35.7	-32.7	13.4	0.16	3253	20.7	79.3	6.6	72.7
Luxembourg	15.1	5.4	-7.1	2.4	0.9	1.00	429	69.6	30.4	13.7	16.7
Netherlands	2.5	1.9	-6.0	-7.0	-6.2	0.67	5435	66.4	33.6	11.0	22.6
Portugal	2.8	1.6	3.6	-11.0	-20.4	0.23	484	61.2	38.8	2.4	36.4
Spain	4.1	10.0	-33.2	-47.2	3.7	0.16	2199	35.2	64.8	4.7	60.0
Sweden	1.2	6.2	9.9	-3.3	6.3	1.02	5831	67.4	32.6	12.5	20.1
United Kingdom	4.0	8.5	-0.2	-0.1	27.8	0.72	17881	59.9	40.1	3.9	36.2
Australia	0.9	6.0	11.4	8.8	-4.5	0.34	4851	86.0	14.0	3.0	11.1
Canada	-2.6	5.4	-2.6	2.9	-11.4	0.27	4911	72.1	27.9	6.4	21.5
Japan	-0.7	-2.3	-9.3	-1.1	36.6	0.23	11786	74.8	25.2	5.0	20.2
New Zealand	2.6	5.4	10.4	4.1	-1.9	0.26	457	76.7	23.3	10.3	13.0
Norway	1.4	4.4	-5.5	1.1	16.4	1.07	5581	77.3	22.7	11.3	11.4
Switzerland	0.5	4.6	12.4	5.7	3.4	0.47	3198	78.8	21.2	6.6	14.6
United States	-1.8	9.5	-0.1	-2.5	1.3	0.19	31545	83.9	16.1	3.5	12.6

Source: UN/DESA, based on OECD/DAC online database, available from http://www.oecd-ilibrary.org/statistics.
a Excluding flows from France to the Overseas Departments, namely Guadeloupe, French Guiana, Martinique and Réunion.

Table A.20

Total net ODA flows from OECD Development Assistance Committee countries, by type, 2004–2013

	Net disbursements at current prices and exchange rates (billions of dollars)									
	2004	2005	2006	2007	2008	2009	2010	2011	2012	2013
Official Development Assistance	80.1	108.3	105.4	104.9	122.8	120.6	129.1	134.7	126.9	134.8
Bilateral official development assistance	54.8	83.1	77.5	73.7	87.1	83.9	91.0	94.4	88.6	93.4
in the form of:										
Technical cooperation	18.7	20.8	22.4	15.1	17.3	17.6	18.0	17.8	18.3	0.1
Humanitarian aid	5.2	7.2	6.8	6.5	8.8	8.6	9.3	9.7	8.5	10.6
Debt forgiveness	8.0	26.2	18.9	9.7	11.1	2.0	4.2	6.3	3.3	..
Bilateral loans	-2.8	-0.8	-2.4	-2.2	-1.1	2.5	3.3	1.7	2.4	..
Contributions to multilateral institutions[a]	25.4	25.2	27.9	31.2	35.7	36.6	38.1	40.2	38.4	41.4
of which are:										
UN agencies	5.2	5.5	5.3	5.9	5.9	6.2	6.5	6.6	6.6	7.3
EU institutions	9.0	9.4	10.1	12.0	13.5	14.2	13.6	13.7	12.0	12.9
World Bank	6.4	5.3	7.2	6.2	8.6	7.6	9.1	10.2	8.8	10.2
Regional development banks	2.3	2.2	2.5	2.4	3.2	3.1	3.2	4.1	3.9	3.9
Others	2.5	2.7	2.7	4.7	4.4	5.4	5.7	5.7	7.4	..
Memorandum item										
Bilateral ODA to least developed countries	16.0	15.9	17.4	19.7	23.5	24.4	28.5	31.0	27.7	..

Source: UN/DESA, based on OECD/DAC online database, available from http://www.oecd.org/dac/stats/idsonline.

a Grants and capital subscriptions. Does not include concessional lending to multilateral agencies.

Table A.21
Commitments and net flows of financial resources, by selected multilateral institutions, 2004–2013

Billions of dollars

	2004	2005	2006	2007	2008	2009	2010	2011	2012	2013
Resource commitments[a]	55.9	71.7	64.7	74.5	135.2	193.7	245.4	163.8	189.8	130.8
Financial institutions, excluding International Monetary Fund (IMF)	45.7	51.4	55.7	66.6	76.1	114.5	119.6	106.8	96.5	98.8
Regional development banks[b]	21.9	23.7	23.8	31.9	36.7	55.1	46.2	46.9	43.0	45.8
World Bank Group[c]	23.7	27.7	31.9	34.7	39.4	59.4	73.4	59.9	53.5	53.0
International Bank for Reconstruction and Development	10.8	13.6	14.2	12.8	13.5	32.9	44.2	26.7	20.6	15.2
International Development Association	8.4	8.7	9.5	11.9	11.2	14.0	14.6	16.3	14.8	16.3
International Financial Corporation	4.6	5.4	8.2	10.0	14.6	12.4	14.6	16.9	18.2	21.4
International Fund for Agricultural Development	0.5	0.7	0.7	0.6	0.6	0.7	0.8	1.0	1.0	0.8
International Monetary Fund	2.6	12.6	1.0	2.0	48.7	68.2	114.1	45.7	82.5	19.6
United Nations operational agencies[d]	7.6	7.7	8.3	6.3	10.5	11.0	11.6	11.3	10.8	12.4
Net flows	-19.3	-38.8	-24.7	-4.4	43.4	54.6	64.6	78.7	35.1	8.8
Financial institutions, excluding IMF	-9.3	1.6	6.3	13.6	24.5	22.6	27.2	38.0	26.3	22.2
Regional development banks[b]	-6.4	-1.5	3.2	6.2	21.4	15.7	9.9	10.5	8.6	5.7
World Bank Group[c]	-2.9	3.1	3.1	7.4	3.1	6.9	17.2	27.6	17.7	16.5
International Bank for Reconstruction and Development	-8.9	-2.9	-5.1	-1.8	-6.2	-2.1	8.3	17.2	8.0	7.8
International Development Association	5.3	5.4	7.3	7.2	6.8	7.0	7.0	9.1	7.8	7.0
International Financial Corporation	0.7	0.6	0.9	1.9	2.4	2.1	1.9	1.2	1.9	1.6
International Fund for Agricultural Development	0.1	0.2	0.2	0.2	0.2	0.2	0.2	0.3	0.3	0.2
International Monetary Fund	-10.0	-40.4	-31.0	-18.0	18.9	32.0	37.4	40.7	8.9	-13.4

Sources: Annual reports of the relevant multilateral institutions, various issues.

a Loans, grants, technical assistance and equity participation, as appropriate; all data are on a calendar-year basis.

b African Development Bank (AfDB), Asian Development Bank (ADB), Caribbean Development Bank (CDB), European Bank for Reconstruction and Development (EBRD), Inter-American Development Bank (IaDB).

c Data is for fiscal year.

d United Nations Development Programme (UNDP), United Nations Population Fund (UNFPA), United Nations Children's Fund (UNICEF), and the World Food Programme (WFP).